1 MONTH OF
FREE
READING

at
www.ForgottenBooks.com

By purchasing this book you are eligible for one month membership to ForgottenBooks.com, giving you unlimited access to our entire collection of over 1,000,000 titles via our web site and mobile apps.

To claim your free month visit:
www.forgottenbooks.com/free965998

ISBN 978-0-260-71619-4
PIBN 10965998

© 1985 NCNA

ISSN 0039-9620

TAR HEEL NURSE

Vol. 47, No. 1   OFFICIAL PUBLICATION OF THE NORTH CAROLINA NURSES ASSOCIATION   January-February 1985

Nurses gear up for 1985 legislative session

By Hazel Browning

The 1985 session of the North Carolina General Assembly promises to be a very active one for NCNA. The session began on February 5. Several issues important to nurses and nursing are expected to be considered.

November 6 elections brought a change in many House and Senate seats, so there will be a number of new legislators on the scene. It will be the responsibility of NCNA's registered lobbyists, as well as all nurse lobbyist members to get to know the new legislators and present to them our perspective on issues. In addition, we will have to maintain and improve our relationship with returning legislators.

Key issues expected to arise in the 1985 session will directly or indirectly impact on the practice of nursing and the nursing profession. You are encouraged to acquaint yourself with these issues and make every effort to acquaint your individual legislators with the nursing perspective on these issues. Grassroots lobbying efforts are more effective than any other lobbying strategy. The March 12 workshop, "A Day at the Legislature", will feature more details about these issues.

Local Boards of Health—Refer to the September-October issue of the *Tar Heel Nurse* to review a resolution on this issue approved by the 1984 NCNA House of Delegates. NCNA will work with other concerned groups to prevent an extension of legislation enabling county commissioners to take over the duties and authority now under the purvue of local and district boards of health. The "whereas" clauses of the resolution explain the rationale for this position.

Public Health Nurses Dispensing—Many of this state's impoverished population receive their only health care through health department services. Often, medicinal therapy is needed (for birth control, treatment of sexually transmitted diseases, control of communicable diseases like tuberculosis, etc.). Just as often, these clients cannot afford the price of medicine. While health departments frequently have the medication available on site, nurses need clear legal authority to dispense medications. Without such authority, the client will suffer from lack of treatment and the public health will be jeopardized by uncontrolled communicable diseases.

NCNA staff members have been working for more than a year with other groups concerned about this problem, including representatives from the county commissioners group, health directors, the state health director and chief nurse, and representatives from both the Pharmacy Association and the Board of Pharmacy. The group is currently reviewing a proposed legislative bill that would regulate certain drug and devise dispensing practices in local health departments. The proposed language would allow RNs with special training for drug and device labeling and packaging to dispense a specified formulary from local health departments. Restrictions are written in to allow the Board of Pharmacy to approve the RN training criteria and the formulary, and it provides for a pharmacist-manager to review dispensing records weekly and provide consultation where appropriate.

Third Party Reimbursement for Nurses—In the 1983 session of the General Assembly, Representative Al Adams introduced House Bill 1223 which would have autho- *(continued on page 7)*

Nurses plan to "mug" legislators

If you attended the recent NCNA convention you might recall seeing coffee mugs imprinted with the NCNA logo in the Finance Committee booth. Even though the mugs and coffee beans sold well, there were several left at the close of the convention.

You might also recall that Carolyn Goforth, chairman of the NCNA Committee on Legislation, issued a challenge to all districts during the closing session of the House of Delegates. Carolyn suggested that each district purchase coffee mugs for the members of the General Assembly who live in their area. The mugs would be "stuffed" with a tea bag, a pouch of Sanka, and a calling card reading "Nurses make House and Senate calls."

The idea was appealing to many NCNA members and to the Board of Directors. Soon after the close of the 1984 NCNA convention, the Board of Directors met, discussed the project further and approved implementation of the "Mug Your Legislator" project.

The project will be implemented on March 12 as a part of the "Day at the Legislature" workshop. The 170 legislators have been assigned to our 34 NCNA districts according to the legislator's county of residence. Districts are the focal point of this project. Many districts have assisted financially by purchasing mugs for each legislator living in their area. In addition, most districts will identify their "muggers"— nurses from the district who plan to attend the March 12 "Day at the Legislature" workshop and who will deliver an NCNA mug to their legislators.

The mugs will be stuffed with a tea bag, a packet of Sanka, and envelopes of cream and sugar. Cards have been printed showing the NCNA logo and address, and a caption reading, "Nurses make House and Senate calls." District members will sign the cards to identify themselves to their legislators.

With any luck, the "Day at the Legislature" workshop will again draw a large crowd. As many as 350 nurses will converge on the State Legislative Building during the afternoon hours on March 12 to meet with their elected representatives. What an icebreaker—an NCNA coffee mug, a gift from an NCNA district, to deliver to elected officials and get the meeting started off right!

Message from the President
Judith B. Seamon

Great expectations for health care and nursing in North Carolina have been the hallmark of NCNA. In recent years we have seen many of our great expectations become great realities. I firmly believe it is our desire and intention to continue to expect and realize many more accomplishments for health care and nursing in North Carolina.

If, however, we are to translate our desire and intention into reality, then we must face and resolve one extremely critical issue—namely, the accrual of adequate financial resources to support qualified staff and the programs of NCNA.

We currently have very qualified staff and an extensive number of relevant and credible programs. Our staff salaries are not, however, commensurate with their qualifications and our programs are not as comprehensive and numerous as they could be if we had greater financial resources.

The answer is very simple—increased membership! Our membership dues provide the "hard monies" to support the ongoing programs of our association. The Finance Committee and the Board of Directors are being very responsible in keeping our organization in the "black" by budgeting only the "hard monies" for support of staff and essential programs.

We can solve this problem by each of us accepting the responsibility to recruit at least one new member. That alone would double our membership!

We have a great heritage and are seeing a remarkable return on the investments of our own time, efforts and money as well as that of many members who preceded us. Each of us must do his/her part in seeing that NCNA continues to have the resources necessary to turn our great expectations into great realities for health care and nursing in North Carolina.

Primary care nurses plan spring workshop in Raleigh

The Primary Care Nurse Practitioner Conference Group has planned a spring continuing education workshop to be held at the North Raleigh Hilton on April 18-20. The 2 1/2 day workshop will feature a keynote address about health care financing, the changing health care industry and what the role of the nurse practitioner is likely to be in those changing times. An opening reception sponsored by Ross Labs will be held on the evening of April 18.

Clinical sessions will be the focus during Friday, April 19. A kaleidoscope of programs will give participants a broad exposure to present day clinical concepts on topics like family planning, dermatology, breast disease, cardiovascular update, etc. Friday's session will also include a trade show with representatives of drug companies and an evening banquet honoring Audrey Booth on her retirement.

During the half day session on Saturday, Wade Smith, legal counsel for NCNA, will be among the session leaders. Smith will address the process of investigations of nurse practitioner practice settings by the Board of Medical Examiners. What are the nurse practitioner's rights and respon-

sibilities during investigation? Come to the workshop and learn all about it!

Workshop flyers will be mailed during February to nurse practitioners across the state. If you are a nurse practitioner and would like more information about this workshop, you may contact Laurie Ferris at (919) 966-3638.

NCNA staff members receive citation

Frances Miller, executive director, and Hazel Browning, associate executive director, were recipients recently of the North Carolina Distinguished Service Award.

Jimmy Green, then Lieutenant Governor, issued the awards in December citing the recipients' "integrity, knowledge and sincere commitment to the fundamental principles of responsible and democratic government." Miller and Browning are registered lobbyists for the North Carolina Nurses Association and, as such, are actively engaged in presenting nursing's perspective on issues before the North Carolina General Assembly.

ACTIONS OF THE BOARD

Actions of the Board
The Board of Directors, at a meeting on November 14, 1984, took the following actions:

● Took several actions directed at clarifying the NCNA position on the credentialing of nurses in advanced practice as prerequisite for third-party reimbursement.

● Supported the nominations of Ellie White for the ANA Cabinet on Nursing Practice and Annette Frauman for the Cabinet on Nursing Research.

● Declined to fund the publishing of a directory for a group of nurse specialists.

● Designated proceeds from the 1984 convention fund-raising projects to the ANA Delegate Fund.

● Referred to the Convention Program Committee recommendations regarding convention registration fees.

● Authorized appointment of an ad hoc committee to develop guidelines on the rights of RNs to accept or refuse a work assignment and to make recommendations with regard to their utilization and distribution.

● Authorized a subcommittee to pursue ANA accreditation as a provider and approver unit and referred to the Finance Committee a request that $2,500 be budgeted in 1985 to cover the application expenses.

● Appointed Joyce Gainey to the Nurse PAC and Convention Program Committees.

● Recommended Russell Eugene Tranbarger for appointment to the ANA Committee on Credentialing.

● Appointed Linda Wallace as NCNA advisor to the N. C. Association of Nursing Students for a term expiring in April 1987.

● Appointed Sharon Rupp to the Commission on Practice.

● Appointed Peggy Norton to the Joint Practice Committee.

● Appointed W. Frank Ausband to the Committee on Human Rights.

● Declined to support the Oklahoma Nurses Association call for a special meeting of the ANA House of Delegates regarding the presidential endorsement by the ANA Board of Directors.

● Voted to renew NCNA membership in the ANF Century Club.

● Changed the name of the Committee on impaired Nurses to the Peer Assistance Program Committee.

● Amended and approved a philosophy statement developed by the Peer Assistance Program Committee.

The Executive Committee reported to the Board that it had taken the following actions at a meeting on January 4, 1985:
(continued on page 7)

Campaign to explore ways of curbing health-care costs

By Katherine Smart
N.C. Foundation for Alternative Health Programs, Inc.

Would you be willing to pay more of your medical bills yourself in exchange for lower insurance premiums?

Or do you think medical costs should be reduced by charging higher insurance premiums to smokers and other people who practice poor health habits?

Those are the kinds of questions that Triangle and Fayetteville area residents will get to answer this spring in a public opinion survey on the rising costs of health care.

The survey, called "Health Vote '85," will take the form of a ballot to be distributed April 15, 1985, in Raleigh, Durham, Chapel Hill, Fayetteville and the surrounding areas.

Thousands of ballots will be inserted in newspapers and distributed at shopping centers. No special registration will be required. Citizens will simply vote for the solutions they think can best solve the problem of rising health-care costs.

But before they do, the N.C. Foundation for Alternative Health Programs Inc. in Raleigh, which is sponsoring the vote, is going to launch a special, six-week information campaign.

NCNA's Districts Eleven, Thirteen, and Fourteen are participating in the project by recruiting members to complete the speaker training sessions, scheduling training sessions, and scheduling programs on the Health Vote project for community groups. District Eleven, for instance, has identified 70 civic and community organizations to contact concerning programs during the project period.

The involved districts also are recruiting workers to hand out ballots at shopping centers on April 15.

A meeting is planned by District Eleven with UNC-N.C. Memorial Hospital Health Maintenance Clinic (FNP-managed clinic) to develop media spots for publicity.

The "Health Vote '85" campaign, which will begin March 1, 1985, will be designed to help people explore the problem of high medical costs and consider the pros and cons of at least a dozen possible solutions.

Besides health insurance, topics covered may include the use of alternative healthcare facilities and non-physician health care providers, Medicare, duplication of services and preventive medicine, said Nan Rideout, vice president of the foundation.

Rideout said the pros and cons of the issues will be presented through public meetings and talks, a half-hour television documentary, a newspaper insert, radio and TV programs and newspaper articles.

"Health Vote '85 will be a way for people to learn more about health cost issues from creditable, objective sources and make their interests known to health care providers, elected officials and other people who have some control over those costs," Rideout said.

"The campaign does not push a particular answer or point of view. We want people to look at all the issues, mull them over, talk about them and come to their own decisions on what they think should be done."

The Foundation for Alternative Health Programs is an independent, non-profit agency established in 1982 on the recommendation of a legislative commission. Its goal is to stimulate private programs that can help curb the state's health costs.

It is launching "Health Vote '85" with the help of The Public Agenda Foundation, a non-profit, non-partisan research and educational organization in New York City that pioneered the first Health Vote campaign in Des Moines, Iowa, in 1982.

That campaign drew 30,000 returned ballots and has prompted Public Agenda to support several 1985 campaigns, including ones in Minneapolis-St. Paul, Minn.; Dayton, Ohio; Kansas City, Mo.; and Peoria, Ill.

Public Agenda officials hope the campaigns will help form a national consensus on how to stem medical inflation and encourage people who regulate health care to consider solutions that people prefer.

Rideout said newspapers and radio and TV stations are supporting the campaign and will spread information on the health-care issues.

The issues and the ballot questions, she said, will be determined by a board of 30 to 40 advisers made up of average citizens, community leaders, public health officials, health-care providers and people from civic groups, insurance companies and health-care facilities. NCNA's representative on the Advisory Board is Marjorie Bye of Raleigh.

"So often people are suspicious of what they read because they're not sure where it's coming from," Rideout said. "But in this campaign, they can depend on information that represents all points of view."

There are no statewide figures on the per capita costs of health care in North Carolina, but Rideout said some companies have found the costs to be lower here than in other states.

"The kicker in that finding," she said, "is that some studies have shown that the rate of increase in medical costs is higher in the Southeast than in many other parts of the country."

Between 1966 and 1978, the U.S. as a whole averaged an 11.6 percent increase in personal health-care costs, but that average was 12.6 percent in the Southeast and 12.2 percent in North Carolina. Rideout said that some companies in the state have seen their medical insurance costs jump as much as 75 percent in a single year.

"We have more to gain by stemming the rapid rate of increase now than by waiting until we get into a crisis, where the absolute level is up with everybody else," she said.

The Foundation needs volunteers to distribute ballots and help with office and community work. For information, call (919) 821-0491.

CALL FOR SHARING
Want to be a leader? Act now!

As a part of a special problem-solving conference to be held in Winston-Salem in November, nurses are invited to submit a brief summary of ideas they have seen effectively implemented by front-line nurses that address the pressures nurses have in their work settings.

If you are aware of, or have been involved in successful projects that have helped nurses to increase job satisfaction, cope more effectively, have a stronger voice in decision-making, or strengthen their professional impact, please contact Faye Haas, RN, MSN, Staff Development Department, North Carolina Baptist Hospital, Winston-Salem, North Carolina 27103, (919) 748-3434, for details about how you can share with other nurses.

You may be selected to present your ideas at the NurseCare Conference to be held November 12-13 at the Graylyn Conference Center of Wake Forest University, Winston-Salem, where grass-roots nurses will meet together to study effective problem-solving strategies for dealing with professional issues.

A day at NCNA headquarters

By Hazel Browning

"Normal office hours are 8:30 a.m. to 4:30 p.m., Monday through Friday." That's a standard part of the message we leave on the NCNA answering machine when the office is closed for a holiday ... but it's hard to find a "normal" day at NCNA.

Many mornings find at least one staff member in before 8:30. Pat Bryan, administrative assistant, usually rides in to work with her husband, John. Since his hours don't coincide with our 8:30-4:30 schedule, Pat often gets a lot of work done during the quiet hours of the early morning.

But, when 8:30 comes around, the staff have learned to be ready for *anything!*

Since many of our members have never been to the headquarters building and, therefore, don't know what "those folks in Raleigh" do, we included this article for your information. Staff members pinpointed a day on the calendar and kept a "diary" of their activities on that day. This article is a compilation of those diaries and is intended to help you, our members, understand what goes on at your headquarters.

8:30 a.m. ... RING! "Good morning, Nurses Association, this is Pat." "..."

"You will need to call the Board of Nursing to renew your license. You have reached the North Carolina Nurses Association, the voluntary organization for professional nurses. The Board of Nursing is the licensing agency and their number is 828-0740."

That scenario is a routine occurrence at NCNA. On the average, we get about ten such calls each day.

When the front door swings open for the second time this morning, Dot Bennett, administrative assistant, comes in to start the day after driving from her home in Fayetteville. She is soon followed by Betty, Hazel, and Frankie.

Warm up the computer, the copy machine, the coffee pot and hold on — the day has begun.

Ordering and sorting the mail is an early morning priority, since there always seems to be pieces of mail that need immediate attention. Dot and Pat do this activity together, with one person opening and sorting while the other records any checks received. This two-person system is a part of our internal control. On the average, we receive 30-40 pieces of mail each day, and everyone usually gets a stack to deal with.

. Once that job is completed, Dot settles down in front of the word processor (she's our resident expert). The task at hand this morning is entering a memo to North Carolina nurses who belong to ANA Councils requesting their input on the process of nominations. The memo is simple enough; it's the lists of 13 different council memberships that have to be entered by name and address that's so time consuming. By 4:30 p.m. today, these 120 memos, with the appropriate council list attached, must be in the mail, since the response time is just around the corner.

Pat's typewriter is already talking! She's busy working on a stack of memos and letters (18 to be exact), that Frankie, Hazel and Betty generated yesterday. Naturally, there is an assortment of enclosures that need to go with this correspondence, and we always keep a file copy of all correspondence, so she's frequently traveling up and down the hall to the copy machine.

Interspersed among these tasks, Dot and Pat answer the in-coming telephone calls which, on the average, number between 40 and 50 per day. There are lots of calls that they (thankfully) handle themselves, such as the calls from nurses who want to renew their licenses. We occasionally get calls from nurses who want membership information and an application form, and we have a standard packet that these persons recieve. There are many other calls, however, that are forwarded on for a response from Betty, Hazel or Frankie.

A major undertaking

Betty has been immersed for almost two weeks now in a major project—an application for ANA approval to NCNA for continuing education provider and approver status. Take it from the rest of the staff, that's a major undertaking. She has been copying stuff from all kinds of files, cutting and pasting like a maniac and has even been pecking on a typewriter at intervals. She's working with a subcommittee of the CERP Committee under a February deadline. Well, Betty is back on that this morning, deleting parts, adding new parts—all with scissors and tape—in hopes that she can sit down at the word processor this afternoon (with Dot as her coach) to feed in this information. her work is frequently punctuated by calls coming in about CERP programs. Betty staffs the CERP Committee, monitors and maintains all CERP records and responds to all kinds of requests for information and assistance from continuing education providers ... that's part of what she does.

If a legislative workshop for 350 people is going to "come off" on March 12, there are a lot of details to work out ahead of time. That project has occupied a lot of Hazel's time for the past week. This morning, the tasks on the "to do" list include writing a letter of invitation for the luncheon to a senator; working on arrangements to typeset and print a reception invitation to legislators; being sure the workshop flyer gets to the mailer; working with the printer on a format for the NCNA "Guide to Lobbying" handout for the workshop; proofing the typesetting of 170 legislators' names, districts, and addresses; and sorting and compiling maps of six different floors of the legislative buildings in preparation for copying.

Meanwhile, Frankie has already responded to "emergency" items from the morning mail by writing three letters, marking some materials to go in the tile and copying appropriate pieces of correspondence to go to NCNA officers. The phone, of course, has been ringing off the hook. This particular morning, Frankie dealt with phone calls from the following:

• an impaired nurse.

The telephone starts our day. By 8:30 a.m., Pat's perky voice is responding to inquiries.

Dot is working on a letter at the computer ... or is the computer working on Dot?

- the NCNA president re: (1) scheduling a work day at headquarters; (2) some correspondence she wants us to get out; (3) an agenda for a committee meeting next week; and, (4) some additional items for the Board of Directors meeting.
- a nurse from a local hospital's inservice education department seeking information about MCH legislation (referred this one to Hazel).
- a nurse practitioner requesting Frankie's article included in a recent issue of *Business and Health* magazine.
- a Board member re: next Board of Directors agenda and her absence from that meeting.
- Judith Ryan, ANA Executive Director, re: Frankie's recent article in *Business and Health* magazine.

In addition, Frankie placed (1) a call to the NCNA president-elect (since Hettie wasn't in, she requested a call-back); and, (2) called in a reservation to a local restaurant for a dinner meeting this evening.

Another project that requires lots of time and energy at the beginning of each new year is the compilation of our accomplishment sheet, "What NCNA Has Done For You in 1984". The staff have poured through calendars and files to put these together, and the 1984 edition is in the final editing stage on this particular day. The document is 13 typed pages, and Frankie requires that each staff member read it in its entirely looking for errors and/or omissions. So, during the day it moves from Frankie's desk, to Hazel's, to Betty's, and finally lands back on Pat's desk for the corrections/additions that have been marked in the process.

Surveys and more surveys

State Nurses Associations (SNAs) frequently survey other SNAs about their activities. On this day, Frankie responds to a questionnaire about SNA activities on health hazards in the workplace. That requires pouring over files and checking through convention proceedings.

Since Frankie is the executive director, she gets the privilege of responding to staff inquiries about a WIDE variety of things. The executive director is responsible to the Board of Directors for the operation of headquarters and the entire NCNA program and activities. Consultations with staff are an everyday occurrence. This day brought staff inquiries to Frankie re: copy services, workshop materials, the association bank accounts, and the need for a new bulletin about legislative activities.

Late in the morning, Dot finished the letter and lists of ANA Council members, ran a copy off the computer, and dashed to the copy center with yet another "emergency job".

"I have to have it by 3:00 pm. It must go out today." Back at the office, she passed the time by typing and copying minutes from a recent committee meeting and other miscellaneous correspondence.

Pat has pulled the mailing cards for the legislative workshop flyer and explained the mailing to our mail service representative when he came in to pick them up. There's a shortage in the supplyroom on CERP packets, so she put together a few more—90, to be exact. That meant running 6 pages through the mimeograph machine for 90 copies each, collating, stapling and storing those.

It seems that money matters are a daily concern at NCNA also. Why, on this day alone, Pat called the auditor about letters of confirmation and bank confirmations, prepared letters and bank confirmations for the auditor, prepared invoices and wrote semi-monthly checks, reconciled 3 bank accounts and prepared a quarterly report for 1 of those accounts, reconciled the Nurse-Pac bank statement and prepared that account's monthly statement of condition, and prepared a rough draft of the NCNA county property tax listing! That also means that Frankie had to proof and sign the confirmation letter, review and sign invoices and checks, and review (with Pat) the personal property tax forms.

Frankie and her cane go scooting down the hall at the stroke of 12 noon. She has a lunch appointment with representatives from two other associations to discuss plans for a joint meeting of three executive boards in February. Everyone nods goodbye rather absent-mindedly. Now, this is concentration!

"It's 12:30 p.m. Doesn't anyone around here get hungry?" After that remark breaks the concentrated silence of the office, everyone realizes they are indeed, hungry. Hazel takes orders for the sandwich shop and dashes off. Lunch is delayed further by a quick stop at the copy center to get a cost estimate on typesetting and printing the reception invitations and to pick up materials left earlier for printing. The "lunch hour" is a quick soup and sandwich break around the kitchen table with everyone talking at once, it seems, to share what they're involved in today. Twenty or 30 minutes later, everyone is back "in the groove" in their respective offices.

Betty has Dot cornered around the IBM-PCXT working on a draft of the ANA application. Hazel has a typesetter cornered in her office trying to talk him into a better price on typesetting the reception invitation. Pat

is responding to a variety of requests that came in by phone or mail this morning. On this day, that included requests from 7 nurses for membership information, requests for information/articles to be sent to various people, a request from one district member for 50 membership applications. Later, she processed 3 new member applications.

Needed it yesterday

During the afternoon, Hazel waded through a pile of things that had accumulated on her desk. A scribbled note to send information to the nurse who called in this morning about MCH legislation—that meant pouring through six files from the 1983 and 1984 legislative session, pulling appropriate documents, copying those, returning originals to their proper place and labeling the copies to be mailed. That has to go out today because—like everyone else—the nurse needed it YESTER-DAY! Another scribbled note required a call to the Board of Nursing to check on the agenda for the next Board meeting. One NCNA staff member usually attends part or all of Board of Nursing meetings to monitor Board decisions and help keep our members apprised of important decisions.

The ANA Board of Directors meeting summaries are scanned by all staff members. Hazel fell heir to that 100-page document on this date, reviewed the contents and passed it on to Betty. A summary of Legislative Research Commission Activities for 1983-85 came off the press recently. Since part of Hazel's staff responsibility is to monitor legislation, the summary needed prompt attention. The NCNA Committee on Legislation will meet soon, and they may need to be apprised of anything hidden in this 81 page summary. So ... Hazel set about studying that.

Somewhere in the middle of all of this, Frankie and her cane, came

Everybody consults with Frankie ... constantly!

Hazel finalizes some workshop plans—the telephone again.

... and again! This time it's Betty consulting with a C.E. provider about applying for credit.

The telephone usually ends our day, too. It's ring catches Betty before she can get out the door.

zipping back down the hall, her luncheon over and her brain running about a mile ahead of her feet. She set quickly about several afternoon tasks which included the following:

- preparing materials to update personnel policies reflecting recent Board actions.
- talking with an ITT representative about new telephone equipment.
- collecting materials for a meeting the following day with the NCNA president.
- investigating an invoice she had questions about.

One thing that punctuates a lot of time at headquarters is the process of assembling and compiling articles for the Tar Heel Nurse. On this particular day, we were getting close to deadline for copy on the January-February issue, so Frankie (the editor) spent some time collecting and sorting assignments for staff for this edition.

Betty and Dot found a stopping point on the ANA application during the late afternoon. Betty had to fly back to her office because she had a lot of materials to assemble for the Ad Hoc Committee on Structure, which will be meeting soon. Dot, meanwhile, dashed back to the copy center, picked up copies of the memo and lists of ANA Council members and dashed back to begin collating, folding and stuffing those.

Is it a plane ... ?

By 4 p.m. Dot was found seated on the floor in the front office with a stack of 120 memos, 13 stacks of lists and 13 stacks of envelopes madly stuffing the mailing. "Can you help? These have to get out today". That question brought Hazel and Betty to their knees in the floor to help collate, fold and stuff and brought Pat to the workroom, where she made the postal machine sing as she sent the envelopes for this mailing through the machine along with the other 40 or 50 pieces of mail we'd accumulated to send out today. By 4:20 p.m., everything was folded, stuffed, licked and stamped and Pat was a visual blur as she dashed out to the post office to have our mail get in the 4:25 p.m. collection.

Remember the prologue of this article? That sentence about office hours being 8:30-4:30? Well, again, it's hard to find a normal day at NCNA, and this day was no exception. With the ANA Council mailing crisis behind us, Betty and Dot settled down to work "just a few more minutes" on the ANA application. The next time they looked up, it was 5:45 p.m. Pat, the perpetual visual blur, had zipped back in from the post office and jumped right in typing materials for the Board of Directors meeting packets (gotta go in the mail tomorrow, right?) as well as some copies needed for the Committee on Legislation meeting. Frankie

wasn't about to give up the progress she was making on the next issue of the Tar Heel Nurse (as exemplified by the clutter of papers spread from one end of the library tables to the other) so she stayed with it, until 5:40 p.m. And Hazel was deeply involved in trying to find names and addresses for sales representatives from about 50 drug companies. She's trying to plan a trade show for the Primary Care Nurse Practitioner Conference Group's spring workshop. She made about 15 calls to companies, nurse practitioners, etc., looking for information. In doing all that, she realized she hadn't received menus from the hotel yet. Those menus need to be selected soon, so she placed a call to the hotel salesperson with a request for same.

Down deeper in the stack that had accumulated on her desk, Hazel uncovered a couple of pieces of information she thought might be helpful to the chairman of the MCH division. With those copies and a note attached, she officially started the stack of mail to go out tomorrow—before today was even finished!

The "see you tomorrows" began ringing out when Frankie called it a day at 5:40 p.m. Pat, Dot, Betty and Hazel were not far behind—just long enough to turn off the computer, the xerox machine, the coffee pot and the lights.

As the foursome headed for the door, a sound broke the fatigued silence.   5:49 p.m. ... RING!

All four looked at each other simultaneously ... "Shall we pretend we didn't hear it?" was the unspoken question—but none of them could do it.

"Good afternoon, Nurses Association, this is Betty."

"... "

"You will need to call the Board of Nursing to renew your license. You have reached the North Carolina Nurses Association, the voluntary organization for professional nurses. The Board of Nursing is the licensing agency and their number is 828-0740."

By 7 p.m., Frankie and Hazel are together again (it's a good thing they like each other, don't you think?) but at a hotel restaurant, this time. It was a dinner meeting with representatives from another agency to discuss common concerns and issues.

During dinner, the many tiny peas that were pushed around in plates were clearly not as numerous as the many thoughts that were running around in the heads of those seated at the table. By 9:45 p.m. the meeting broke up and, for NCNA staff, another day was over.

RNs will elect two board members

Two registered nurses are to be elected this year to the Board of Nursing for three-year terms beginning January 1, 1986.

One nurse educator and one community health nurse are to be elected. Currently holding these positions are R. Leigh

Andrews, educator, eligible for nomination, and Olga C. Hoskins, community health nurse, not eligible for nomination.

Petitions nominating qualified nurses must be postmarked on or before April 1, 1985.

All registered nurse nominees must hold a current North Carolina license, have at least five years' experience as a registered nurse, and have been engaged in nursing

for at least three years immediately preceding election. Nurse educators must have baccalaureate or advanced degree.

NURSE TO NURSE

By Carolyn Billings, Chairman
Commission on Member Services

I talk a lot about nurse-pride. In fact, I've been accused of being an ivory-tower idealist. Maybe so. I *do* have a tendency to see Nursing through rose-colored glasses. To me nurses are the healers, the relationship experts, the last hope for humane health care. Nurses after all, have the right background. Who else is better prepared to understand the total bio-psycho-social-spiritual-cultural person—the Unitary Man? Who else has the opportunity and the inclination for a completely therapeutic use of self—through gentle touch, through sensitive inquiry and understanding, through interpersonal awareness and skilled nurturance? There is more potential in the nursing act than in any other—potential for the patient's affirmation of self and mobilization of his or her own restorative energy.

But every now and then it hits me. Like a sudden cold wash of chilling Winter air. It frosts me to my core and then leaves me with the deep sickness of helpless despair and a powerful swelling of frustrated disappointment and overwhelming rage.

It usually begins with a story about someone's bad experience with nurses. That story and its telling stirs up uneasy memories of my own. One such memory is of my weakened and emaciated father suffering from chronic pain who spent two days without any nourishment in a major medical center. Two days without food because nobody noticed that lab tests and x-rays were scheduled in tandem and he was either NPO or away from his bedside for diagnostic studies at tray-time. When he finally complained of dizzyness (having been without appetite for over a year and consequently not hungry), the mealtime events were retraced and the "Primary Nurse" who was responsible for coordinating his total care huffily remarked that he hadn't told *her* he *wanted* anything to eat. The problem finally identified, he waited an additional three hours because "it wasn't time for trays just yet".

The most recent story to leave me awash with shame and anger about nursing comes from a friend. Her father was recently hospitalized with a stroke. Her experience was a nightmare. Not only was there no coordinated plan of care or consistent nursing caregiver, no personalized approach or recognition of the person behind the CVA diagnosis, but complication after compounding complication resulted from inept and careless nursing activity. The most dramatic examples of

this were persistent global use of narcotics in response to any patient problem from restlessness to reflux vomiting, and oral medications administered improperly and without regard for left-sided paralysis, swallowing difficulties, and a supine position. The results: a weakened, unresponsive patient whose recovery time was compromised by excessive sedation and severe esophagitis caused by caustic medicinal chemicals lodged in various locations down the esophageal passage. His transfer to a Rehab Center after unnecessary delay was accompanied by tears of relief when the staff there actually *looked at* him, *spoke to* him, and nursed the *patient* rather than the IV bag or catheter. (The worst of us can make the rest of us look so good!)

Oh, there are reasons; there are always reasons. And there are two (at least) sides to every story. But can there really be any justification?

Sometimes I just want to give up on us. There are so many nurses and there is so little *nursing*. That's when I desperately grope for a hopeful sign. This time fate puts me on a train between New York and Philadelphia. I sit down beside a young R.N. who is working, she tells me, as a hemodialysis nurse in a local unit in Philly. She is alive with excitement over her work. She talks about her patients with a full awareness of the totality of their lives. She tells me with light shining in her eyes how much she loves her job, how she enjoys the regular consistent contact with the same group of patients—the challenge in it—the completeness of their relationship—and how she believes that her work with her dialysis patients affects their entire lives. "I am their Comforter, their Counselor, their Helper, their Friend", she says. "I wouldn't want to do anything else. *Nursing is my thing!"*

Later, after she departs, I look out the window of the still moving train and send her a silent thank-you. Nurses are *my* people and Nursing is *my* thing. I'm grateful to feel good again—about them both!

Notice!

Bring this issue with you to the "Day at the Legislature" workshop on March 12. You will need the Guide to Lobbying Section that appears in this issue.

Nurses gear up
from page 1

rized direct third party reimbursement to selected nurse providers. That bill did not pass; however, language was included in an insurance law study bill to allow a legislative committee to study reimbursement to health care providers, including nurses. The study committee met periodically during the past eight months but focused its attention primarily on auto insurance.

NCNA has continued to work on this important issue. Currently, a subcommittee and NCNA staff members are working with legal counsel to determine the next step toward the goal of achieving legislative sanction to directly pay nurse providers for the services they render. Specific elements of the bill have not been finalized. This issue will be discussed further at the March 12 workshop and will be covered in future issues of the *Tar Heel Nurse.*

Administrative Procedures Act (APA) Recodification—Please refer back to your July/August 1984 issue of the *Tar Heel Nurse.* This issue was not resolved in the 1984 session and is expected to return for consideration in 1985. At this point, we do not know what form any action about the APA will take. This topic will be discussed at the March "Day at the Legislature" workshop.

Action of the Board
from page 2

● Recommended to the Board adoption of a philosophy statement prepared by the Ad Hoc Committee on ANA Accreditation, and requested the Ad Hoc Committee to prepare (1) a modification of the NCNA organizational chart that reflects structural unit relationships more specifically, and (2) a policy on NCNA's participation in single offerings/programs as a co-provider.
● Denied a request that NCNA provide legal counsel to a group of members and directed that a policy be developed for presentation to the Board of Directors on use of NCNA legal counsel.
● Requested that a list be prepared for the board of organizations to which NCNA belongs and pays dues and recommended that the board review the list to establish priorities.
● Reviewed proposed amendments to rules and regulations of the Board of Nursing and determined that there are no questions raised requiring NCNA to give testimony.

Multiply Membership

Lindeman poses questions nurses must answer

By Sue Morgan
Delegate, District Twenty-Six

As keynote speaker at the 1984 NCNA convention, Carol Lindeman, R.N., Ph.D., F.A.A.N., reviewed several of the historical aspects of nursing that reflect some of the reasons there have been and now are conflicts in nursing practice.

Dr. Lindeman is dean, School of Nursing, and associate director, nursing services, University of Oregon Health Sciences Center.

It is her belief that nursing is a socially relevant practice with roots linked to societal need as evidenced in the care of soldiers by Florence Nightingale; that research and evaluation of nursing activities were built into the group of tasks rather than in knowledge; that control of nursing education has been in the hands of employers so that one serves the other; that nurses have not controlled their own practice; and, that nurses seemed to have a feeling that they have devaluated what they do—an internal devaluation, reinforced by devaluation of women in general—an external devaluation.

Dr. Lindeman feels that World War II helped nursing begin to make changes in both education and practice. The knowledge explosion of recent years and the move from an industrial to an informational system, are also major impactors on the profession. We are still dealing with conflicts, however, and some questions need to be answered with regard to nursing.

Who owns the knowledge? Access to knowledge is no longer open only to a specified few. Clients are becoming almost as knowedgeable as practitioners. This may call for a new definition of a professional—one who not only has the knowledge, but knows how to use it.

What is the role of the health professional in a society of people who value self-care? Nursing has long had the value of self-care, but it has been an empty value in that we continue to make the patient dependent. Whose needs are we meeting?

Who will control the practice of nursing? We need to make society say that nurses are to be involved in the control of nursing practice. The practice of competent nurse midwives and nurse practitioners has been hampered by society and politics. Nurses must be involved on the boards that exercise control.

What range of services are we going to provide and to support? Shall we promote dental hygienists who foster dental health or dentists who promote dental disease? We must be relevant, because society demands it.

Dr. Lindeman tells us that if we are going to be successful as nurses in the Brave New World, that there are some things we will have to do. She notes that times have never been better for nurses, but we must still make changes in some of the conceptions we have of ourselves.

Dr. Lindeman says:
We have to be willing to believe that nursing is a KNOWLEDGE-BASED discipline. The difference is in the knowing, rather than in the doing.

We must become recognized as significant decision-makers.

We must have a change in nursing education from the doing to the thinking, producing life-long learners.

We have to come to understand that research and knowledge are critical developments.

We must have nursing controlling nursing and the authority to deal with our practice.

We must change our conceptions dealing with leadership and understand that leadership exists at the grassroots level and within nursing in our own institutions.

This article is reprinted with permission of the author from the District Twenty-Six Newsletter.

AMERICAN JOURNAL OF NURSING COMPANY
and
NORTH CAROLINA NURSES ASSOCIATION

——————— 1985 ———————
Award for Excellence in Writing

Purpose
This award is intended to encourage members of the North Carolina Nurses Association to write for publicaton.

The Award
An award of $100 and a certificate suitable for framing will be presented to the winning author.

The Rules
All members of the North Carolina Nurses Association who hold membership during 1985 are eligible, except for employees of the American Journal of Nursing Company and the North Carolina Nurses Association headquarters staff.

The writing submitted must be in prose, prepared for publication but unpublished, not to exeed 3,000 words on nursing; written for nurses, members of other healthcare disciplines or for the general public. *Particularly, participants are encouraged to write articles or reports on nursing projects, innovations in nursing practice, and data collected to improve nursing care.* A research paper, such as a master's thesis, should be rewritten from a research format to an article format to be considered. Articles with more than one author will be eligible only if all co-authors are NCNA members. Entries are to be typed, double spaced on one side of 8½ x 11 white paper. Upon receipt of the entry at state headquarters office, it becomes the property of the North Carolina Nurses Association until it is returned to the writer.

The Judges
Manuscripts shall be judged and the winning entry selected by a committee of members of the North Carolina Nurses Association to be appointed by the president, one of whom shall be the editor of the North Carolina Nurses Association's official publication.

Deadline
No special entry forms or application blanks are necessary. Entries should be sent to: NCNA, P.O. Box 12025, Raleigh, NC 27605, postmarked not later than August 1, 1985.

Think Membership

Headquarters
bulletin board

NCNA's structural unit nominating committees (13 in all) will be meeting through the coming few months to prepare ballots for their biennial elections. Every structural unit with open membership (divisions, conference groups, forums, sections) is important and has its special interest to pursue through NCNA. Leadership is needed, so if you are asked to run for office, we hope you will give it serious consideration. Even if you can't run for office, give some thought to qualified candidates and assist the nominating committee of your structural unit by suggesting names for the ballot.

●

An article, "Nurse Providers: A Resource for Growing Population Needs," by Executive Director Frances N. Miller appeared in the January/February 1985 issue of *Business and Health*, published by the Washington Business Group on Health. The article is based on testimony prepared early in 1984 for the North Carolina General Assembly Legislative Study Committee on Medical Cost Containment. Willis Goldbeck, who spoke at the 1984 NCNA convention, is the magazine's publisher.

●

The Public Relations and Membership Comittees designed an exhibit about NCNA for display at the annual convention in early Feburary of the North Carolina Association of Nursing Students. The exhibit depicted members involved in a variety of Association programs and activities and was accompanied by handouts on membership benefits and NCNA services.

●

During the last two weeks of January, 12 members from throughout the state acted as a response group to ANA's analysis of the principles and issues of the Health Policy Agenda for the American People, a project initiated by the American Medical Association Board of Trustees in 1982. The project is a private and public health sector effort to develop a long term, consistent approach to the health care issues facing the nation. ANA has reviewed the Health Policy Agenda and submitted a document to state nurses associations for comment. The 12 NCNA members worked in six teams of two

members each to review and comment on each of six segments of the document. Their comments will be compiled at headquarters into a response to ANA.

●

Pat Bryan and Dot Bennett attended workshops in January on word processing and data base management. At the word processor workshop (for first-time users) the participants had hands-on experience in creating, revising, editing, and printing a document/file. The data base management workshop was an introduction to data file processing, report forms, programming, and manipulating data.

●

An ad hoc committee has been working diligently to prepare an application from NCNA for ANA certification as a continuing education provider and approver. The deadline for the application is February 10, 1985. The earliest decision will be in August. The hard-working ad hoc committee is chaired by Margaret Raynor. Other members are Ginger Sandlin and Joanne Corson. Betty Godwin is the NCNA staff person working with the group.

Medical Facilities Plan projects needs, issues

The 1985 State Medical Facilities Plan, signed by Governor James B. Hunt, Jr., in December, is available for distribution.

The Plan contains need projections and policy considerations for the following types of health care facilities: hospitals (including rehabilitation facilities), nursing homes, home health agencies, psychiatric facilities, chemical dependency facilities, intermediate care facilities for the mentally retarded, end stage renal dialysis stations.

In addition, the Plan contains detailed inventory and utilization information on the health care facilities and services listed above, as well as information on ambulatory surgical facilities, facilities offering intensive residential treatment and detoxification services for chemical dependent individuals, rural health clinics and selected hospital services.

The plan, including the appendices, is 486 pages and the cost is $40.00 plus $5.00 for shipping and postage (if mailed) for a total of $45.00. Make check payable to: Health Planning Section, Division of Facility Services, P.O. Box 12200, Raleigh, N.C. 27605.

BEFORE YOU MOVE ...
... please let us know! To be sure you don't miss copies of TAR HEEL NURSE, send change of address to NCNA, P. O. Box 12025, Raleigh, NC 27605.

CAMPS SEA GULL/SEAFARER NURSES

NORTH CAROLINA
NURSES ASSOCIATION

103 Enterprise Street ● P.O. Box 12025 ● Raleigh, North Carolina 27605 ● Telephone (919) 821-4250

Guide to lobbying

This special section is your lobbying guide for the 1985 session of the North Carolina General Assembly. It contains our goals for this year's lobbying effort, lobbying do's and don't's, guides on how to contact your lawmaker, and names and addresses of members of the 1985 General Assembly, along with maps showing the new house and senate districts. House and Senate districts are different in most cases. Locate your county on each map to find the names of your representatives in the House and your senators.

Keep this guide handy for easy reference throughout the session. Add to your file future issues of the Legislative Bulletin and the Tar Heel Nurse.

Lobbying goals

1. Every nurse a lobbyist. The nurse lobbyist (that's you) provides the one-to-one contact between NCNA and the lawmaker. You, the nurse lobbyist, can influence his/her vote because you are his constituent.

2. Feedback system. An equally important lobbying goal is that every nurse lobbyist will communicate to headquarters in Raleigh data obtained and responses received from the lawmaker. We must have this important feedback to assist us in assessing our progress and devising actions.

3. At least one informed registered nurse serving as liaison throughout the session for each lawmaker. This liaison nurse is to communicate frequently with the lawmaker and encourage the lawmaker to consult with the liaison nurse about nursing legislation.

Responsibilities of the nurse lobbyist

1. To make periodic and timely contact (personal visits whenever possible) with the legislator to explain the NCNA position on the issues and to report back to NCNA headquarters the results of the contacts.

2. To contact the legislator directly before key committee or floor votes. The professional lobbyist in Raleigh usually alerts the member lobbyists as to timing of these contacts.

3. To collect and maintain information about the legislator, such as commitment to NCNA issues, voting records, committee assignments, bills sponsored.

4. To seek support for NCNA's position from other constituents or sympathetic groups who may be especially influential with the legislator.

Contacting your legislator

Personal contact with your representative or senator is the most effective way to promote your legislative interests and concerns. All legislators appreciate hearing from their constituents. Opinions of constituents on any issue assist the legislator in making decisions about the actions he/she will take in support or opposition (or for compromise) regarding that issue.

Face-to-face contact with your legislator is the most effective way to make your opinions known to the legislator. When this is impossible, a telephone call or personal letter also can be effective. During the legislative session, members of the General Assembly spend nearly every weekend in their home communities. Call on them personally or telephone them at their home or place of business. Legislators' telephone numbers at the State Legislative Building can be obtained through (919) 733-4111.

Use the following guide in addressing letters to legislators:

The Honorable _____
North Carolina House of Representatives
State Legislative Building
Raleigh, N.C. 27611

The Honorable _____
North Carolina Senate
State Legislative Building
Raleigh, N.C. 27611

When you make a visit

Make an appointment and go with one or more other nurses if possible. Keep the visit brief and to the point. Be friendly—you'll probably be visiting again in the future, and you want the legislator to be receptive. Be sure to express appreciation for the appointment. If the legislator asks questions you can't answer, say you don't know but you will get the answer and communicate it to him/her. Be respectful of the office and responsibility the legislator holds, but don't be intimidated—he/she is a citizen in your community just as you are.

When you make a phone call

When time is short a telephone message is sometimes the best way to communicate, especially when you know the legislator personally or you have established previous face-to-face contact. If you cannot talk to the legislator directly, deliver your message to a member of his staff. Be sure you identify yourself clearly to the answering party and clearly identify the issue you are addressing.

When you write a letter

1. Address the letter properly.

2. Use your own stationery. Use your own words. Form letters are ineffective.

3. Write legibly or type your letter.

4. Sign your full name and show your address on the letter.

5. Do not write on "behalf of NCNA"—write on behalf of YOURSELF.

6. Know your subject. Identify the bill by number or name, if you can.

7. Stick to one subject. This makes your position easier to understand and adds weight to the message.

8. Keep it brief. One page should be enough. One sincere paragraph could be enough. You don't have to analyze and explain the entire bill.

9. Be concise. Summarize your position in the first paragraph. use the remainder of the page for explanation and supporting remarks.

10. Be factual. If you have expert knowledge, share it. Do not offer arguments that cannot be substantiated. Personalize the effect of the legislation, if possible, telling how you see the legislation affecting you, your practice, your community.

11. Be reasonable and polite, but communicate that you would like to know your legislator's position on the legislation.

12. Write while there is still time for the legislator to take effective action.

13. Say "thank you" for a favorable vote to let your legislator know you appreciate a job well done.

Lobbying tips

DO be knowledgeable about the subject you discuss with your legislator to gain and keep his/her confidence.

DO make periodic contact with the legislator. One letter or telephone call won't establish a legislator-constituent relationship.

DO furnish the legislator with your address and telephone number.

Avoid threats or demands. It will turn the legislator off. Be polite and fair.

Avoid being nasty about people whose views differ from yours.

Avoid excessive pressure for a commitment from the legislator. Remember that lawmakers may not be ready to express specific commitment on a bill, but this does not minimize the value of your contact in helping the lawmaker to reach a decision.

Sources of information

A Bill Status Desk is in operation during the 1985 session. By calling (919) 733-7779, writing, or visiting this desk, anyone may obtain information on the current status and legislative history of any bill introduced. The desk is located in Room 2226 (Legislative Library) of the State Legislative Building. The service is available 9-5:30 on weekdays and 7-9 on Monday evenings.

Anyone may obtain a single copy of any bill introduced in the 1985 session at no charge. A bill may be picked up at Room 2022. To request a copy of a bill by mail, send a stamped self-addressed envelope to: Printed Bills, State Legislative Building, Raleigh, N.C. 27611. Bills requested should be identified by house of origin and number (e.g., House Bill 21). A single copy of a Bill may be requested by telephone at (919) 733-5648.

A final word ...

Legislation becomes law through compromise. Legislators want to pass laws that are as non-controversial as possible. They are skilled at finding the common ground for agreement. They will be seeking to satisfy all interested parties. Lobbying involves the art of compromise—accepting refinements of thought, clarifying language, giving here to gain there. Compromise in lobbying is inevitable.

PRE-REGISTRATION
"A DAY AT THE LEGISLATURE"
March 12, 1985

NOTE: Fee includes workshop materials, coffee break, lunch, and reception for legislators.

Name _____ Phone (W) _____ (H) _____

Address _____

( ) RN   ( ) NCNA Member   ( ) Non-Member   ( ) LPN   ( ) Student

Pre-registration Fee: ( ) $30 member workshop fee (includes reception)
( ) $40 non-member workshop fee (includes reception)
( ) $20 special fee for students in any nursing education program (limit - 50 students at this special rate. **See special notice on brochure)
( ) $20 special fee for *reception only*

NO REFUNDS AFTER FEBRUARY 26   Amount Enclosed $ _____
Pre-registration deadline: March 1. *All on-site fees will be $5 higher than those listed above.

Make check payable to NCNA and mail to: NCNA, P.O. Box 12025, Raleigh, NC 27605

North Carolina Senate

1st District (1):
MARC BASNIGHT
Box 1025
Manteo, N.C. 27954

2nd District (1):
J. J. "MONK" HARRINGTON
P.O. Drawer 519
Lewiston-Woodville, N.C.
27849

3rd District (1):
JOSEPH E. "JOE" THOMAS
P.O. Box 337
Vanceboro, N.C. 28586

4th District (1):
A. D. GUY
306 Woodlawn Drive
Jacksonville, N.C. 28540

5th District (1):
HAROLD W. HARDISON
P.O. Box 128
Deep Run, N.C. 28525

6th District (1):
R. L. "BOB" MARTIN
P.O. Box 387
Bethel, N.C. 27812

7th District (1):
J. A. "CHIP" WRIGHT
P.O. Box 4412
Wilmington, N.C. 28403

8th District (1):
HENSON P. BARNES
707 Park Avenue
Goldsboro, N.C. 27530

9th District (1):
TOM F. TAFT
P.O. Box 588
Greenville, N.C. 27834

10th District (1):
JAMES E. EZZELL, JR.
201 Forest Hill Avenue
Rocky Mount, N.C. 27801

11th District (1):
JAMES D. SPEED
Route 6, Box 542
Louisburg, N.C. 27549

12th District (2):
ANTHONY E. "TONY" RAND
1600 Morganton Road
Fayetteville, N.C. 28305

LURA S. TALLY
3100 Tallywood Drive
Fayetteville, N.C. 28303

13th District (2):
KENNETH C. ROYALL, JR.
64 Beverly Drive
Durham, N.C. 27707

RALPH A. HUNT
433 Pilot Street
Durham, N.C. 27707

14th District (3):
JOSEPH E. "JOE" JOHNSON
P.O. Box 750
Raleigh, N.C. 27602

WILLIAM W. "BILL" STATON
205 Courtland
Sanford, N.C. 27330

WILMA C. WOODARD
P.O. Box 189
Garner, N.C. 27529

15th District (1):
ROBERT D. "BOB" WARREN
Route 3, Box 25
Benson, N.C. 27504

16th District (2):
RUSSELL G. WALKER
1004 Westmont Drive
Asheboro, N.C. 27203

WANDA H. HUNT
P.O. Box 1335
Pinehurst, N.C. 28374

17th District (2):
J. RICHARD CONDER
1401 Carolina Drive
Rockingham, N.C. 28379

AARON W. PLYLER
2170 Concord Avenue
Monroe, N.C. 28110

18th District (1):
R. C. SOLES, JR.
P.O. Box 6
Tabor City, N.C. 28463

19th District (1):
ROBERT G. "BOB" SHAW
P.O. Box 8101
Greensboro, N.C. 27419

20th District (2):
MARVIN M. WARD
641 Yorkshire Road
Winston-Salem, N.C. 27106

TED KAPLAN
P.O. Box 5128
Winston-Salem, N.C. 27113

21st District (1):
JOHN M. JORDAN
P.O. Box 128
Saxapahaw, N.C. 27340

22nd District (1):
JAMES C. "JIM" JOHNSON, JR.
29 Church Street, South
Concord, N.C. 28025

23rd District (2)
ROBERT VANCE SOMERS
240 Confederate Avenue
Salisbury, N.C. 28144

PAUL S. SMITH
P.O. Box 916
Salisbury, N.C. 28145

24th District (2):
W. D. "BILL" GOLDSTON
P.O. Box 307
Eden, N.C. 27288

WELDON R. PRICE
North Scales Street
Reidsville, N.C. 27320

25th District (3):
J. OLLIE HARRIS
P.O. Box 627
Kings Mountain, N.C. 28086

HELEN RHYNE MARVIN
119 Ridge Lane
Gastonia, N.C. 28054

MARSHALL A. RAUCH
1121 Scotch Drive
Gastonia, N.C. 28052

26th District (2):
T. CASS BALLENGER
P.O. Box 2029
Hickory, N.C. 28601

WM. W. "BILL" REDMAN, JR.
Route 2, Box 43
Statesville, N.C. 28677

27th District (2):
DONALD R. KINCAID
P.O. Box 988
Lenoir, N.C. 28645

DANIEL R. SIMPSON
P.O. Drawer 1329
Morganton, N.C. 28655

28th District (2):
ROBERT S. SWAIN
Route 5, Box 1112
Asheville, N.C. 28803

DENNIS J. WINNER
67 Stratford Road
Asheville, N.C. 28804

29th District (2):
CHARLES W. HIPPS
505 N. Main Street
Suite 305
Waynesville, N.C. 28786

R. P. "BO" THOMAS
P.O. Drawer 220
Hendersonville, N.C. 28739

30th District (1):
DAVID R. PARNELL
P.O. Box 100
Parkton, N.C. 28371

31st District (1):
WILLIAM N. "BILL" MARTIN
P.O. Box 21363
Greensboro, N.C. 27420

32nd District (1):
WENDELL H. SAWYER
P.O. Box 148
Greensboro, N.C. 27402

33rd District (1):
MELVIN L. WATT
951 S. Independence Boulevard
Charlotte, N.C. 28215

34th District (1):
JAMES D. "JIM" MC DUFFIE
819 Eastway Drive
Charlotte, N.C. 28205

35th District (1):
LAURENCE A. "LARRY" COBB
1014 Law Building
Charlotte, N.C. 28202

North Carolina House of Representatives

1st District (2):
CHARLES D. EVANS
P.O. Box 909
Nags Head, N.C. 27959

VERNON G. JAMES
Route 4, Box 265
Elizabeth City, N.C. 27909

2nd District (1):
HOWARD B. CHAPIN
212 Smaw Road
Washington, N.C. 27889

3rd District (3):
GERALD L. ANDERSON
P.O. Box 568
Bridgeton, N.C. 28519

CHRIS S. BARKER, JR.
3911 Trent Pines Drive
New Bern, N.C. 28560

DANIEL T. LILLEY
P.O. Box 824
Kinston, N.C. 28501

4th District (3):
W. BRUCE ETHRIDGE
Route 2, Box 27
Swansboro, N.C. 28584

J. PAUL TYNDALL
414 Woodhaven Drive
Jacksonville, N.C. 28540

GERALD B. HURST
1 Amelia Lane
Jacksonville, N.C. 28540

5th District (1):
C. MELVIN CREECY
P.O. Box 526
Rich Square, N.C. 27869

6th District (1):
L. M. "MUTT" BRINKLEY
P.O. Box 3105
Ahoskie, N.C. 27910

7th District (1):
FRANK W. BALLANCE, JR.
P.O. Box 358
Warrenton, N.C. 27589

8th District (1):
J. L. MAVRETIC
Rt. 3, P.O. Box "1984"
Tarboro, N.C. 27886

9th District (2):
WALTER B. JONES, JR.
302 Hillcrest Drive
Farmville, N.C. 27828

EDWARD N. "ED" WARREN
227 Country Club Drive
Greenville, N.C. 27834

10th District (1):
WENDELL H. MURPHY
Route 1, Box 76-E
Rose Hill, N.C. 28458

11th District (2):
H. MARTIN LANCASTER
P.O. Box 916
Goldsboro, N.C. 27530

CHARLES D. WOODARD
209 Walnut Creek Drive
Goldsboro, N.C. 27530

12th District (2):
MURRAY P. POOL
P.O. Box 779
Clinton, N.C. 28328

EDD NYE
P.O. Box 8
Elizabethtown, N.C. 28337

13th District (2):
HARRY E. PAYNE, JR.
P.O. Box 1147
Wilmington, N.C. 28402

A. M. "ALEX" HALL
223 Ashford Avenue
Wilmington, N.C. 28405

14th District (1):
E. DAVID REDWINE
P.O. Box 1238
Shallotte, N.C. 28459

15th District (1):
RICHARD WRIGHT
6 Orange Street
Tabor City, N.C. 28463

16th District (3):
DANIEL H. DEVANE
P.O. Drawer N
Raeford, N.C. 28376

JOHN C. HASTY
P.O. Box 338
Maxton, N.C. 28364

SIDNEY A. LOCKS
P.O. Box 290
Lumberton, N.C. 28358

17th District (1):
C. R. EDWARDS
1502 Boros Drive
Fayetteville, N.C. 28303

LUTHER R. JERALDS
319 Jasper Street
Fayetteville, N.C. 28301

18th District (3):
R. D. "DON" BEARD
2918 Skye Drive
Fayetteville, N.C. 28303

WILLIAM E. CLARK
109 Magnolia Avenue
Fayetteville, N.C. 28305

HENRY M. TYSON
Route 7, Box 284
Fayetteville, N.C. 28306

19th District (2):
BOB R. ETHERIDGE
Box 295
Lillington, N.C. 27546

DENNIS A. WICKER
1201 Burnes Drive
Sanford, N.C. 27330

20th District (2):
GEORGE W. BRANNAN
309 Maplewood Drive
Smithfield, N.C. 27577

BARNEY PAUL WOODARD
Box 5
Princeton, N.C. 27569

21st District (1):
DANIEL "DAN" BLUE, JR.
2541 Albemarle Avenue
Raleigh, N.C. 27610

22nd District (3):
JOHN T. CHURCH
420 Woodland Road
Henderson, N.C. 27536

JAMES W. CRAWFORD, JR.
509 College Street
Oxford, N.C. 27565

WILLIAM T. WATKINS
P.O. Box 247
Oxford, N.C. 27565

23rd District (1):
H. M. "MICKEY" MICHAUX, JR.
1722 Alfred Street
Durham, N.C. 27713

24th District (2):
ANNE C. BARNES
313 Severin Street
Chapel Hill, N.C. 27514

JOE HACKNEY
104 Carolina Forest
Chapel Hill, N.C. 27514

25th District (4):
BERTHA M. HOLT
P.O. Box 1111
Burlington, N.C. 27215

J. FRED BOWMAN
814 N. Graham-Hopedale Road
Burlington, N.C. 27215

TIMOTHY H. MC DOWELL
Route 6, Box 96
Mebane, N.C. 27302

ROBERT L. MC ALISTER
Route 1, Box 336
Ruffin, N.C. 27326

26th District (1):
HERMAN C. GIST
442 Gorrell Street
Greensboro, N.C. 27406

27th District (3):
MARGARET P. KEESEE-
FORRESTER
204 N. Mendenhall Street
Greensboro, N.C. 27401

ALBERT S. LINEBERRY, SR.
300 Meadowbrook Terr.
Greensboro, N.C. 27408

FRANK J. "TRIP" SIZEMORE, III
711 Greene Street
Greensboro, N.C. 27401

28th District (2):
RICHARD E. CHALK
427 Wright Street
High Point, N.C. 27260

STEPHEN W. "STEVE" WOOD
P.O. Box 5172
High Point, N.C. 27262

29th District (1):
MICHAEL "MIKE" DECKER
6011 Bexhill Drive
Walkertown, N.C. 27051

30th District (1):
WILLIAM T. "BILL" BOYD
1315 N. Shore Drive
Asheboro, N.C. 27203

31st District (1):
JAMES M. CRAVEN
P.O. Box 44
Pinebluff, N.C. 28373

32nd District (1):
DONALD M. "DON" DAWKINS
Route 3, Box 358
Rockingham, N.C. 28379

33rd District (1):
FOYLE HIGHTOWER, JR.
715 East Wade Street
Wadesboro, N.C. 28170

34th District (4):
DWIGHT W. QUINN
213 S. Main Street
Kannapolis, N.C. 28081

JOE R. HUDSON
Route 3
Waxhaw, N.C. 28173

TIMOTHY N. "TIM" TALLENT
210 Corban Avenue, S.E.
Concord, N.C. 28025

COY C. PRIVETTE
306 Cottage Drive
Kannapolis, N.C. 28081

35th District (2):
BRADFORD V. LIGON
Route 12, Box 460
Salisbury, N.C. 28144

CHARLOTTE A. GARDNER
1500 W. Colonial Drive
Salisbury, N.C. 28144

36th District (1):
RAYMOND "RAY" WARREN
10003 Grand Junction Road
Charlotte, N.C. 28212

37th District (3):
BETSY L. COCHRANE
Box 517
Bermuda Run
Advance, N.C. 27006

CHARLES L. CROMER
Route 4, Box 362
Thomasville, N.C. 27360

JOE H. HEGE, JR.
1526 Greensboro Street
Lexington, N.C. 27292

38th District (1):
HAROLD J. BRUBAKER
Route 9, Box 268
Asheboro, N.C. 27203

39th District (3):
ANN Q. DUNCAN
4237 Mashie Drive
Pfafftown, N.C. 27040

THERESA H. ESPOSITO
207 Stanaford Road
Winston-Salem, N.C. 27104

FRANK E. RHODES
4701 Whitehaven Road
Winston-Salem, N.C. 27106

40th District (3):
DAVID H. DIAMONT
P.O. Box 784
Pilot Mountain, N.C. 27041

MARSHALL HALL
Route 5, Box 95
King, N.C. 27021

JAMES M. "JIM" COLE
Route 4
Boone, N.C. 28607

41st District (2):
JOHN WALTER BROWN
Route 2, Box 87
Elkin, N.C. 28621

GEORGE M. HOLMES
P.O. Box 217
Hamptonville, N.C. 27020

42nd District (1):
LOIS S. WALKER
611 Woods Drive
Statesville, N.C. 28677

43rd District (1):
C. ROBERT BRAWLEY
Route 5, Box 96
Mooresville, N.C. 28115

44th District (4):
DAVID W. BUMGARDNER, JR.
P.O. Box 904
Belmont, N.C. 28012

WALTER H. WINDLEY
2138 Winterlake Drive
Gastonia, N.C. 28054

DAVID J. NOLES
612 Sherrill Avenue
Lincolnton, N.C. 28092

JOHNATHAN L. RHYNE, JR.
Route 6, Box 538-R
Lincolnton, N.C. 28092

45th District (2):
AUSTIN M. ALLRAN
P.O. Box 2907
Hickory,N.C. 28603

DORIS R. HUFFMAN
Route 4, Box 81
Newton, N.C. 28650

46th District (1):
JAMES F. HUGHES
P.O. Box 277
Linville, N.C. 28646

GEORGE S. ROBINSON
501 Norwood Street, SW
Lenoir, N.C. 28645

CHARLES F. "MONROE"
BUCHANAN
Route 1
Green Mountain, N.C. 28740

47th District (1):
RAY C. FLETCHER
P.O. Box 68
Valdese, N.C. 28690

48th District (3):
JOHN J. "JACK" HUNT
P.O. Box 277
Lattimore, N.C. 28089

EDITH LEDFORD LUTZ
Route 3
Lawndale, N.C. 28090

CHARLES D. "BABE" OWENS
P.O. Box 610
Forest City, N.C. 28043

49th District (1):
ROBERT C. "BOB" HUNTER
P.O. Drawer 1330
Marion, N.C. 28752

50th District (1):
CHARLES H. HUGHES
1208 Highland Avenue
Hendersonville, N.C. 28739

51st District (4):
MARIE W. COLTON
392 Charlotte Street
Asheville, N.C. 28801

NARVEL J. "JIM" CRAWFORD
15 Edgemont Road
Asheville, N.C. 28801

GORDON H. GREENWOOD
P.O. Box 487
Black Mountain, N.C. 28711

MARTIN L. NESBITT
6 Maple Ridge Lane
Asheville, N.C. 28806

52nd District (2):
CHARLES M. BEALL
Route 3, Box 322
Clyde, N.C. 28721

LISTON B. RAMSEY
P.O. Box 337
Marshall, N.C. 28753

53rd District (1):
JEFF H. ENLOE, JR.
Route 1, Box 38
Franklin, N.C. 28734

54th District (1):
JOHN B. MC LAUGHLIN
8801 Grier Road
P.O. Box 158
Newell, N.C. 28126

55th District (1):
C. IVAN MOTHERSHEAD
1815 Queens Road
Charlotte, N.C. 28207

56th District (1):
JO GRAHAM FOSTER
1520 Maryland Avenue
Charlotte, N.C. 28209

57th District (1):
L. P. "ROY" SPOON
7028 Folger Drive
Charlotte, N.C. 28211

58th District (1):
RUTH M. EASTERLING
811 Bromley Road #1
Charlotte, N.C. 28207

59th District (1):
JAMES F. "JIM" RICHARDSON
1739 Northbrook Drive
Charlotte, N.C. 28216

60th District (1):
HOWARD C. BARNHILL
2400 Newland Road
Charlotte, N.C. 28216

61st District (1):
CASPER HOLROYD
1401 Granada Drive
Raleigh, N.C. 27612

62nd District (1)
J. RAY SPARROW
1119 Queensferry Road
Cary, N.C. 27511

63rd District (1):
MARGARET "PEGGY" STAMEY
6201 Arnold Road
Raleigh, N.C. 27607

64th District (1):
BETTY H. WISER
404 Dixie Trail
Raleigh, N.C. 27607

65th District (1):
AARON E. FUSSELL
1201 Briar Patch Lane
Raleigh, N.C. 27609

66th District (1):
ANNIE BROWN KENNEDY
3727 Spaulding Drive
Winston-Salem, N.C. 27105

67th District (1):
C. B. HAUSER
2072 K Court Avenue, NW
Winston-Salem, N.C. 27105

68th District (1):
PAUL PULLEY
P.O. Box 3600
Durham, N.C. 27701

69th District (1):
GEORGE W. MILLER, JR.
3862 Sommerset Drive
Durham, N.C. 27707

70th District (1):
MILTON F. FITCH, JR.
516 S. Lodge St.
Wilson, N.C. 27893

71st District (1):
LARRY E. ETHERIDGE
1406 Downing St.
Wilson, N.C. 27893

72nd District (1):
ALLEN C. BARBEE (D)
P.O. Box 339
Spring Hope, N.C. 27882

BUY YOUR NEW VEHICLES AT FLEET SALES COST

- Eliminate new vehicle negotiating
- Save significantly
- Forward inquiry form below
- Order vehicle of your choice
- (6) to (8) week Mfr. cycle
- No hidden costs

National Fleet Sales Corp.

115 E. Pennsylvania Ave.
Southern Pines, NC 28387

- If you wish to **AVOID** capital commitment you may **LEASE** this same vehicle
- No down payments. (Such funds are more productive for you in cash generation or money market fund.)
- Great flexibility at end of lease. Eliminate residual by buying, selling or refinancing the vehicle.

- **NEW DOMESTIC CARS, VANS, PICK-UPS & LIGHT TRUCKS**
- Participate as NCNA member in Fleet Sales Savings
- **PURCHASE** all of your vehicles for $97.50 over invoice except for Cadillacs & Lincolns. These are but $362.60 over invoice.
- Vehicles delivered to local market areas with no charge.

National Fleet Sales Corp.

The National Fleet Sales Corp. is a North Carolina corporation chartered for national sales coverage for the PLS Sales Corp. of Oregon. National Fleet Sales Corp. will purchase your vehicle for you. Delivery will normally be through a local dealer, usually less than 25 miles from the purchaser. Warranties and associated responsibilities are a function and obligation of the car manufacturer. The delivering dealer has the responsibility of providing such service, for which he is compensated by the manufacturer.

Vehicles of your choice

This program is restricted to domestic cars, vans, pickups, and light trucks. These vehicles are ordered on the factory and will be built to your exact specifications. You must be very specific when selecting options. Vehicle changes may be processed until the order has been factory preferenced for production. Thereafter purchaser is bound in all respects.

Pricing policy

No hidden costs — no add-ons for advertising, no dealer preparation charges, no new accessory installations by the delivering dealer. Any factory rebates or incentive program savings provided through the dealer organization will be passed on to purchaser.

Compare prices

Select the vehicle of your choice and specific options you want. Get a price quote from your local dealer. Then send the Inquiry Form below to NCNA. National Fleet Sales Corp. will respond to you directly with the NFSC price quote. You can then purchase through NFSC at significant savings.

Inquiry Form

Return to:
NCNA, P. O. Box 12025
Raleigh, NC 27605   purchase (   )   or lease (   )   (please check)

Name	Address	Phone

Vehicle(s) of your choice (model, make)

Options desired: _____

(This is not an offer to buy. It is a request for a price quote from National Fleet Sales Corp.)

New membership benefit—exciting vacations!

- Two exciting vacations are advertised in this issue and are available to NCNA members—the gala 7 day/7 night Caribbean Cruise and the 8 day/7 night Alpine Country Tour. A third vacation (London-Paris-Monte Carlo) will be available in November and advertised later.

NCNA has announced the completion of arrangements for these vacations with Trans National Travel of Boston, Massachusetts. These vacations are a special offering to NCNA members, their families and friends. Members of several other state nurses associations will be taking the same vacation tours. A congenial group is assured.

The Caribbean Cruise Vacation

This vacation starts with jet transportation to Miami (except dockside departures) where you and your luggage will be transferred to the ship. Once aboard, members will soon discover why a cruise is so restful and relaxing.

If you wish, for example, there's breakfast in bed, and room service is available 24 hours a day. Cruise passengers are treated to a delicious array of eight gourmet meals and snacks throughout the day—and night. Deck sports are available as well as a gymnasium, swimming pools and a sauna.

There's also celebrating galore with a Welcome Aboard Rum Swizzle Party, the Captain's Cocktail Party, and the Gala Farewell Dinner. For tripping the light fantastic, there's music and dancing every night as well as two entirely different nightclub shows.

Nassau, San Juan and St. Thomas—the most exciting ports in the Caribbean—are the ports of call we'll be visiting. For exploring, sightseeing, fabulous shopping and incredible beaches, the exotic atmosphere in each port is available without the hassle of packing and unpacking.

The Alpine Country Tour

The Alpine Country Tour begins in Frankfurt, where the old and new of the city are a happy combination. Nearby the Rhine River Valley reveals its beauty, an inspiration for generations of poets and artists. Ancient castles, cobblestoned streets, and soaring cathedrals dot the landscape.

Then it's on to Munich, the capital of warm-hearted Bavaria where rare treasures fill the museums and old-fashioned fun is the rule. Delicious dining and fine wines and beers are also local specialties. A one-night stay in the Black Forest rounds out a delightful week.

A six-night extension takes you high in the Swiss Alps amid majestic mountain peaks in St. Moritz-Champfer, the resort area favored by the jet set. Too soon you're off to the magical Black Forest of fairytale fame.

Special finds in shopping are local wares, such as cuckoo clocks, cheeses, handmade crystal, watches, and antiques. Throughout Europe, American travelers will appreciate that, thanks to the strength of the dollar, they are able to see more, do more and buy more at prices that are amazing.

The Alpine Country Tour offers many included features such as Welcome Arrival Get-Togethers in Frankfurt, Munich, St. Moritz-Champfer and the Black Forest. All hotels are modern and comfortable, with all the conveniences needed for a relaxing vacation.

Members who are interested in these vacations are urged to watch their mailboxes carefully for more information. Complete details on all prices, departure dates and cities will be coming soon. However, only a limited number of accommodations will be available, so make your reservations early to avoid disappointment.

Calendar of Events

The following "Calendar of Events" will inform members of meetings of NCNA structural units and other related groups and agencies. All structural unit meetings will take place in headquarters unless otherwise indicated.

Meetings of the NCNA Board of Directors, committees and commissions are open to the membership. Members may attend to see the Association in action and to communicate with the elected and appointed officials. Members planning to attend should notify NCNA at least two days prior to the meeting, so that we can plan for adequate seating and plenty of coffee!

Date/Hour	Event
February 20, 9:30 a.m.	Nursing Practice Administrator Section
February 23, 10 a.m.	Conference Group of Psych-Mental Health Nurse Specialists
February 28, 10 a.m.	Peer Assistance Program Committee
March 1	NCNA Executive Committee
March 5, 12-4 p.m.	Executive Committee, Medical-Surgical Division
March 6 - March 8	ANA Board Meeting
March 9, 9:30 a.m.	Federation of Nursing Organizations
March 12	"Day at the Legislature Workshop"
March 13	Commission on Member Services
March 14	Ad Hoc Committee on Structure
March 15, 9 a.m.	NCNA Board of Directors
March 20	Commission on Practice
March 22, 10 a.m.-3 p.m.	Commission on Education
March 28, 10 a.m.-2 p.m.	Peer Assistance Program Committee
March 29	NCNA Executive Committee
April 1	Commission on Member Services
April 5	Holiday, Office Closed
April 8	Holiday, Office Closed
April 17, 9:30 a.m.-12 N	Nursing Practice Administrators Section
April 18	Ad Hoc Committee on Structure
April 19, 9 a.m.	NCNA Board of Directors
April 23, 10 a.m.-2 p.m.	Peer Assistance Program Committee
April 24, 1 p.m.-4 p.m.	Headquarters Committee
April 29	Ad Hoc Committee on Workshop Planning

 **on Districts**

by Betty Godwin

November district meetings across the state were planned for those who attended the NCNA Convention to share their experiences with those members unable to attend. This type of sharing rewards those members, unable to attend, for their support of fellow members who represented the district.

It seems that most districts set aside some time for fun and relaxation during the usual meeting times in December. Particularly, for NCNA members, the holiday season comes at the best time of the year. Members are recovering from convention, and this year, from the general elections. December and January are months that allow districts to slow the momentum just enough to regroup and begin plans for the new year.

There are several districts with exciting activities on their calendars. Districts Eleven, Thirteen and Fourteen are involved in a community project, "Health Vote '85", sponsored by the N.C. Foundation for Alternative Health Programs. See the article in this issue for more information about "Health Vote '85."

There are several districts that have selected this time of year to focus on membership recruitment. District Thirty-one designated their January meeting as "non-member" night. Judy Seamon was the speaker and shared information about certification. District Eight targeted potential members from senior nursing students by having members Sheila Bryson and Cheryl Workman attend the Nursing Career Day at North Carolina State A & T University. This Career Day, on November 14, 1984, was for area university senior nursing students. District Eight is planning a reception at Wesley Long Hospital in the near future to recruit new members.

Nursing Board names associate director

Mary Ann Brewer has been appointed associate director of the North Carolina Board of Nursing.

Brewer has been employed by the Board since 1980 as educational consultant. Prior to joining the Board staff, she had experiences in associate degree, diploma, and baccalaureate educational programs and in various clinical settings. She also served a four-year term as a member of the Board of Nursing.

Tranbarger runs for Cabinet office

Russell Eugene Tranbarger of Greensboro is the only NCNA member on the ANA 1985 ballot. Tranbarger is one of seven candidates for three positions on the Cabinet on Nursing Services.

Elections will be held at the ANA House of Delegates meeting July 22-25 in Kansas City.

ANA councils are in the process of nominating for their executive and nominating committees. A number of NCNA members are considering offering their names for these positions.

Warm welcome to new staff member

Dorothy D. Bennett of Fayetteville joined the NCNA staff on December 1, 1984, as an administrative assistant.

Dot and the computer and word processor arrived at about the same time. Fortunately, they were not strangers, and Dot quickly showed us how useful our new equipment can be.

Prior to joining the NCNA staff, Dot worked for IBM in Fayetteville and prior to that experience was executive secretary for Fayetteville Ambulatory Services. Part of her IBM duties was to demonstrate the word processor to customers.

She has a daughter who graduates from high school this year. Dot will be moving to Raleigh in a few months. Dot fits right in with our staff, and we welcome her to NCNA!

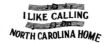

RESOLUTIONS PROCEDURE

The Committee on Resolutions functions throughout the biennium in receiving and studying proposed resolutions submitted to it.

A resolution is a main motion put before the policy-making body on a subject of great importance, expressed in formal wording. A resolution adopted by the House of Delegates of the North Carolina Nurses Association establishes or makes known the position of the Association on matters of state and/or national scope and significance affecting nurses, nursing, and the health needs of the public.

Substantive resolutions are those which deal with basic principles and policies of the Association or with issues of national concern to nurses as practitioners and citizens. These resolutions are thoughtfully and carefully developed in advance of a convention for presentation to the House of Delegates. These may include recommendations for legislation or for joint or separate action with other organizations on matters of mutual interest.

Deadline—Substantive resolutions must be submitted to the Committee on Resolutions by May 15, preceding the fall convention.

Emergency resolutions are those whose significance could not have been apparent by the deadline date and which, because of timeliness, require immediate action.

Deadline—Emergency resolutions must be submitted no later than 5 p.m. on Wednesday, October 25, 1985, at the convention.

Initiation of Resolutions—Resolutions may be submitted to the Committee on Resolutions by individual members, the NCNA Board of Directors, district associations, any structural unit of the Association, or may be initiated by the Committee on Resolutions.

Disposition—The Committee on Resolutions will review resolutions for content, relevance, appropriateness, timeliness, and scope. The Committee may edit, rewrite, or combine resolutions.

The Committee will report to the Board of Directors in advance of the convention a recommendation for approval or disapproval of each resolution received by the deadline date. The Committee may recommend referral of a resolution to an appropriate committee or other structural units of the Association.

All resolutions received by the Committee shall be reported to the House of Delegates with the Committee's recommendation.

All resolutions approved by the Committee will be put before the House of Delegates for vote.

Originators of resolutions will be advised whether their particular resolution has been approved, disapproved, or substantially changed. Reasons for not approving resolutions will be stated.

Copies of substantive resolutions approved for presentation to the House of Delegates will be distributed in advance of the convention to district associations and to delegates.

Guidelines for writing resolutions are available from the Resolutions Committee at NCNA headquarters.

NEWS BRIEFS

● The Third National Symposium on The Impaired Nurse, "Re-en-try.—Professional Issues: Rights and Obligations," will be held May 1-4, 1985, in Atlanta. Sponsored by Emory University Nell Hodgson Woodruff School of Nursing, Georgia Nurses Association, and Georgia Board of Nursing, the symposium will address the social, legal, and economic issues related to re-entry, along with rights and obligations of the nurse and the profession to society. Contact: Rose C. Dilday, Continuing Education Program, Emory University School of Nursing, Atlanta, Georgia 30322.

● "Collaborative Practice: A Professional Practice System", March 28-29 in Hartford, CT, will present the global concept of collaboration in theory and its application in action, as demonstrated in Hartford Hospital's project. Fee is $195. Contact William Kennedy, Educational Facilities, 560 Hudson Street, Hartford, CT 06106.

● The first conference of the N.C. Coalition for High Blood Pressure Control, "Working Together for High Blood Pressure Control," will be held March 15, 1985, at the Raleigh Hilton. Contact Debra Wilcox, Lenoir County Health Department 200 Rhodes Avenue, Kinston 28501.

● ANA is one of six national groups co-sponsoring the 1985 National Nurse Practitioner Forum, "Coalition for Practice: Future Markets, Future Models," May 3-5 at the Hyatt Regency in Chicago. Keynote Speaker Lucie S. Kelly, Ph.D., R.N., F.A.A.N., will discuss "Shaping the Future through Coalitions in Practice." Other topics will be: professional/legal regulation, prospective payment, image marketing, political influence, and diagnostic classification. Fee for ANA members is $225, and registration deadline is April 5. Contact: Marketing, ANA, 2420 Pershing Road, Kansas City, Missouri 64108.

● The North Carolina League for Nursing will hold its annual meeting March 14-15, 1985, at the Greensboro Sheraton. Topic is "Maintaining Quality of Care in an Era of Cost Containment."

● *Pages from Nursing History,* a collection of articles originally published in *Nursing Outlook, American Journal of Nursing,* and *Nursing Research,* is available at $7.95 from AJN Company, Educational Services Division, NO66, 555 West 57th Street, New York, NY 10019. The theme is important women contributing to nursing's history.

● The ANA Council on Continuing Education is inviting nominees for its $500 scholarship to be awarded in 1985 to a council affiliate who is pursuing graduate education in nursing. Deadline for applications is March 31. Applications are available from ANA.

● A conference on "Transculturalism—Impact on Health Care System," will be held April 15-16, 1985, in Nashville, TN, sponsored by Vanderbilt University School of Nursing, Center for Continuing Education, Nashville. Contact Director, Center for C.E., Vanderbilt University School of Nursing, 515 Godchaux Hall, Nashville, TN 37240.

● March 8, 1985, is the deadline for abstracts for a December 4-7, 1985, conference sponsored by the ANA Council of Nurse Researchers. Theme is "Nursing Research: Integration into the Social Structure." Contact: Karen Wasinger, Council Services, ANA.

● NAACOG will hold its Fifth National Meeting June 2-6, 1985, at the New Orleans Hilton. The theme is "Charting a Course Toward Excellence."

● The 1985 John W. Umstead Lecture Series will be held March 13-15 at the Radisson Plaza Hotel, Raleigh. Topic is "Family Violence: Its Impact, Management and Prevention."

(Cont. on page 20)

NCNA professional items for sale

Portfolios (black with gold NCNA logo) . . . . $5 (reduced!)
Paperweights with NCNA logo $4
Cross Pens (black) with NCNA logo $18.50
NCNA Logo Cross Stitch Graph $1.50
NCNA Logo Cross Stitch Kits . . . . $5 (reduced!)
　(Logo, graph, cloth, thread)
History of Nursing in North Carolina Books:
　Hardback $3
　Paperback $2
　Update (Highlights 1935-1976) $1
NCNA Coffee Mugs
　(clear glass embossed with red NCNA logo) $3.25
Nursing: A Social Policy Statement $2
Perspectives on the Code for Nurses $2

Please order from:　N.C. Nurses Association
　　　　　　　　　　　P.O. Box 12025
　　　　　　　　　　　Raleigh, NC 27605

Spotlighting minority nurses in NCNA

The Human Rights Committee Corner

by
Dr. Johnea D. Kelley
Chairperson, Human Rights Committee

The program focus for the February meeting of District Eleven will be a salute to black nurses of the District and the NCNA. The salute will consist of a biographical profile and visual image of the nurse honorees. More than 15 nurses will be honored during the hour long program. They all are involved in nursing practice, education, or administration. All have made significant contributions to the profession in one or more areas and have invested personal time in community activities. Most reside and work in the counties that make up District Eleven.

This program is the first of its kind in any district and is very timely, because February is Black History month. It is a time for remembering and recognizing the achievements and contributions of black people's progress, albeit in the profession of nursing or any other area of work.

Additionally, this is an opportunity for your NCNA Human Rights Committee to become familiar with the honoree's strengths and contributions; to serve as a catalyst in seeking election or appointment of black nurses to offices in the Association; and to encourage membership and participation in the districts and at the state level.

The Human Rights Committee of NCNA salutes District Eleven on its quantum leap forward to recognize these nurses during Black History month. Among these are:

Ms. Thelma Brown
Ms. Elizabeth Burkett
Ms. Gwendolyn Andrews
Ms. Gwendolyn Jones
Ms. Joan Martin-Jones
Dr. Inez Tucker
Ms. Ernestine Small
Ms. Mary Baldwin
Ms. Dorothy Cox
Ms. Patricia Blue
Ms. Cathy Hughes
Ms. Helen Miller
Dr. Johnea D. Kelley
Ms. Evelyn Wicker
Ms. Maude Speakman

We hope you'll see your colleagues at work in all levels of activities in the Association. Look for the Human Rights Committee's Corner in future issues of the *Tar Heel Nurse.*

Twelve win free convention registration

Prior to the 1984 NCNA Convention, the Membership Committee conducted a membership recruitment project—"Five for Free"—free convention registration for the member recruiting five new members. Twelve members came out winners!

Receiving free convention registration were: Greta Powell, Kay Helfrich, Gwendolyn Waddell, Debbie Hutchinson, and Joanne Beckman, all of District Eleven; Donna Jackson, District Thirty-Three; Judith Kuykendall, District Thirty; Debbie Craver, District Nine; Linda Wright, Carol Koontz, and Mary Estep, all of District Two; and Carolyn Billings, District Thirteen.

News Briefs
(Continued from page 19)

● Papers presented at the 1983 Scientific Session of the American Academy of Nursing are available in a publication, *Nursing Research and Policy Formation: The Case of Prospective Payment* (Pub. No. G-164) from the ANA Publications Unit at $10.

● The National Directory of Hispanic Nurses is now being updated. All Hispanic nurses interested in being listed are requested to contact Dr. Ildaura Murello-Rohde, 300 West 108th Street, Apt. 12A, New York, NY 10025.

NORTH CAROLINA NURSES ASSOCIATION
P O Box 12025
Raleigh North Carolina 27605

Vol. 47, No. 1   January-February 1985

Official Publication of the North Carolina Nurses Association, 103 Enterprise St., Raleigh, N.C. Tel. (919) 821-4250. Published 6 times a year. Subscription price $12 per year, included with membership dues. Indexed in *Cumulative Index to Nursing and Allied Health Literature* and available in MICROFORM, University Microfilms International.

JUDITH B. SEAMON .... President
HETTIE L. GARLAND .... President-Elect
GALE B JOHNSTON .... Vice-President
SALLY S TODD .... Secretary
CAROL A OSMAN .... Treasurer

Staff

FRANCES N. MILLER ..... Executive Director
HAZEL BROWNING .... Assoc. Exec. Director
BETTY GODWIN .... Asst. Exec. Director
PATRICIA W. BRYAN ..... Administrative Asst.
DOROTHY BENNETT .... Administrative Asst.

● 1985 NCNA

ISSN 0039-9620

[TAR HEEL
NURSE

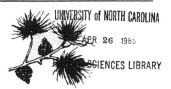

Vol. 47, No. 2   OFFICIAL PUBLICATION OF THE NORTH CAROLINA NURSES ASSOCIATION   March-April 1985

May 6 is National Nurses' Day

"Nursing care makes the difference" is the message of National Nurses' Day, May 6, 1985. Nurses in North Carolina will join nurses across the country in marking this event.

ANA President Eunice Cole, R.N., targets competition in health care and the availability and affordability of health care services as critical national issues. "These questions that are only lately receiving attention from multiple segments of society have long been of concern to nurses," she said. "On National Nurses' Day, we rededicate ourselves to providing quality nursing care services to the public at prices they can afford."

District associations have received a National Nurses' Day promotional kit from ANA containing suggestions about the various ways nurses contribute to health care delivery to "make a difference;" guidelines for working with the media; suggested local activities to increase nursing's visibility in the community; a statistical fact sheet on nursing and an annotated bibliography of specific references to document the message that "nursing care makes the difference."

Legislative update

NCNA monitors several bills moving through General Assembly

By Hazel Browning

Since convening on February 5, the North Carolina General Assembly members have been quite busy. As of this writing, 230 House bills and 107 Senate bills have been introduced.

A 1985 version of the recodification of the Administrative Procedures Act has been introduced as House Bill (HB) 52 and assigned to the Judiciary 4 committee. Rep. Billy Watkins (D-Oxford) is the bill sponsor. This issue has been reviewed in past issues of the *Tar Heel Nurse* since it first surfaced in the 1984 short session. At that time, much concern was voiced on behalf of most occupational licensing boards, since the bill introduced in the short session took away the licensing board's authority to discipline its own licensees. The current bill, HB 52, includes similar language. Some events have occurred since the bill's introduction which indicate that the concerns voiced on behalf of the nursing profession and the Board of Nursing are being resolved.

On March 5, members of all four House Judiciary committees met to discuss HB 52. The bill sponsor discussed a proposed committee substitute for HB 52. Since the proposed substitute has not been adopted by the committee, it has not been available in the printed bills office and lobbyists have not had an opportunity to review it. The bill sponsors tell us, however, that the substitute exempts the *(continued on page 5)*

(continued on page 5)

(Top) Rep. Richard Wright, Tabor City, listens to Annie Hayes, Whiteville.

Some 380 nurses and legislators enjoyed a reception on March 12 at the end of a busy day of briefing on legislative issues and visits in the State Legislative Building. Left, nurses chat with Rep. Raymond Warren of Charlotte.

Message from the President
Judith B. Seamon

From all reports, the Day at the Legislature workshop was a resounding success and served not only as an opportunity to learn more about legislative issues and lobbying skills, but also provided a forum for nurses to demonstrate with confidence the legislative knowledge and skills they have already acquired.

The development of sound political process and power is a major facet of professionalism in nursing. It allows us to have a major influence in determining policies and decisions that affect our profession and health care. Clearly we have developed the correct perspective about political power and influence and are becoming increasingly skilled in using it to enhance the consumers' voice in their health care choices and to liberate nursing practice from unnecessary and unfair constraints.

It has long been our responsibility to be accountable as health care professionals. Learning to use the political process is a major part of that responsibility. Let's keep up the good work by staying informed and acting when necessary. Most importantly, let's continue to move in the direction of becoming increasingly proactive and less reactive.

EDITORIAL

Frances N. Miller
Executive Director

The Invisible Nurses

NCNA makes a persistent effort to have registered nurses appointed to advisory and policy-making bodies. Our spokesmen call attention time and time again to nurses as a rich resource to the state and local communities in health care matters and other efforts to improve the quality of life.

Nurses have had some success in gaining those appointments and a variety of leadership roles on a state level as well as in their own communities. But all too often they seem to be invisible **as nurses,** whether serving on a statewide advisory committee, a conference planning committee, a local mental health board, a PTA executive committee, a local government task force, or a county volunteer organization board of directors.

What's our complaint? When these boards, committees, and task forces are listed—in the press, in conference printed programs, in annual reports, in minutes of meetings—more times than not the nurses' names appear without the "R.N." One has to know them through some other context to know they are nurses. Physicians and dentists almost always are listed with the M.D., or D.D.S. You know right away that here is a physician or dentist giving his/her time to a group working for the public good.

Why is a professional identity not equally important to registered nurses? Let's make it important enough that registered nurses will see to it that the R.N. appears after their names to make nursing more visible. Wherever the hundreds of you are giving your time, skills, and knowledge to community and health-related activities—be proud of your professional identity. Put the R.N. after your name!

Correction

The Resolutions Procedure printed in the January-February *Tar Heel Nurse* contained a great big typo in the deadline for submitting emergency resolutions for consideration of the 1985 House of Delegates.

The deadline is 5 p.m. on Wednesday, October 23.

Think Membership

Dear Editor:

This letter is a response to the article entitled *"Buyer's Uninformed on Insurance Benefits"* that appeared in the September-October issue of the *Tar Heel Nurse.* Since the appearance of that article, I have attended the Commission on Member Services meeting (February 6, 1985) to further explore the basis for the article.

As a nurse consultant for an insurance company, I am frequently asked by insureds about their coverage for private duty nursing services. Like any other covered benefit in a contract, covered and non-covered situations exist. Insureds are encouraged to inquire about covered expenses **before** services are rendered in order to prevent a possible costly denial. Part of my job is to review private duty nursing claims. One of the main reasons for private duty nursing denials is directly related to the **level of care** the nurse delivered. For example, I have reviewed nurses' notes where the private duty nurse "sat" with a patient while the floor nurse administered medications, suctioned the patient, and performed other necessary care for the patient. (Of course, other nursing functions include periodic assessments and **ability** to intervene when necessary).

When a private duty nurse is receiving the payment for the services, she should be accountable for the care she gives.

If professional nurses are better able to decide what level of care is needed, then we should push for those changes. Until then, nurses can educate health care consumers about levels of care normally covered and possibly prevent a costly private duty nursing claim denial.

IF SOME insurance companies are not informing their buyers about covered and non-covered services, let's strive to change this practice for the sake of our consumers. Let's not categorize **ALL** insurance companies as being neglectful.

Fay Harris, R.N., M.S.N.

Lieutenant Governor addresses NCNA workshop

Some 180 registered nurses and student nurses met on March 12 at the Holiday Inn State Capital in Raleigh to participate in the NCNA "Day at the Legislature."

Lieutenant Governor Bob Jordan was the luncheon speaker. In his address he identified major issues facing the 1985 General Assembly and urged nurses to be an active group in the legislative arena. He commended nurses for past legislative achievements. Other special luncheon guests were Senator Wilma Woodard (D-14th Senate District), and Wade Smith, legal counsel for NCNA and current chairman of the N.C. Democratic Party.

During the morning briefing session, participants heard members of the NCNA Committee on Legislation discuss current legislative issues of interest to nurses: Carolyn Goforth, Committee chairman, Estelle Fulp, Alene Watson, and Martha Henderson. Frances Miller, executive director, discussed legislative strategies.

Participants spent the afternoon session at the Legislative Building, observing House and Senate sessions and meeting with their area legislators. At 5 p.m., a reception was held at the Holiday Inn State Capital honoring members of the General Assembly and the Council of State. More than 380 people attended. Photographs included in this issue of the *Tar Heel Nurse* speak much louder than words. Everyone had a wonderful time!

The workshop was a stimulating learning experience for those who attended. Many thanks to the subcommittee chaired by Estelle Fulp for planning another successful "Day at the Legislature" workshop.

Scenes at 'Day at the Legislature'

Alene Watson, left, member of the Committee on Legislation, gets an earful from Rep. Peggy Stamey, Raleigh.

Senator Donald Kincaid, Lenoir, is intent in a conversation with two of his nurse constituents.

President-Elect Hettie Garland visits with Rep. Jim Crawford and Rep. Marie Colton, both of Asheville.

Rep. Dave Bumgardner, Belmont, meets some of his constituents at the reception.

Workshop scheduled in May on 'Silent Workplace Hazards'

As technology advances nurses must become increasingly aware of and take necessary precautions to protect themselves from hazards within their daily work environment. It was the recognition of this issue of increasing concern that prompted the Commission on Member Services to host a session at the 1984 convention that addressed this topic. Based on the numerous verbal and written evaluative comments, the Workshop Planning Committee is offering a day-long program to give you the opportunity to explore this area in more detail.

Dr. Jerry J. Tulis, director of the Bio-hazard Science Program, School of Public Health, University of North Carolina in Chapel Hill, will begin the program. Dr. Tulis has presented lectures nationally on this topic. He will cover a broad spectrum of hazards that are found throughout the hospital environment. Dr. Bonnie Rodgers, faculty at UNC-CH School of Nursing, will concentrate on necessary precautions nurses should employ when administering neoplastic drugs. The program will be completed by Dr. Julie Falconer, a nurse and the associate director of Employee Occupational Health Medicine at Duke Medical Center. Dr. Falconer will complement the other faculty by expanding on the implications for nurses concerning workplace hazards.

The focus of the workshop will be on hazards found in the hospital setting. As nurses know, these hazards are by no means limited to this setting. Among the numerous areas of concern are infectious diseases, radiation, anesthetic gases, electrical equipment, drugs, etc. There are special groups of nurses who have particular concerns that will be addressed, such as the pregnant nurse.

The workshop is scheduled for May 17, 1985, at the Wake AHEC Auditorium, Wake Medical Center in Raleigh. Registration begins at 8:30 a.m., and the program will extend from 9 a.m. until 3 p.m. The registration fee is $25 for members, $35 for non-members, and $10 for full-time nursing students. **Registration deadline is May 3, 1985.** No refunds for cancellations after May 13, 1985, but substitutions are welcome.

Registration Form

Name _____

Address _____ Phone No. (home) _____ (work) _____

Employer and Position _____

_____ Member   _____ Non-Member   _____ Full-time student

_____ Amount Enclosed

*Return registration to: Attn: Registration, NCNA, P.O. Box 12025, Raleigh, NC 27605.

NEWS BRIEFS

● "Oncology Nursing Society Tenth Anniversary Congress," Houston, TX, May 15-18, 1985. For information contact Nancy Berkowitz, Oncology Nursing Society, 3111 Banksville Rd., Suite 200, Pittsburgh, PA 15216)

● The Seventh Annual Continuing Education Conference, "Enrichment-Practice - Issue - Confrontation" sponsored by the Florida Nurses Association will be held May 16-17, 1985, in Orlando, Florida. For information contact Paula Massey, associate executive director, Florida Nurses Association, P.O. Box 6985, Orlando, Florida, 32853 or call 305-896-3261.

● The 1985 National Nurse Practitioner Forum, "Coalition for Practice: Future Markets, Future Models," will be held May 3-5, 1985, in Chicago, Illinois. For information contact ANA, 2420 Pershing Road, Kansas City, MO 64108.

● The ANA Council on Psychiatric and Mental Health Nursing Practice has announced plans to co-sponsor a conference for psychiatric nurses in Israel, following the 18th quadrennial Congress of the International Council of Nurses. This two-day meeting will focus on New Trends in Psychiatric Nursing and Psychiatric Nursing in the Community, June 26-27, 1985. For information contact Kenness International, Inc., One Park Ave., New York, New York, 10016; 800-235-6400 or 212-684-2010.

● The Second Annual North Carolina Health Promotion and Wellness Institute will be held June 23-28, 1985 in Raleigh, NC, on the campus of Meredith College. The institute is sponsored by Wake Area Health Education Center and Meredith College, along with several cc-sponsors including state government health agencies, academic institutions, and industries. For information contact Wake AHEC, 3000 New Bern Ave., Raleigh, 27610; 919-755-8018 or 919-755-8522.

● "Nurses in Business" is a conference for nurses who own their own business, offer "on-the-side" consultation or education services, or want to start a business. It will be held May 16-17, 1985, in Atlanta, GA., by the Continuing Education Program, Nell Hodgson Woodruff School of Nursing, Emory University. The program includes topics on home health, education and consultation, finance, tax planning, organizational structures, networking and marketing. The early registration fee is $135 (by April 26); $145 thereafter. Contact the School of Nursing at Emory University, Atlanta, GA 30322 for further information.

● The Maternal-Child Health Committee of the Massachusetts Nurses Association has developed several pamphlets which highlight parent/child interactions during play activities at different stages of development. Future pamphlets will be available focusing on pre-school, school age, and adolescent children. Single copies are free at present, and bulk prices available upon request. (Contact Massachusetts Nurses Association, 376 Boylston Street, Boston, MASS. 02116 or call 617-482-5465)

Booth retirement set for May

Audrey Booth is retiring in May as associate dean of the UNC-CH School of Nursing. She will be honored at a reception on April 30, hosted by the UNC-CH School of Nursing. UNC-CH nursing alumni honored her recently with the Alumnus of the Year Award.

Booth's contributions to nursing in North Carolina have been numerous— chairman of the N.C. Board of Nursing, director of Statewide AHEC Nursing Activities; member of the Joint Practice Committee of NCNA and the N.C. Medical Society, and currently a member of the NCNA Subcommittee on Third Party Reimbursement.

She hopes to have time after retirement for hobbies and becoming more involved in political activity.

Legislative Update from page 1

occupational licensing boards from requirements that contested cases be heard by an independent administrative judge, except in the case of license revocation. In such cases, the licensee would have the option of appealing the case to an administrative judge for a trial *de novo*, allowing both the defendant and the plaintiff to plea their case as if it had never been tried.

Future issues of the *Tar Heel Nurse* will track this legislation.

HB 84, an act clarifying the Health Maintenance Organization (HMO) statute, was introduced on February 18 by Rep. Gerald Anderson (D-New Bern). The bill came out of the House Insurance Committee quickly and passed the full House with ease.

Lobbyists sought to impress upon Senate Insurance Committee members that this "simple little 9-line bill" had far reaching effects. The bill as passed by the House would exempt HMOs from all provisions of Chapter 90, which includes the statutes regulating health care service occupations such as nursing, medicine, dentistry, pharmacy, etc., as well as the Controlled Substances Act and other health care regulations. HMOs have been exempt from provisions of Chapter 90 relating to the practice of medicine for some time to avoid the problem of "corporate practice of medicine."

A subcommittee of the Senate Insurance Committee heard objections of several associations, including NCNA, and adopted a substitute bill that exempts HMOs only from the medical and dental practice acts. The substitute bill was reported to the full committee on March 19 and given a favorable report by the full Senate Insurance Committee. It passed the Senate on March 20 and goes to the house for concurrence.

The NCNA Committee on Legislation and Board of Directors have endorsed a committee substitute for Senate Bill 39, An Act to Make the Use of Seat Belts in Motor Vehicles Mandatory. The bill was introduced by Senator Bob Warren (D-Benson). As the title indicates, the bill mandates the use of seat belts in motor vehicles for all persons over the age of 2. Certain exemptions apply for handicapped persons, rural letter carriers, motorcycles, persons making frequent stops and leaving the vehicle but not driving in excess of 20 m.p.h. and motor vehicles with a seating capacity of less than 4 or more than 9. A nine-month period is allowed for warning violations and, after such time, violators will pay a fine of $25. No driver license points will be assessed on violators' driving records.

A press release has been prepared announcing NCNA's endorsement of this legislation. Sarah Pike Brown, R.N., of Raleigh, represented NCNA in presenting testimony at a public hearing on the bill held at the Legislative Building on March 20.

The NCNA Board of Directors has endorsed a committee substitute for SB 18, an act to establish the N. C. Center for Missing Children. Senator Charles Hipps (D-Waynesville) introduced this legislation on February 8. The bill provides for a resource center focusing on protection of missing children and coordinates all state activities with respect to them.

Two bills have been introduced in the House of Representatives calling for abolishment of the Pay Equity Advisory Committee. HB 126 was introduced on February 26 by Rep. Michael Decker (R-Walkertown) and on March 18, Rep. Richard Wright (D-Tabor City) introduced HB 236.

The pay equity issue is one that is of interest to nursing since our profession is by far predominantly female. We need to support the efforts of such people as Senator Wilma Woodard, who has consistently championed this cause for women and equality in North Carolina by speaking out in favor of pay equity. Every member of the House and Senate should receive letters from their nurse constituents **opposing** HB 125 and HB 236. If HB 126 or HB 236 passes, our state, especially the female sector, will have lost a major achievement of the last session of the General Assembly.

A bill to recodify the Mental Health Law was introduced in late February. A Joint Committee of the House and Senate has been appointed to consider the legislation.

The bill to authorize direct reimbursement to certain nurses is still in the draft stage. Future issues of the *Tar Heel Nurse* will include more information on this issue.

By now, every NCNA member should have received the first issue of *Nurses' Notes from the Capital.* This new service to subscribers is designed to keep you abreast of legislative issues of concern to nursing. The newsletter will be mailed every 2 weeks throughout the legislative session. The newsletter is available to students who are members of NCNA or NCANS at member rates. Use the form below and subscribe today!

SUBSCRIPTION FORM . . . .
Nurses' Notes from the Capital

Name _____

Address _____

_____

Telephone (H) _____ (W) _____

NCNA MEMBER _____ (Rate — $5)

NON-MEMBER _____ (Rate — $40)   AMOUNT ENCLOSED $ _____

COMPLETE AND RETURN FORM WITH APPROPRIATE SUBSCRIPTION FEE *TODAY* TO:
NCNA, P.O. BOX 12025, RALEIGH, NC 27605

Tell Us If You Are Interested . . . .

The Medical-Surgical Division is planning a continuing education program, "Living With Pain", as a result of positive evaluations from a similar program held at the 1984 convention.

Help the Division in successful planning by completing this short survey and return by May 15.

_____ Yes   _____ No   Would you be interested in attending a program that focuses on key concepts of pain control as they relate to nursing practice areas including adult medical-surgical, home care, critical care, pediatrics, etc.?

_____ Yes   _____ No   Would you be willing to pay a registration fee between $20 -$40 (lunch included)?

Indicate your preference for program dates:

_____ October 22, 1985 (day prior to beginning of 1985 convention)

_____ January 17, 1986

_____ February 21, 1986

Complete and return to NCNA, P.O. Box 12025, Raleigh, NC 27605 by May 15.

The ABC's of Finance for Nurse Managers
Accounting, Budgets, Control

Description: THIS IS A WORKSHOP ABOUT THE *BUSINESS* OF NURSING

Until nurse managers can design and control their budgets, they will be unable to control their practice.

- Can you talk with your administrator, accountant or comptroller using *their* language?
- Can you use the terms *asset, liability, depreciation, zero-based budget, accrual* with confidence?
- Can you defend your budget requests in terms of return on investment?
- Can you use your current budgeting process as a managerial tool?
- Can you read and understand a balance sheet and income statement?

The purpose of this workshop is to guide participants through the basics of the budgeting and accounting process by defining terms and decoding financial jargon. Through lecture, small group discussion and case studies participants will have the opportunity to apply the budgeting and accounting process within a nursing context and will gain confidence in their abilities to interact with financial managers.

Target Audiences:
This workshop is designed for directors of nursing, supervisors, head nurses, and others with management responsibilities. This is an excellent opportunity for many nurses not currently involved in nursing financial management, but who are interested in pursuing a career that involves management, or who are involved in education.

Objectives:
At the conclusion of the workshop, participants will be able to:
1. Define selected accounting terms.
2. Identify several types of budgets.
3. Describe the budgeting process.
4. Name three variances to use in budget analysis.
5. Identify components of a balance sheet and income statement.
6. Recognize the role of budgeting within the context of the prospective reimbursement environment.
7. Practice the budgeting process using case studies.

Faculty

SALLY S. TODD, R.N., M.S.N.
Sally Todd is the founder and owner of Sally S. Todd & Associates, an organization that offers management training for nurses and other health care professionals. She has worked in a number of nursing positions, including head nurse in a critical care unit. She has held faculty positions at Case Western Reserve University, Duke University, and the University of North Carolina-Chapel Hill.

JOSEPH H. TODD, C.P.A.
Joe Todd is a partner in the certified public accounting firm of Todd & Rivenbark. He was previously associated with the international firm of Deliotte Haskins & Sells in their Atlanta office. His practice currently brings him into contact with a number of clients in the health care field. He has taught accounting and tax courses at North Carolina State University.

Dates and Location:
June 24, 1985   Mountain AHEC, Asheville, N.C. 8:30 a.m. - 4:00 p.m.
July 8, 1985   Wake AHEC, Raleigh, N.C. 8:30 a.m. - 4:00 p.m.

Registration Fees:
Members $25   Non-Members $35
Full Time Students $10

Registration fees include workshop materials and breaks. *A thorough workshop manual will be provided for each participant.*

Registration deadline: June 17 for the Asheville location and July 1 for the Raleigh location. No refunds within 72 hours of workshop but substitutions are welcome.

Workshops are produced in association with Nursing Education at Mountain and Wake Area Health Education Centers.

CERP credit pending.

Pre-registration Form

Name _____

Address _____ Home Phone _____ Work Phone _____

Employer and Position _____

_____ Member ($25)   _____ Non-Member ($35)   _____ Full Time Student ($10)

Indicate location you will attend
_____ June 24, 1985, Mountain AHEC in Asheville, N.C.   _____ July 8, 1985, Wake AHEC in Raleigh, N.C.
Registration Deadline is June 17, 1985   Registration Deadline is July 1, 1985

Amount enclosed $ _____

Return to: ATTN: Registration, NCNA, P.O. Box 12025, Raleigh, NC 27605

Focus on Districts

by Betty Godwin

Districts Three, Eight, Nine, and Thirty-One deserve a "round of applause" for their successful program, "Professional Issues in Nursing." The program was co-sponsored with NCNA Workshop Planning Committee and produced in association with the Nursing Division of Northwest AHEC.

The program was presented by Carolyn Billings, R.N., M.S.N., C.N.S., on February 12, 1985, at Babcock Auditorium in Winston-Salem. There were questions about whether, with the present economy, nurses could take time from work to attend a program that was not of a clinical nature. Thanks to the efforts of the co-sponsoring districts, 45 nurses attended!

By co-sponsoring the workshop, the district presidents—Kay Jackson of District Three, Patti Hunsucker of District Eight, Debbie Craver of District Nine, and Loucille Swaim of District Thirty-One—agreed to help coordinate and publicize the event. Each district contributed $50 for workshop production cost, and were able to send a district "representative" at no charge. This representative agreed to assist on-site if needed. The representatives were Glenyce Fulton, District Nine; Debbie Kiser, District Three; Cynthia Bussey, District Eight; and Loucille Swaim, District Thirty-One.

The evaluations were outstanding. Patti Hunsucker, president of District Eight, summarized the experience nicely in her March newsletter message as follows:

"If you were unable to attend Carolyn Billings' workshop, 'Professional Issues in Nursing,' you had better watch out! Those of us who braved the threatening snow to attend really did get inspired. She told us that she hoped she could "light a little flame" inside of us, and she certainly succeeded."

District One has a "success story" to share about a continuing education program. On March 7, 1985, the Nursing Practice Committee of the District, chaired by Shirley H. Tenney, sponsored a dinner symposium, "The Impaired Nurse: Nurses Helping Nurses." The meeting was held at the Mountain AHEC Auditorium in Asheville, NC. There were 153 participants! These included nursing students and nurses from hospitals, community health care agencies, and long-term care facilities. The meeting featured recovering nurses, nurse administrators, a member of the North Carolina Board of Nursing, and a nurse investigator from the State Bureau of Investigation.

Alise Irwin, president of District One, left the program beaming with pride that members of District One have proven to be "Brave nurses in a new World"!

District Thirty-Four will hold its Second Annual Nursing Symposium, "Our Professional Organization—Responsibilities and Privileges," on May 14 in the AHEC building adjacent to Catawba Memorial Hospital in Hickory. The speaker will be NCNA President Judy Seamon. Dinner is at 6 p.m., and the program begins at 7 p.m.

Retiring dean named editor

Dr. Eloise R. Lewis

Dr. Eloise R. Lewis will retire from her position as dean of the UNC-G School of Nursing on June 30. She will be honored at a reception on the UNC-G campus on March 30.

Dr. Lewis was appointed as the first dean of the school in 1966. Prior to that appointment she was associate professor at UNC-CH School of Nursing. She is a past president of NCNA, NCLN, and the American Association of Colleges of Nursing and past chairman of the N.C. Board of Nursing.

She has been appointed to a five-year term as editor of the new Journal of Professional Nursing to begin publication soon for the AACN.

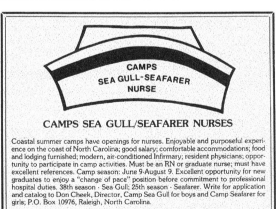

Education Notes

by Nancy Sumner, Member
Commission on Education

Nurses continue to grapple with the issue of how nurses should be educated. We have been dis-*cuss*-ing the issue for years. Florence Nightingale made nursing education more formalized, and the Goldmark Report of 1923 identified the importance for nursing education to take place in institutions of higher learning. But nursing, a woman-dominated profession, has certainly suffered because of the status of women in society. There are many reports in the literature, as late as the 20th century, that education was harmful to a woman's mind and body. Women were carefully taught subservience to men. Lack of education and a role based on obedience combined to make nursing an unattractive occupation. We won't even mention the pay scale!

These societal factors, however, are changing and so must nursing education and practice. Men and women enter nursing and plan to participate until retirement—it is a career. Working conditions are improving, and more emphasis is being placed on being educationally prepared for a position, instead of perpetuating the Peter Principle.

It is this last area to which I would direct the reader's attention—educational preparation for a position. Nurses have long been divided on this issue, and the opportunists are taking advantage of our lack of unity. There is a pervasive lack of trust among nurses, based frequently on differing educational backgrounds. We seem to be busy protecting our historical turf while the opportunists are eroding the progress we have fought so hard to gain.

Your NCNA Commission on Education is very concerned about the increasing numbers of programs at the baccalaureate and master's levels being developed for "health care professionals." These programs are not designed for nurses and often do not broaden the nursing knowledge base one has from previous educational experiences. Nursing has developed to a point where we are no longer subservient either in practice, or by law. We are held accountable for our actions, and it is dangerous to purport to practice at an advanced level on knowledge gained in a lower level of education. Evidence of this came in a recent announcement from ANA that applicants for 6 of the 17 certification examinations will be required to hold a baccalaureate or higher degree **in nursing** beginning in 1986.

No other profession recognizes degrees outside the discipline as preparation for practice. If nursing is to meet the challenge of the future, each nurse should select continuing education experiences and degree awarding curriculums with the idea of being educationally prepared for the position he or she holds or seeks.

To make this possible, nurses must come together and determine position requirements. Nurses are confused, the public is confused, the legislators are confused! What is nursing education? Nurses from every area of practice and education must collaborate and reach some middle ground so that we can move forward.

For the present, when choosing an educational experience ask yourself:

1. What is my long range professional goal? If you can't answer this one, it will be difficult to answer the rest!
2. How will this experience help me meet my goal?
3. Does the program meet current standards of **nursing** education or practice such as those published by NLN and the N.C. Board of Nursing.

The potential student should explore the status of accreditation or the accreditation application as part of assessing the program. Baccalaureate programs designed exclusively for registered nurses are not required to be approved by the North Carolina Board of Nursing since the program is not preparing students for licensure. There are several of these baccalaureate programs being developed and implemented in North Carolina that have not acquired accreditation from the National League for Nursing. Programs are not eligible for accreditation until the first class graduates; however, perspective students should determine the school's plans to apply for accreditation. Accreditation by NLN is important, since many graduate nursing programs and the military service may require graduation from an accredited program, and since accreditation signifies program quality.

4. Does the program build on my nursing knowledge and provide for expansion of my nursing data base?

Other questions related to accessability, cost, and prerequisites will depend on the program and the individual. Planning for education is much like planning a vacation; answers to all the other questions rest on, "where do you want to go?". But your educational decisions have a far more lasting impact.

The Winner!

Eunice Paul, Charlotte, received the $25 award from the Public Relations Committee for the winning public service announcement for Nurses' Day, May 6.

Notice: *Leadership Orientation Day*

June 3, 1985
NCNA Headquarters
10 a.m. - 3 p.m.

Target Audience: New and outgoing district officers and committee chairmen. Other members interested in preparing for district leadership are encouraged to attend.

Purpose: To assist those of you who accept leadership responsibilities at the district level by acquainting you with the organizational system of NCNA and providing some "how to" tips on fulfilling leadership responsibilities.

*The Council of District Presidents will meet during lunch. It is suggested that district presidents bring a "bag lunch."

OPPORTUNITIES FOR THE REGISTERED NURSE IN BACCALAUREATE EDUCATION IN NURSING IN NORTH CAROLINA

This publication contains revised information about programs offering opportunities for baccalaureate education for registered nurses in North Carolina, following the initial effort which was published by NCNA in 1977. The information was furnished and approved for publication by 15 programs in the state. This information was compiled by the NCNA Commission on Education.

The need for a single source of information about pathways to baccalaureate nursing education for the registered nurse in North Carolina is on the increase. This revision was completed in continuing recognition and support for graduates and students of diploma and associate degree nursing programs interested in earning a baccalaureate degree in nursing. The sources of motivation to seek the baccalaureate degree continue to be varied—among which are career advancement, personal satisfaction, and job security.

The publication of this information is intended to make the career journey easier and more pleasant. **(Inquiries for more specific information should be directed to the respective schools of nursing.)**

March, 1985

OPPORTUNITIES FOR THE REGISTERED NURSE IN BACCALAUREATE EDUCATION IN NURSING IN NORTH CAROLINA

General Information:

1. All baccalaureate programs in nursing admit graduates of diploma and associate degree programs.
2. Part-time study of nursing courses is possible in all baccalaureate programs in nursing except UNC-CH and for the senior year at Winston-Salem State University.
3. Specific course requirements for each program may be found in school catalogs.
4. Living accommodations and financial aid information may be found in the individual school catalog.
5. Nursing and non-nursing courses are available during weekdays for both fall and spring terms in all baccalaureate programs in nursing. Contact individual schools for the availability of summer courses.
6. See list of programs for national (NLN) and state (N.C. Board of Nursing) accreditation status.
7. Admission requirements include the following items unless otherwise specified:
   a. Transcripts of high school, college, and nursing course credits.
   b. S.A.T. or A.C.T. scores.
   c. Current RN licensure or eligibility for NC registered nurse licensure.

Name and Address of School or Department	Dean or Chairperson	Accrediting Bodies	Deadline for Completed Application	Total S.H. Required	S.H. in Residency	Advanced Placement — Non Nursing Courses	Advanced Placement — Nursing Courses	Additional Course Times — Evening Non-Nursing	Additional Course Times — Evening Nursing	Additional Course Times — Saturday Non-Nursing	Additional Course Times — Saturday Nursing
Atlantic Christian College Department of Nursing Wilson, N.C. 27893 (919)237-3161 Ext. 342,345	Dr. Sue Hunter, Chairman	NLN N.C. Board of Nursing	March 1 for admission to nsg. courses	124	Credit for nsg courses at ACC meets the residency requirement	CLEP	Placement/Challenge Exams	Nursing courses are provided with minimal classroom attendance and flexible scheduling of clinical experiences.			No
East Carolina University School of Nursing Greenville, N.C. 27834 (919)757-6061	Dr. Emilie D. Henning, Dean Barbara Oyler, Asst. Dean of of Student Services	NLN N.C. Board of Nursing	March 15 for fall admission	131 (subject to change)	30	CLEP & other exams	Proficiency exams (Maximum 38 s.h.- subject to change)	Yes	Yes	No	No
Lenoir-Rhyne College Department of Nursing Hickory, N.C. 28603 (704)328-7281	Linda Reece, Acting Chairperson	NLN N.C. Board of Nursing	6 months prior to semester sought	128	12	CLEP & other exams	Written & clinical assessment Challenge exams	Yes	No	No	No
N.C. A&T University School of Nursing Greensboro, N.C. 27411 (919)379-7751	Mrs. Marietta C. Raines, Dean	NLN N.C. Board of Nursing	May 30 (Flexible)	126	36	CLEP & other exams	Challenge Exams	Yes	No	Yes	No
N.C. Central University Department of Nursing P.O. Box 19798 Durham, N.C. 27707 (919)683-6322	Dr. Johnea D. Kelley, Chairperson	NLN N.C. Board of Nursing	July 1 for Fall Admission	130	N/A	CLEP	Dept. of Nursing Challenge Exams	Yes	No	Yes	No
Queens College The James D. Vail III Bachelor of Science in Nursing Program 1900 Selwyn Avenue, Charlotte, N.C. 28274 (704)337-2276	Dr. Carolyn Jones, Chairman	NLN N.C. Board of Nursing	Open	128	60	CLEP	NLN Profile II	Yes	No	Yes	No
UNC at Chapel Hill	Dr. Laurel	NLN	Process	120	30	CLEP &	*	Yes	Yes	No	No

Name and Address of School or Department	Dean or Chairperson	Accrediting Bodies	Deadline for Completed Application	Total S.H. Required	S.H. in Residency	Advanced Placement		Additional Course Times			
						Non Nursing Courses	Nursing Courses	Evening Non-Nursing	Nursing	Saturday Non-Nursing	Nursing
Charlotte, N.C. 28223 (704) 597-4650	Acting Dean	of Nursing	Semester Admission					after 3:30 p.m.			
*After first semester in program students are given a comprehensive examination which measures prior learning from work, life and educational experiences; successful completion earns students up to 24 s.h. of the required nursing credit.											
UNC-G School of Nursing, Greensboro, N.C. 27412-5001 (919) 379-5010	Dr. Eloise R. Lewis, Dean	NLN, N.C. Board of Nursing	Dec. 15	122	30	CLEP	Challenge Exams (Maximum 20 s.h.)	Yes	No	Yes	No
UNC-Wilmington School of Nursing, 601 South College Road, Wilmington, N.C. 28403-3297 (919) 395-3784	Dr. Marlene M. Rosenkoetter, Dean *	N.C. Board of Nursing *	Feb. 15	124	30	Yes	Pending Approval	Yes	Yes	No	No
*Plan to seek NLN accreditation in 1987 when first class graduates.											
Western Carolina University, Department of Nursing, Cullowhee, N.C. 28723 (704) 227-7467	Ms. Vivian Deitz, Interim Department Head	NLN, N.C. Board of Nursing	Feb. 15 Oct. 15	128	30	CLEP & other exams	Exams (Maximum 16 s.h.)	Yes	Yes	No	No
Winston-Salem State University, Division of Nursing & Allied Health, Winston-Salem, N.C. 27110 (919) 761-2170	Mrs. Sadie B. Webster, Director	NLN, N.C. Board of Nursing	March 15	127	30	CLEP	Challenge Exams (Maximum 35 s.h.)	Yes	Yes (Contingent Upon Demand)	No	No

NEW PROGRAMS DESIGNED EXCLUSIVELY FOR REGISTERED NURSES SEEKING A BACCALAUREATE DEGREE IN NURSING

Name and Address of School or Department	Dean or Chairperson	Accrediting Bodies	Deadline for Completed Application	Total S.H. Required	S.H. in Residency	Advanced Placement		Additional Course Times			
						Non Nursing Courses	Nursing Courses	Evening Non-Nursing	Nursing	Saturday Non-Nursing	Nursing
Gardner-Webb College, Davis School of Nursing, P.O. Box 268, Boiling Springs, N.C. 28017 (704) 434-2361	Dr. Janie Carlton, Chairman	*	Prior to Semester Sought	64	30	CLEP	Department Challenge Exams	Yes	No	No	No
*Application has been made for NLN accreditation; site visit is scheduled for Fall, 1985											
NOTE: RN students have a choice of two locations; the program is offered at Gardner Webb College, Boiling Springs, N.C. and at Davis School of Nursing, Statesville, N.C.											
Meredith College, Office of Continuing Education, 3800 Hillsborough Street, Raleigh, N.C. 27607-5298 (919) 829-8353	Dr. Ellen Ironside, Associate Dean for Continuing Education	SACS	Applications accepted for Fall, Spring, Summer, beginning in Summer 1985	124-127	18 Meredith 30 Duke	Credit by examination possible for up to 30 s.h. of nursing and some non-nursing		Yes	Yes	No	No
Wingate College, Wingate, N.C. 28174 (704) 233-4061 Ext. 197	Dr. Geraldine N. Jordan	SACS *	None	125	30	CLEP, (15 s.h.)	Validate 33 s.h.	Yes	Yes	No	No
*Plan to seek NLN accreditation as soon as the first class graduates; tentative plans for 1986.											

ACTIONS OF THE BOARD

The Board of Directors at a meeting on January 25, 1985, took the following actions:

• Adopted a policy on use of NCNA legal counsel, stipulating that the mechanism for offering assistance on specific legal issues of concern and interest to nurses as individuals is continuing education experiences, which are supported by registration fees. The policy stipulates also that NCNA does not provide legal counsel to individuals.

• Adopted a budget for 1985 that reflects the following cost-containment measures: continue membership only in those organizations that help NCNA meet its priorities and provide useful networks (discontinuing membership in the Conference for Social Service, N.C. Health Council, Child Advocacy Council, ANF Century Fund, N.C. Hospice); reduction in all possible line items; elimination of staff development funds; use of available cash resources; and elimination of contribution to the Building Conservation Fund. The budget also is based on a 5% increase in membership during 1985.

• Decided that no travel funds are to be allowed for staff to travel away from headquarters for routine meetings of committees and other structural units.

• Reviewed drafts of bills on direct third party reimbursement for nurses, to be sponsored by NCNA, and on dispensing of medications by public health nurses, to be sponsored by the Association of County Commissioners.

• Authorized publication of a legislative bulletin on a regular basis to be available to nurses on a subscription basis.

• Approved continuing 1984 policies on representatives at conventions from schools of nursing.

• Suggested Dr. Laurel Copp for the AJN Company Board of Directors.

• Voted to support Russell Eugene Tranbarger's candidacy for the ANA Cabinet on Nursing Services.

• Authorized the Committee on Membership to proceed with a video tape membership recruitment project.

• Approved a draft of NCNA's response to ANA's National Plan on Entry into Professional Practice.

• Reappointed Kathy Collins as NCNA representative to the Committee on Practice and Education, N.C. Conference of Public Health Directors, Supervisors, and Consultants.

• Authorized appointment of an ad hoc committee to explore NCNA's role as catalyst in the development of a systematic statewide plan for nursing education.

• Authorized the Commission on Education to proceed with a project to publish the list of RN-BSN programs in the *Tar Heel Nurse*.

• Accepted a philosophy statement, policy on co-sponsorship of continuing education offerings, and a revised organizational chart as prepared by the Ad Hoc Committee preparing the application for ANA accreditation as a C.E. provider and approver unit.

• Nominated Senator Wilma Woodard for the N.C. Women's Forum Gail Bradley Award.

• Appointed Barbara Bennett and Judy Schlichting to the Committee on Peer Assistance Program.

At a meeting on February 15, 1985, the Board took the following actions:

• Set subscription rates for the biweekly legislative bulletin.

• Reviewed a new draft of the third party reimbursement bill and suggested revisions.

• Voted to support the Association of Nurse Anesthetists in sponsoring a bill on hospital patients' bill of rights and suggested seeking co-sponsorship with the Hospital Association.

• Directed that agenda materials for board meetings be received at least one week in advance.

• Endorsed the Member Loan Program of Trans National, formerly marketed by ANA.

• Recommended to the ANA Board of Directors that a registration fee reflecting costs of materials be charged to delegates, alternates, and observers at the 1985 ANA convention.

• Endorsed the proposal of Michigan Nurses Association for certification for RNs in continuing education.

• Referred the issue of endorsement of liability insurance plans to the Commission on Member Services for study and recommendation.

• Appointed Mary Lou Moore to the Ad Hoc Committee to explore establishing a foundation.

• Authorized the Division on Gerontological Nursing Practice to develop a "Gerontological Nurse of the Year" award.

• Referred to the Executive Committee a member request for reconsideration of the policy regarding registration fee for members of planning committees attending NCNA workshops and conferences.

• Directed that a mechanism be developed to cost out the activities and services of NCNA for the purpose of gathering information.

At a meeting on March 1, 1985, the Executive Committee took the following actions:

• Voted to recommend to the board revision in the Policy on Reimbursement for Presenters at NCNA convention.

• Voted to recommend to the board revision in the Policy on Reimbursement for Members of Committees Planning Workshops, Programs, and Conventions.

• Selected names and alternates for appointment to the Ad Hoc Committee on Credentialing.

• Selected names and alternates for appointment to the Ad Hoc Committee on Statewide Planning for Nursing Education.

• Recommended names of members to be interviewed for the Membership Committee's VCR.

• Voted to allocate $500 for representative(s) of the Committee on Peer Assistance Program to attend a conference on the Impaired Nurse in Atlanta.

Brooks proposes rules on OSHA standards

NCNA has been notified by the N.C. Department of Labor that Commissioner John C. Brooks' proposed amendments to rules related to the OSHA Hazard Communication ("Right-to-Know") Standard include nurses among those health professionals authorized for access to trade secret information in non-emergency standards.

NCNA urged this rule change in testimony presented by Rachel Allred,Greensboro, at public hearings last fall. Federal rules do not include nurses as health professionals authorized for access to trade secrets.

Public hearings on the proposed amendments will be held in five cities around the state during April.

ANA Board receives report on titling

The ANA Cabinet on Nursing Education has presented its titling report to the ANA Board of Directors recommending that the title for individuals prepared with a baccalaureate degree in nursing will be Registered Nurse (R.N.) and the title for individuals prepared with an associate degree in nursing will be Registered Technical Nurse (R.T.N.)

The report will be forwarded to the Reference Committee and will be discussed at a Reference Committee hearing at the 1985 House of Delegates.

NCNA hopes to receive the report in time for discussion at delegate meetings prior to the July ANA House of Delegates meeting.

AMERICAN JOURNAL OF NURSING COMPANY
and
NORTH CAROLINA NURSES ASSOCIATION
1985
Award for Excellence in Writing

Purpose

This award is intended to encourage members of the North Carolina Nurses Association to write for publication.

The Award

An award of $100 and a certificate suitable for framing will be presented to the winning author.

The Rules

All members of the North Carolina Nurses Association who hold membership during 1985 are eligible, except for employees of the American Journal of Nursing Company and the North Carolina Nurses Association headquarters staff.

The writing submitted must be in prose, prepared for publication but unpublished, not to exceed 3,000 words on nursing; written for nurses, members of other health care disciplines or for the general public. *Particularly, participants are encouraged to write articles or reports on nursing projects, innovations in nursing practice, and data collected to improve nursing care.* A research paper, such as a master's thesis, should be rewritten from a research format to an article format to be considered. Articles with more than one author will be eligible only if all co-authors are NCNA members. Entries are to be typed, double spaced on one side of 8½ x 11 white paper. Upon receipt of the entry at state headquarters office, it becomes the property of the North Carolina Nurses Association until it is returned to the writer.

The Judges

Manuscripts shall be judged and the winning entry selected by a committee of members of the North Carolina Nurses Association to be appointed by the president, one of whom shall be the editor of the North Carolina Nurses Association's official publication.

Deadline

No special entry forms or application blanks are necessary. Entries should be sent to: NCNA, P.O. Box 12025, Raleigh, NC 27605, postmarked not later than August 1, 1985.

GERONTOLOGICAL NURSING DIVISION
of the
NORTH CAROLINA NURSES ASSOCIATION
announces the
Gerontological
Nurse of the Year Competition - 1985

Recognition of a registered nurse in North Carolina who has demonstrated excellence in gerontological nursing practice.

Award: Recognition for outstanding Gerontological nursing practice.

Entry Process:

1. Candidate must be a registered nurse in North Carolina working within the area of gerontological nursing. Membership in NCNA is required.
2. Nomination for award may come from any source (colleague, supervisor, physician, district nurses association, etc.)
3. Application must be completed by candidate.
4. Selection will be based on identified guidelines.
5. Award will be given at the discretion of the selection committee only if the applicant meets the criteria for excellence in gerontological nursing practice.

Deadline for Entry: August 1, 1985

Selection: To be made by the Gerontological Nursing Division, North Carolina Nurses Association.

Award will be presented at the 1985 convention of the North Carolina Nurses Association, October 23-26, at the Hyatt, Winston-Salem, NC.

Application Forms and Criteria Available From:

Gerontological Nursing Division
North Carolina Nurses Association
Post Office Box 12025
Raleigh, NC 27605

MEDICAL-SURGICAL NURSING DIVISION
of the
NORTH CAROLINA NURSES ASSOCIATION
announces the
Medical-Surgical
Nurse of the Year Competition - 1985

Recognition of a registered nurse in North Carolina who has demonstrated excellence in Medical-Surgical nursing practice.

Award: Recognition for outstanding Medical-Surgical nursing practice.

Entry Process:

1. Candidate must be a registered nurse in North Carolina working within the area of Medical-Surgical nursing. Membership in NCNA is required.
2. Nomination for award may come from any source (colleague, supervisor, physician, district nurses association, etc.)
3. Application must be completed by candidate.
4. Selection will be based on identified guidelines.
5. Award will be given at the discretion of the selection committee only if the applicant meets the criteria for excellence in Medical-Surgical nursing practice.

Deadline for Entry: August 1, 1985

Selection: To be made by the Medical-Surgical Nursing Division, North Carolina Nurses Association.

Award will be presented at the 1985 convention of the North Carolina Nurses Association, October 23-26, at the Hyatt, Winston-Salem, NC.

Application Forms and Criteria Available From:

Medical-Surgical Nursing Division
North Carolina Nurses Association
Post Office Box 12025
Raleigh, NC 27605

NORTH CAROLINA NURSES ASSOCIATION
and
THE NATIONAL FOUNDATION—MARCH OF DIMES
announces the
Maternal-Child Health
Nurse of the Year Competition - 1985

Recognition of a registered nurse in North Carolina who has made significant contribution to Maternal-Child Health.

Award: $500 for continuing education activities toward improvement of Maternal-Child Health

Entry Process:

1. Candidate must be a registered nurse in North Carolina working within the area of Maternal-Child Health. Membership in NCNA is not required.
2. Application must be filled out by the individual nurse. Sponsors may request that nurse(s) make application. Self-declared candidates are also appropriate.
3. Selection will be based on criteria stated on the reverse side of nomination/application form.
4. Two letters of recommendation must be provided by persons knowledgeable of candidate's professional MCH contribution

Deadline for Entry: August 1, 1985

Selection: To be made by the Maternal-Child Health Nursing Division, North Carolina Nurses Association.

Award will be presented at the 1985 convention of the North Carolina Nurses Association, October 23-26, at the Hyatt, Winston-Salem, NC.

Application Forms and Criteria Available From:

Maternal-Child Health Nursing Division
North Carolina Nurses Association
Post Office Box 12025
Raleigh, NC 27605

NURSE TO NURSE

By Carolyn Billings, Chairman
Commission on Member Services

Dear Front Line Nurse:

Whether you are in hospital nursing, public health, home health, or any other employment setting, if you are a **hands-on caregiver**, this column is especially for you. Over the past year I have written about the needs of nurses in their work-settings, some of the issues that confront nursing practice today, some of the ideals that we struggle to fulfill, and some of the realities that hold us back.

The Commission on Member Services is the body within NCNA that is charged with the responsibility of dealing with the workplace concerns of our members and the profession at large and with their economic and professional welfare. When the Commission drafted the resolution on the right of the RN to refuse a work assignment and advocated its passage by the 1984 Convention delegates, it was in response to concerns raised by staff nurses and nurse-managers who were struggling with how to deal with some of the consequences of the economic squeeze their hospital employers were feeling.

These nurses asked for the voice of NCNA to support them in their right and responsibility to assure safe nursing care to their patients. Since the passage of the resolution, an ad hoc committee has been formed to prepare guidelines to help nurses to determine when it is appropriate to refuse or accept an assignment and the alternatives and consequences attached to such decision-making.

Last year the Commission was approached by a group of private duty nurses who were frustrated with constraints placed on their practice by insurers who insist on physician gate-keepers to determine the need for and appropriateness of their nursing services. These nurses believe that the assessment of the need for nursing care and the determination of which level of nursing care is most required is a nursing assessment, not a medical one. The Commission supported these nurses in that position and sent a letter to the Insurance Commissioner in their behalf. We are continuing to develop strategies for action to help these nurses advocate for their proper role in the health care market, and to assist consumers in understanding what their health care insurance coverage will and will not buy.

The Commission sponsored a work-shop on Health Hazards in the Work Setting for nurses at the 1984 Convention in Asheville. Because it was so well received there, and seems to be such an important need for the protection of the health and safety of our nursing colleagues, the Workshop Planning Committee is developing a special workshop on that topic to be offered soon.

Over the biennium, Commission members have worked to update and revitalize the Association's position on employment standards for nurses. This position statement has now been completed and was approved by the NCNA Board of Directors. It will appear in the next issue of the *Tar Heel Nurse* (watch for it!), and we hope it will be published in brochure form and circulated to employers of nurses within the next several months.

As a Commission, we have dealt with and acted on a number of other matters affecting the welfare of nurses like you. We hope that you are finding our support of practical use to you. Because we have so little opportunity to hear from you directly, we don't always know what help you need most. The Commission meets every month. The time of our meetings is posted in the *Tar Heel Nurse*. If you have work setting concerns which you believe the Commission should be addressing, contact me through NCNA, and we will put your item on our agenda. You and your colleagues can attend that meeting to participate in discussion or one of us will contact you to hear in detail your problem and recommendations. You can initiate contact with me directly or through your District president.

It's important to us that we feel that we are responding to the needs of our membership. We don't always know. Will you tell us?

Sincerely,
Carolyn

Workshop Planning Committee Calendar of Scheduled Events

May 17, 1985, 8:30 a.m. - 3:00 p.m.
"Silent Workplace Hazards", Raleigh (See announcement in this issue)

June 24, 1985, 8:30 a.m. - 4:00 p.m.
"ABC's of Finance", Asheville (See announcement in this issue)

July 8, 1985, 8:30 a.m. - 4:00 p.m.
"ABC's of Finance", Raleigh (See announcement in this issue)

August 8, 1985, 8:30 a.m. - 4:00 p.m.
"Discharge Planning", Hickory, In association with Northwest AHEC
Presented by: Gail Hardy
$30 Member, $40 Non-Member, $10 Full Time Students

September, 1985
"Laws Affecting North Carolina Nurses, 1985"
Greenville, Greensboro, and Hickory
In association with Eastern, Greensboro, and Northwest AHECs
*Specific dates, times, locations, and fees to be announced

---------- —Response Form - Clip and return —— Response Form - Clip and Return— ----------

Name _____

Address _____
_____

Please send me brochures for the following programs:
(check as many as you like)

_____ "Silent Workplace Hazards"

_____ "ABC's of Finance"

_____ "Discharge Planning"

_____ "Laws Affecting North Carolina Nurses, 1985"

Return response to: ATTN. Betty Godwin, NCNA, P.O. Box 12025, Raleigh, NC 27605

TV stations receive 'Ask Your Nurse' spots

Seven TV Stations in North Carolina have received a 30-second public service announcement, "Ask Your Nurse," distributed by the National Council on Patient Information and Education.

The PSA encourages consumers to ask their nurse for information about prescription drugs. NCPIE is addressing a serious national problem: up to 50% of the 1.38 billion prescriptions filled each year are used improperly.

NCPIE has prepared a booklet, "A Sourcebook for Nurses: Counseling Patients About Their Medicines," available for $3 each from NCPIE "Give the Answers" Campaign, P.O. Box 1080 TV, Purcellville, VA 22132-1080.

The text of the "Ask Your Nurse" PSA is: "Every day, millions of Americans rely on medicine to relieve pain, fight disease, reduce the stress of illness day in and day out. But every day, people can be hurt by what they don't know; by taking their medication with the wrong food, and wrong liquid, or even other medications. If you're taking medication, **ask your nurse** or other health professionals about when and how to use it. Remember, the more you know about the medicines you take the better they'll help take care of you."

The following TV Stations have received the PSA: WBTV-TV, WPCQ-TV, and WSOC-TV, Charlotte; WPTF-TV and WRAL-TV, Raleigh; WTVD-TV, Durham; WGHP-TV, High Point. Call the station manager and urge use of the PSA, explaining the importance of its message for consumers.

Delegate meeting set for May 8

NCNA's first meeting of ANA delegates and alternates to prepare for the 1985 ANA convention will be held at 10 a.m. on Wednesday, May 8, at NCNA headquarters.

Members are urged to attend to discuss the issues with our delegates.

Members also are encouraged to communicate directly with delegates about any issue coming before the 1985 ANA House of Delegates. The delegates are:

Judith B. Seamon, P.O. Box 3486, Morehead City 28557
Barbara Jo McGrath, 3685 Kale Drive, Lumberton 28358
Carol A. Osman, 113 Shirley Drive, Cary 27511
Hettie L. Garland, 22 Woodbury Road, Asheville 28804
Connie B. Wolfe, P.O. Box 2724, Shallotte 28459
Estelle Fulp, 2836 Wycliff Road, Raleigh 27607
Sheila P. Englebardt, 818 Walker Avenue, Greensboro 27402
Wanda L. Boyette, Assistant Administrator, Sampson County Memorial Hospital, Clinton 28328
Cathy C. Hughes, 9120 Steelberry Drive, W., Rt. 4, Charlotte 28208
Eris H. Russell, P.O. Box 98, Black Mountain 28711

**WATCH THE
MEMBERSHIP THERMOMETER**

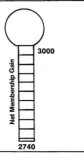

Net Membership Gain

3000

2740

Calendar of Events

The following "Calendar of Events" will inform members of meetings of NCNA structural units and other related groups and agencies. All structural unit meetings will take place in headquarters unless otherwise indicated.

Meetings of the NCNA Board of Directors, committees and commissions are open to the membership. Members may attend to see the Association in action and to communicate with the elected and appointed officials. Members planning to attend should notify NCNA at least two days prior to the meeting, so that we can plan for adequate seating and plenty of coffee!

Date/Hour	Event
April 10, 10 a.m.	Executive Committee, Maternal-Child Health Division
April 10, 10 a.m.	Ad Hoc Committee on Statewide Planning for Nursing Education
April 15, 10 a.m.	Public Relations Committee
April 17, 9:30 a.m.	Executive Committee, Nursing Practice Administrator Section
April 18, 10 a.m.	Ad Hoc Committee on RN Work Assignments
April 19, 9 a.m.	NCNA Board of Directors
April 22, 10 a.m.	Committee on Legislation
April 22, 10 a.m.	CERP Committee
April 23, 10 a.m.	Peer Assistance Program Committee
April 24, 1 p.m.	Headquarters Committee
April 25, 1:30 p.m.	Joint Practice Committee
April 29, 9:30 a.m.	Ad Hoc Committee on Foundations
April 29, 10 a.m.	Workshop Planning Committee
April 30, 10 a.m.	Ad Hoc Committee on Structure
May 6	National Nurses' Day
May 7, 10 a.m.	Commission on Member Services
May 8, 10 a.m.	ANA Delegate/Alternate meeting
May 9, 10 a.m.	Ad Hoc Committee on Structure
May 13, 10 a.m.	Executive Committee, Gerontological Division
May 16, 12 Noon	Membership Committee
May 17, 8:30 a.m.	Convention Program Planning Committee
May 17, 8:30 a.m.	NCNA Workshop, "Silent Workplace Hazards," Wake AHEC
May 20, 10 a.m.	CERP Committee
May 21, 10 a.m.	Ad Hoc Committee on RN Work Assignments
May 23, 9:30 a.m.	Commission on Practice
May 24, 10 a.m.	Committee on Legislation
May 24, 10 a.m.	Commission on Education
May 29, 9:30 a.m.	Executive Committee, Nursing Practice Administrator Section
May 30, 10 a.m.	Peer Assistance Program Committee
May 31, 9 a.m.	NCNA Board of Directors
June 3, 10 a.m.	District Leadership Day

Western Union   *Telegram*

ALL NCNA MEMBERS:
CONGRATULATIONS STOP YOU CAN AGAIN GET FREE NCNA
CONVENTION REGISTRATION INCLUDING MEALS STOP RECRUIT
5 NEW MEMBERS FROM APRIL 15 THROUGH SEPTEMBER 16,
1985 STOP THIS OFFER CAN SAVE YOU BIG BUCKS STOP SEE
DETAILS BELOW STOP JOIN US IN WINSTON-SALEM AS OUR
GUEST STOP

Sender: MEMBERSHIP COMMITTEE

THAT'S RIGHT! By recruiting 5 new full pay members (or any combination of new members paying half-price and/or quarter-price dues equivalent to 5 full pay members) you can enjoy the 1985 NCNA convention, including meal functions, as a guest of NCNA. Please follow these guidelines to insure accurate record-keeping and a smoothly run contest.

You, the nurse recruiter, are responsible for:

1. Writing "Recruited by" and your name on *all three* copies of each application used.
2. Ensuring that applications are completed fully and correctly (those with missing information, i.e., license number, *cannot* be processed—only processed applications will be counted as new members).
3. Ensuring that applications are mailed to NCNA Headquarters, P.O. Box 12025, Raleigh, NC 27605 *and* are received on or before September 16, 1985.
4. Mailing your completed recruiter form to NCNA Headquarters on or before September 16, 1985.

You will be notified when the applications of "your" new members are received and processed.You will also be advised of any deficiencies in a prospective member's application (that prevents processing) so that *you* may contact them to correct it.

Winners will be notified between September 17 and October 23, 1985. Remember! A new member is a nurse who has not been a member of NCNA or another state nurses association for at least six months.

RECRUITER FORM

NAME OF RECRUITING MEMBER _____ DISTRICT _____

ADDRESS _____ PHONE (H) _____

(W) _____

NEW MEMBERS (NAME, ADDRESS, PHONE NO., DUES CATEGORY, —FULL, HALF, QUARTER— AND DISTRICT

1. _____

_____

2. _____

_____

3. _____

_____

4. _____

_____

ADD ADDITIONAL PAGE IF NEEDED
*RETURN FORM BY SEPTEMBER 16, 1985 TO NCNA, P.O. BOX 12025, RALEIGH, NC 27605

NORTH CAROLINA NURSES ASSOCIATION

WHAT NCNA HAS DONE FOR YOU
AND FOR NURSING IN 1984

In Legislation
• Monitored legislation throughout the 1984 session of the General Assembly for implications for nursing.
• Provided information to members of the General Assembly about nursing needs and goals.
• Adopted a position opposing legislation that allows county commissioners to assume the functions and authority of local boards of health, mental health, and social services.
• Drafted a bill to sponsor in the 1985 General Assembly for direct third-party reimbursement for nurses.
• Presented testimony on the cost-effectiveness of registered nurses as health care providers to the Legislative Study Committee on Medical Cost Containment. Later adapted the testimony into an article, "Nurse Providers: A Resource for Growing Population Needs," which was published in the national magazine, *Business and Health*. The testimony as published in the *Tar Heel Nurse* won the Region 7 Sigma Theta Tau 1984 media award for its significance to nursing practice.
• Supported a study of the attitudes and beliefs of North Carolina legislators about nursing and the effectiveness of nurse lobbying, and disseminated the survey results to the membership.
• Conducted a workshop to train key nurse specialists and NCNA leadership as lobbyists on the third-party reimbursement issue.
• Updated and refined a "telephone tree" for grassroots lobbying, utilizing the district associations, specialty organizations, and other existing nurse communication networks.

In Political Action
• Distributed a questionnaire prior to the 1984 primary election to all candidates for the North Carolina General Assembly to learn their views on nursing issues.
• Conducted a "Nurse PAC Needs Your Dollar" fund-raising effort.
• Through state and national political action committees provided support services to nurse volunteers in political campaigns.
• Through Nurse PAC and district associations conducted a project of interviewing candidates and increasing the number of nurse voters in the primary and general elections.
• Nurse PAC endorsed 31 candidates for the General Assembly House of Representatives and 9 candidates for the N.C. Senate before the 1984 primary elections; endorsed 16 additional candidates for the House and 11 additional candidates for the Senate before the 1984 general elections; Nurse PAC contributed $3,500 to the 1984 campaigns of political candidates to strengthen nursing's political voice. Endorsements were based on past voting records and information gathered during interviews by district members.

In Practice
• Conducted a statewide competition in collaboration with The National Foundation on Birth Defects for selection of the "March of Dimes Nurse of the Year" to recognize contributions to maternal-infant care.
• Conducted a statewide competition for selection of the Medical-Surgical Nurse of the Year" to recognize outstanding contributions by a medical-surgical nurse to improving patient care.
• Conducted 2 workshops on "Premenstrual Syndrome," using multidisciplinary faculty currently involved in a team practice.

• Conducted a workshop for nurse managers on financial management techniques using a nationally known nurse leader as faculty.
• Conducted 2 workshops on "Essentials of Nursing for Patients with Cancer."
• Through the Primary Care Nurse Practitioner Conference Group conducted continuing education for nurse practitioners on a variety of clinical topics.
• Conducted 3 regional workshops on "Laws Affecting North Carolina Nurses, 1984" with content presented by NCNA legal counsel.
• Made a financial contribution to the American Nurses' Foundation in support of nursing research.
• Responded to specific practice issues and questions from individual nurses.
• Purchased a media package on "Nursing: A Social Policy Statement" (developed by the ANA Congress for Nursing Practice) and made it available to district associations and other nurse groups.
• Convened a statewide meeting of gerontological nurses to discuss concern about the health care of older citizens and to plan strategies for addressing those concerns.
• Convened a second meeting to set priorities for action on health needs of the elderly, attended by representatives of senior citizen groups and more than 30 organizations that work with the elderly.

In Education
• Conducted a Continuing Education Review Program through which 395 continuing education single offerings were reviewed for compliance with professional standards.
• Issued 2 Total Program Approvals and 8 Total Program Renewals through the Continuing Education Review Program.
• Administered the Memorial Educational Fund, which provides low-cost educational loans to registered nurses seeking further education.
• Identified a need for a systematic state-wide approach for nursing education and committed NCNA to serve as a catalyst for addressing this need.
• Publicized a warning to nurses and the public that an NLN accredited B.S. in Nursing is a pre-requisite for admission to most masters in nursing programs and that alternative baccalaureate programs to which nurses are being recruited do not meet this pre-requisite.
• Gathered data on requirements and availability of BSN programs for RNs and made plans for making the information available to nurses.

In Health Planning and Policy Making
• Promoted participation of nurses in local, regional, and state health planning activities.
• Provided information to state agencies, organizations, and statewide media on the role of nurses in delivery of health care.
• Reviewed the State Health Medical Facilities Plan as revised by the State Health Planning Agency and presented written and oral testimony to the State Health Coordinating Council.
• Presented testimony to the Governor's Advisory Council on Aging dealing with standards for homes for the aged and disabled.
• Communicated to the State Commissioner of Insurance concerns about companies and their agents selling hospital insurance policies

that claim to provide the benefit of private duty nursing without explaining the restrictions on such benefit.

● Filed recommendations with appropriate state agencies that the minimum qualification for health care coordinator in Adult Day Health Centers be a registered nurse.

● Maintained organizational membership in Hospice of North Carolina.

● Provided testimony to the State Department of Labor on OSHA standards on hazard communication, protesting the exclusion of nurses from the definition of health professionals.

● Provided a representative on the North Carolina Task Force that participated in the Southeastern Conference on Prescription Drug Abuse.

● Provided nurse representation on the Advisory Committee for the Health Vote project of the North Carolina Foundation for Alternative Health Programs, Inc.

● Developed and disseminated a position statement on "Registered Nurses' Participation in Capital Punishment."

In Improving the Image of Nursing

● Interpreted nursing goals and needs to statewide media, official agencies, and other health organizations.

● Initiated the proclamation of Nurses Week in North Carolina by Governor James B. Hunt, Jr., and promoted the observance throughout the state to acquaint the public with the diversity of nursing today and to spotlight the growing legislative and political power of nurses.

● Protested to the producers of the CBS TV show "ER" the negative depiction of nursing.

● Provided a speaker on comparable worth for the Second Annual Conference of the North Carolina Women's Network.

● Nominated Senator Wilma Woodard and Virginia Stone, R.N., Ph.D., for the "Distinguished Women of North Carolina" awards of the Council on Status of Women.

● Hosted a delegation of nurse educators and administrators from the United Kingdom during their People-to-People visit in the United States.

● Participated in the Wellness Institute, sponsored by Wake AHEC, to promote understanding of the role of the registered nurse as a health care provider in disease prevention and health maintenance.

● Commended nurses who responded to the emergency needs of the victims in the 1984 tornadoes in Eastern North Carolina.

In Services to Members

● Published and distributed six issues of the *Tar Heel Nurse*, a newsletter on nursing news in North Carolina.

● Provided consultation to individual nurses and groups of nurses in relation to practice and employment problems.

● Conducted an annual convention, attended by nearly 400 nurses, on the impact of new technology, economic forces, and politics on the profession.

● Maintained a "Talent Bank" to serve as a resource for nurses and other health care providers about this Association's activities and nursing's goals and health care concerns.

● Sponsored with the American Journal of Nursing Company a statewide competition for selection of the recipient of an award for Excellence in Writing.

● Provided support to the RN bargaining unit at the Durham VA hospital.

● Prepared revisions of the Association's recommended Minimum Employment Standards for publication early in 1985.

● Surveyed nursing practice management nurses concerning their needs that can be addressed by the Nursing Practice Administrators Section.

● Disseminated results of a survey of members to identify employment setting characteristics that foster professional development and satisfaction of nurses.

● Surveyed members who are private duty nurses to determine their needs and desires for an organizational unit within the NCNA structure.

● Supported the individual's right to accept only those assignments for which he/she is adequately prepared and the right to adequate recovery time between shifts; and directed that guidelines to assist all nurses in making these decisions be developed.

● Offered a discount car purchase plan as a membership benefit.

● Offered professional liability insurance at low group rates as a membership benefit.

● Offered a discount on the *American Journal of Nursing* as membership benefit.

In Strengthening the Organization Voice of Nursing

● Provided representation and meeting facilities for the North Carolina Federation of Nursing Organizations.

● Provided speakers on the role of the professional association for schools of nursing and inservice education departments.

● Provided support services to Nurse PAC, political action committee.

● Provided advisors to the North Carolina Association of Nursing Students, meeting facilities for its executive board, and an exhibit at the NCANS convention.

● Conducted 3 meetings of the Council of District Presidents to update district leadership on major projects and priorities.

● Provided representation at meetings of the ANA Constituent Forum.

● Provided representation at meetings of the executive directors of state nurses associations in the Southeast region.

● Provided representation for nursing on the Governor's Long-Term Care Advisory Committee, Joint Practice Committee, Coalition on Sexually Transmitted Diseases, North Carolina Arthritis Program, North Carolina Conference for Social Service, North Carolina Family Planning Council, North Carolina Health Council, North Carolina Health Manpower Council, Medical Care Commission of North Carolina, State Rural Health Task Force, State School Health Education Advisory Committee, the Task Force on Nursing—Program on Access to Health Care, and N.C. Children's Network.

● Developed a position paper on key issues before the 1984 ANA House of Delegates and related them to concepts essential to strengthening the federation adopted in 1982; disseminated the position paper to other state nurses associations and their ANA delegates and worked for the acceptance of the position paper at the ANA convention.

● Added a staff member to administer the Continuing Education Review Program, workshops, and a program of services and leadership development for district associations.

● Took steps to encourage minority representation on the Association's ballot and elevated the Committee on Human Rights to the status of a standing committee.

● Sent representatives to attend meetings of the ANA Board of Directors to foster better understanding of current issues and the new roles of the national and state associations.

● Recommended qualified North Carolina nurses for appointment to a variety of ANA committees.

● Conducted a leadership workshop for more than 120 commission and committee members to orient them to their Association responsibilities and to develop strategies for achieving NCNA's goals for the 1983-85 biennium.

● Conducted a leadership orientation for officers and committees of district associations.

● Instituted a "Personal Board Member" project to strengthen relationships with district associations by close communication between individual Board of Director members and geographic groupings of districts.

● Created a new District Thirty-Four for Catawba County to facilitate participation in Association activities by nurses at the local level.

● Demonstrated support of attendance and participation of student nurses at the NCNA convention by allocating to each school of nursing one student representative at the convention at no registration fee.

● Provided refreshments and encouragement on-site to more than 1,950 new graduates taking the licensure exam at 4 sites across the state.

● Mailed a complimentary copy of the *Tar Heel Nurse* to more than 1,700 newly licensed RNs.

Focus on *Your* Practice

One of the most important roles of NCNA's Commission on Practice is increasing nurses' knowledge of issues which may affect nursing practice. Frequently important issues are discussed in our Commission meetings, but less frequently is information about these issues disseminated throughout the state.

Many of our discussions are initially prompted by a question from a NCNA member. That member, or group of members, receives an answer, but others with similar, although unasked, questions may not. For these reasons, the Commission on Practice will be including this column, "Focus on Your Practice," in this and future issues of the *Tar Heel Nurse*. Please let us know of your response to this column, and also what questions you would like the Commission on Practice to address.

This month's question relates to activities of aides in rest homes. Nurses have been concerned about teaching rest home caretakers (who are frequently aides) to perform certain activities including administration of insulin. However, Board of Nursing rule 0.221 states that repetitive performances do not require an R.N. but may be performed by the patient, a family member, or a caretaker (aide). This includes the administration of insulin, as long as there is consistency in delegating the responsibility. The determination of responsibility is legally made by the patient's physician. Once this determination is made, nurses may appropriately teach patient, family members, or aides to administer insulin or other activities which in other circumstances would be considered the practice of nursing.

High blood pressure to be targeted in May

May is National High Blood Pressure Month. This is the 11th year that community health and service organizations across the country will combine their efforts to increase public awareness about the importance of controlling high blood pressure.

A kit containing media releases, fact sheets, reproducible pamphlets, poster, and order form for free materials is available in NCNA headquarters.

Campaign Committee Aids Tranbarger

A Campaign Committee is being formed to work for the election of Russell Eugene Tranbarger to the ANA Cabinet on Nursing Services. The election will be held in July at the 1985 ANA House of Delegates.

Tranbarger is the only NCNA member on the ANA general ballot this year. Sheila Englebardt is Campaign Committee chairman, and Judy Seamon is co-chairman.

Nurses who want to support our North Carolina candidate may send contributions to Sheila Englebardt, 818 Walker Ave., Greensboro, NC 27402. Indicate the contribution is for the Tranbarger Campaign.

Organ Donor Week set for April 21-27

Celebrate National Organ Donor Awareness Week, April 21-27, by signing a donor card, discussing organ donation with your family and friends, and by designating on your driver's license that you will be a donor.

Contact the transplant coordinator at the major medical center closest to you, your community hospital, or the Josh Brooks Living Memorial Transplant Association, P.O. Box 2018, Laurinburg 28352 or (919)276-7171, to make arrangements for someone to speak to any group interested in learning more about organ donation.

NORTH CAROLINA NURSES ASSOCIATION
P.O. Box 12025
Raleigh, North Carolina 27605

Vol. 47, No. 2   **March-April 1985**

Official Publication of the North Carolina Nurses Association, 103 Enterprise St., Raleigh, N.C. Tel. (919) 821-4250. Published 6 times a year. Subscription price $12 per year, included with membership dues indexed in *Cumulative Index to Nursing and Allied Health Literature* and available in MICROFORM, University Microfilms International.

JUDITH B. SEAMON .... President
HETTIE L. GARLAND .... President-Elect
GALE B. JOHNSTON .... Vice-President
SALLY S. TODD .... Secretary
CAROL A. OSMAN .... Treasurer
                STAFF
FRANCES N. MILLER ..... Executive Director
HAZEL BROWNING .....Assoc. Exec. Director
BETTY GODWIN .... Asst. Exec. Director
PATRICIA W. BRYAN ..... Administrative Asst.
DOROTHY BENNETT .... Administrative Asst.

● 1985 NCNA

L'I B R A R Y

ISSN 0039-9620

JUN 26 1985

⌐TAR HEEL NURSE

Vol. 47, No. 3   OFFICIAL PUBLICATION OF THE NORTH CAROLINA NURSES ASSOCIATION   May-June 1985

Legislative session in full swing

There is a rumor circulating through the halls of the Legislative Building that this session of the General Assembly may adjourn by the end of June or in early July. In addition, May 15 was the deadline for filing proposed legislation. Any bills filed after that date will require a 2/3 vote of both chambers to be enacted into law. In the week preceding May 15, the bill drafting office, which usually receives about 70 requests per week, received more than 300 requests from legislators who were trying to meet the bill filing deadline.

The rumor and the bill filing deadline have moved the legislative treadmill into high gear and legislators and lobbyists are quickening their steps to keep pace. It will be "survival of the fittest" from here to the finish.

■ Senate Bill 470 (SB 470) was introduced by Senator Ted Kaplan (D-Lewisville) on May 3. This is the long-awaited third party reimbursement bill. All members of NCNA have received a special edition of "Nurses Notes From the Capital" describing this proposed legislation. The bill was initially assigned to the Senate Judiciary II Committee and the committee hearing took place on May 14. Committee members heard supportive statements for the bill from Michael Crowell, attorney and lobbyist for NCNA, Judy Seamon, NCNA President, Betty Evans, CRNA, and Linda May, CNM. Although opponents of the bill, including representatives from BCBS and the NC Medical Society, were present, they chose not to speak at this committee hearing. The Judiciary II Committee was very

supportive of the bill and unanimously gave it a favorable report. When SB 470 was reported in to the Senate, it was re-referred to the Senate Insurance Committee. At the time of this writing, it is expected that the bill will be considered by the Senate Insurance Committee on May 28.

■ House Bill 52 (HB 52), as described in the March/April issue of the Tar Heel Nurse, rewrites the administrative procedures act. A committee substitute for HB 52 has passed the House and is now awaiting action from the Senate Judiciary I Committee. The substitute provides that an agency
(Continued on page 7)

NCNA members and staff were recently saddened by the deaths of members of Executive Director Frances Miller's family.
Frankie, our thoughts and prayers are with you.

Health Vote '85 results shows strong support for nurse specialists

More home care instead of hospital or nursing home care for older people and those with long term illness—

Greater use of nurse practitioners and other non-physician providers for primary health care—

These were the two measures to curb health care costs that received the greatest support by 24,000 citizens who cast ballots in the Health Vote '85 campaign recently conducted in the Triangle/Fayetteville area.

Results of the Health Vote ballot were announced May 16 by officials of the Public Agenda Foundation and the North Carolina Foundation for Alternative Health Programs, Inc., co-sponsors of the six-week long citizens information campaign.

"The ballot results clearly indicate that residents of the Triangle (Orange, Durham, and Wake Counties) and Fayetteville want more choice in their health care," said NCNA President Judy Seamon. "We have promoted the greater use of nurses in advanced practice as primary health care

providers and are even now pressing the General Assembly to remove third-party reimbursement barriers for these nurses. The Health Vote results dramatically reinforce our position."

NCNA Districts Eleven, Thirteen, and Fourteen participated in the campaign by scheduling meetings, providing trained moderators, and distributing ballots. Marjorie Bye represented NCNA on the Health Vote Advisory Board.

The thirteen options listed on the ballot and the percentage of voters who voted for offering the options now, included:
1. Prevent duplication of high cost services (such as open heart surgery) and expensive equipment in area hospitals, doctors' offices, and other health care facilities. (52.7%)
2. Have patients pay more of their own medical bills before their insurance coverage begins (say the first $300 or $400 each year), but also provide
(Continued on page 12)

June Challenge!

The Gerontological Division challenges other NCNA Divisions and Conference groups to recruit three new members by July 15.

Update on March Challenge

Carolyn Billings challenged each member of the Board of Directors to recruit one new member by the April 19, 1985 board meeting.

Fourteen (14) new members were recruited to NCNA as a result of that challenge!

Message from the President
Judith B. Seamon

In July, the first annual meeting of the ANA House of Delegates will be held. Your ten elected delegates from NCNA will once again represent you on the vital issues being considered by the national organization.

While some refinement of the new federated structure of ANA will be considered, many other issues essential to professional nursing practice and health care will be of primary importance.

One of the major issues will be the report and recommendations relating to titling and licensure for nursing practice. Resolution of this is one of the most urgent professional issues in nursing.

Broader health care issues such as the Health Policy Agenda for the American People are important because they demonstrate the involvement of nursing at the policy-making level.

Donna Diers in a recent address described the current situation in health care as a revolution, rather than a crisis which is returning nursing to the old days, whether we like it or not. She goes on to say that nursing will have the authority we have been saying we wanted and visibility we have never had before.

Our actions at the 1985 House of Delegates will be an important opportunity for nurses to accept and respond to the current and future challenges in health care. As Diers says—"The future is already with us and we cannot hold it back."

Five N.C. nurses on ANA Council ballots

The nominating committee of each of the 13 ANA councils have completed the slates for the 1985 council elections. Several North Carolina nurses are among the nominees, including:

Dorothy Talbot, Ph.D., R.N., F.A.A.N.; nominee for Chairperson, Council of Community Health Nurses

Marjorie V. Goff, M.S.H.E., R.N.; nominee for Nominating Committee, Council on Continuing Education

Janice Robinson, M.S.N., R.N.; nominee for Nominating Committee, Council on Maternal-Child Nursing

Gwendolyn C. Jones, M.S.N., R.N.; nominee for Member-at-Large, Council on Medical-Surgical Nursing

Mary Brodish, M.N., R.N., C.; nominee for Member-at-Large, Council of Perinatal Nurses

Ballots were mailed to council affiliates in late April.

Nurse Mates sponsor Heart of Gold Competition

Nurse Mates Company is sponsoring another Nurse Mates Heart of Gold award designed to recognize excellence in nursing. The program is open to RNs, LPNs, and student nurses throughout the nation. Patients, families, fellow nursing colleagues, administrators, and hospital staff can initiate nomination of a nurse who they feel has contributed above and beyond her/his normal call of duty and deserves recognition.

Twenty-five semi-finalists in the contest will receive a gold locket and a pair of Nurse Mates. Five finalists will each receive a $2,000 grant and a $1,000 check to the charity/research/educational foundation of his/her choice. One Heart of Gold winner will receive an additional $5,000 plus another $1,000 to the foundation of choice. Nomination forms are available in major hospitals and all Nurse Mate retail stores, or by writing to Nurse Mate Heart of Gold, c/o Lowell Shoe, 8 Hampshire Drive, Hudson, NH 03051.

1985 NCNA Convention program promises to be exciting, enjoyable

The Convention Program Committee has been working diligently for the past few months, planning yet another stimulating and enjoyable convention. The Convention will take place on October 23-26 at the Winston-Salem Hyatt Hotel and Benton Convention Center.

This year's theme is "Professional Power: Pathway to Progress". Barbara Brown, M.S.N., R.N., with Virginia Commonwealth University will present the keynote address, "Power Avenue: Roadway to Professionalism". Evaluation forms from the 1984 convention clearly expressed a desire to hear more from featured speaker Willis Goldbeck. Mr. Goldbeck will return this year to present the October 24 session, "Politics Parkway: Route to Influence". The Biennial Elizabeth Holley Memorial Lecture will feature North Carolina's own Cindy Freund in a session titled "Unity Boulevard: Expressway to Power".

The Convention Program Committee heeded more advice from 1984 convention evaluators who requested that the leisure living activities be maintained and that House of Delegates be planned on consecutive days. "Leisure Lane: Walkway to Wellness" is planned for the afternoon and evening of October 24 and convention participants will be able to relax and enjoy the city of Winston-Salem. House of Delegates sessions are planned for 9:00 a.m.-12:00 noon on Friday, October 25 and 9:00 a.m. until … on Saturday, October 26.

The trade show will be conducted on Thursday this year and the Country Store again promises to be a popular exhibit. District Seven will coordinate the effort and NCNA members are requested to make plans now to contribute more of their crafty talents (see Country Store advertisement in this edition).

Biennial business meetings of structural units will allow for networking and for NCNA members to address the issues of the nursing profession. Biennial election of officers will be held so bring your hard hats to avoid concussions from the campaign signs!

An NCNA Ad Hoc Committee on Structure has spent almost two years studying needed structural changes to better meet the needs of NCNA members. This committee will hold a forum during the 1985 convention to hear input from members about recommended changes. Your voice is needed and welcomed!

Finally, every effort is being made to secure a copy of the highly acclaimed film, "Code Gray: Ethical Dilemmas in Nursing". This AJN Media Award winner takes a thought-provoking look at actual situations where nurses face ethical dilemmas. It is hoped that the film will be available for viewing during several optional time periods during the convention.

All of these plans promise to bring another exciting convention to NCNA nurses! Plan now to attend!

Nurse Practitioner rights addressed by legal counsel

by Hettie Garland

"You have the right to ..." The rights of nurse practioners during an investigation by the Board of Medical Examiners was part of a presentation to the Primary Care Nurse Practitioner Conference Group Spring Continuing Education offering April 18-20, Raleigh. "When the BME comes a callin" was presented on Saturday morning by Mr. Wade Smith, NCNA's legal counsel and lobbyist.

Mr. Smith began this presentation with basic and significant assumptions. The primary one is the Board's statutory authority to conduct routine investigations into practice settings that employ NPs. The purpose is to assure compliance with the rules and regulations that govern the practice of NPs and serves a public purpose in theory. Mr. Smith urged the NPs to be as helpful and cooperative as possible but should not feel intimidated or threatened.

The rights of NPs during an investigation included the rights to request identification, the purpose of the visit, and to delay the interview if it disrupts patient care and other responsibilities. The request to delay should be reasonable, e.g., at the end of the day. NPs should ask any questions necessary to clarify the purpose of the visit and what the investigator wants to accomplish. The NP should also call the primary supervising physician or the back-up physician to inform him of the investigation and arrange for his presence during the interview. NPs should also ask what he found during the visit and request, preferably in writing, a copy of the report that is submitted to the BME.

The investigator is expected to conduct his visit in a professional, reasonable, cooperative, and efficient manner. Also, the investigation is not a "search"; that is, the investigator cannot open drawers and file cabinets or go through personal belongings. In addition, records should not be reviewed if the NP or physician is out of the office. The investigator must serve a subpoena to the physician to remove medical records from the practice setting. Some practice settings follow strict federal and/or professional guidelines concerning confidentiality of patient records. The investigator should be shown a copy of the guidelines, and he should sign the appropriate forms for confidentiality. If he refuses to sign, the BME should be notified. "The investigator is not permitted to violate the rule of reason as a rule of thumb", stated Mr. Smith. NPs are encouraged to use professional judgement if they feel the investigation is not reasonably related to its purpose. If the NP feels that the investigator is not conducting the visit in a reasonable manner, the NP should document the details of the visit and notify the BME.

A professional environment is the first thing that the investigator notes on his arrival at the practice setting; in his opinion, it "sets the stage" for the remainder of the visit. An identification badge, using the full title not just initials, such as FNP, is a must. The investigator will ask the NP to call the supervising physician, and he may use a stop watch to determine how long it takes to reach the physician. He will interview the NP to determine if the role and functions are within the rules and regulations. If several NPs are practicing together, he will want to conduct the interviews separately. Each NP is encouraged to have the supervising physician present during these interviews.

The investigator will ask to see the prescription pad and will take a copy with him. He will also question the NP about the drugs that can and cannot be prescribed by the NPs authorizing number.

The investigator will conduct a patient record audit. He will not let the office procedure, such as re-filing records, thwart this purpose. He will evaluate the record for completeness, e.g. medications listed in the plan of care, for the date of the patient visit, signature of the NP, and countersignature of the physician. If the NPs approval to practice application states that records will be countersigned in 48 hours, the investigator will request "aged" and randomly selected records to evaluate compliance.

The investigation should not take more than half an hour. If the investigation is begun as a result of a complaint, the investigator should discuss the details of the complaint with the NP and physician.

The five big "gotchas" include no identification or a name tag that is incomplete; records that are not properly signed or countersigned, practicing beyond the scope of practice; writing prescriptions outside the formulary; no reasonable access to the supervising physician; and, dishonesty. "An effort to cover something up is, the most important "gotcha," warned Mr. Smith.

Mr. Smith recommended that a checklist be devised and that NPs conduct dry runs for investigations. This would also serve as a legal quality assurance check. He also recommended that NPs develop a mechanism of networking to let others know that an investigation has been conducted. He also assured the NPs that there has been no predetermined pattern to the investigations and that he feels that random, routine investigations are a passing phase.

NPs who had been investigated commented during the discussion that they had had positive experiences with the investigators. They confirmed that, over all, the investigators were courteous and professional.

(Mr. Wade Smith is a partner in the Raleigh-based law firm of Tharrington, Smith and Hargrove.)

Education Notes

Graduate Education for Advanced Practice

**by Sylvenne Spickerman,
Chairman, Commission on Education**

A Master's Degree! In what? Does it matter? More than you probably believe! Upon earning a master's in nursing degree, one experiences many new opportunities, challenges and responsibilities.

This does not mean that all nurses should pursue a master's degree. This decision is an individual one, based upon a person's goals. However, if one wishes to advance in the nursing profession and advanced degree preparation is needed, the decision to pursue a nursing, rather than a non-nursing degree is a crucial choice.

The decision to pursue and earn a graduate degree has major significance in one's life. There must be a financial commitment which can be quite large if one considers the income not earned while in graduate school. Should one choose part-time study in order to. continue full-time employment, matriculation will cover a much longer time period. Graduate school has a major impact on the social life of many graduate students. The assumption of one more role—student—necessitates additional planning and adjustments. However, we know significant worthwhile en-deavors require major commitments. Certainly graduate school for a nurse fits in such a category.

Many, and in some areas most, nurses who consider graduate education concede that the pursuit must be on a part-time basis. The individual believes he/she must remain employed in order to afford graduate school. The most frequent concerns of potential students are 1) how much will it cost? 2) can I earn the degree part-time in the evening? 3) how accessible is a program (job and family responsibilities won't go away)? 4) what are the program requirements? and 5) what differences will it make after I earn the degree?

Considering these factors, the individual prospective student must identify his/her goals and purposes for pursuing graduate education. Professing disillusions about nursing and graduate nursing education obscures direction and impedes setting and achieving goals. *Nursing education is gained in graduate nursing programs.* If one's goal includes continuing in the nursing profession, advanced preparation must be in nursing—nursing practice, nursing education, nursing administration and supervision, and nursing specialization. This belief is pervasive and absolute at the master's level today. Progress is being made, but as yet many people think it is too restrictive to say absolutely nothing except nursing at the doctoral level.

Nursing needs, in fact must have, many more nurses prepared at the masters and doctoral levels if nursing is to compete in the health care arena. For decades, if not centuries, nursing has struggled to define, develop, organize, and enlarge its body of specialized knowledge. This requires nurses with advanced nursing preparation to develop nursing theory as well as to practice, teach, administer, and research nursing.

No group other than nursing that has an entry level below the baccalaureate debates its professional status. Neither does a master's degree outside the discipline enable one to advance in the original interest area. When a person holding an undergraduate degree in social work earns a master's degree in sociology, he/she does not have advanced preparation for social work. Society considers that such a person has made a career change and so expects him/her to earn the doctorate in sociology in order to assume a leadership position in the new discipline. So is the case in nursing. Nurses must accept this fact and act accordingly.

The time was that any graduate degree earned by a nurse was an EVENT. Those days are past. We must live in the present and prepare for the future. For the sake of nursing's future, many more nurse leaders must become prepared in nursing, by nurse faculty. Without this level and extent of preparation, nursing cannot make its contribution to health care in the 21st century.

Think graduate school! Nursing graduate school! In North Carolina that is Duke, East Carolina, UNC-Chapel Hill, UNC-Charlotte, and UNC-Greensboro. For NLN accredited programs in other states contact NLN Headquarters, 10 Columbus Circle, New York, NY 10019.

Reimbursement legislative effort receives support

The North Carolina Chapter of the American College of Nurse Midwives recently issued a very tangible display of support for the third party reimbursement legislative effort—a check for $250. In so doing, the group expressed their appreciation for NCNA's "never failing commitment" to advance the nursing profession.

In addition, NCNA's own Primary Care Nurse Practitioner Conference Group recently conducted a trade show in conjunction with their spring conference. Conference Group Chairman, Judith Roberts, reported the group's decision to contribute the proceeds from that trade show to support lobbying efforts for the reimbursement bill—a contribution of $750!

CAMPS SEA GULL-SEAFARER NURSE

CAMPS SEA GULL/SEAFARER NURSES

Coastal summer camps have openings for nurses. Enjoyable and purposeful experience on the coast of North Carolina; good salary; comfortable accommodations; food and lodging furnished; modern, air-conditioned Infirmary; resident physicians; opportunity to participate in camp activities. Must be an RN or graduate nurse; must have excellent references. Camp season: June 9-August 9. Excellent opportunity for new graduates to enjoy a "change of pace" position before commitment to professional hospital duties. 38th season · Sea Gull; 25th season · Seafarer. Write for application and catalog to Don Cheek, Director, Camp Sea Gull for boys and Camp Seafarer for girls; P.O. Box 10976, Raleigh, North Carolina.

N.C. educator made NCNA membership a top priority

In 1931, Eva Woosley Warren had a B.A. in Biology and a dream of being a nurse. In her family, neither were unusual. Her Moravian parents strongly believed in college education for their four daughters (two were teachers and two were nurses). Eva's father was the "moving force" in her life-long desire for advanced education, and her aunt (also a nurse) had a great influence on her choice of nursing as a profession. So after graduation from the North Carolina College for Women (now UNC-Greensboro), Eva entered the Training School for Nurses of the Jefferson Medical College Hospital of Philadelphia. In 1934, she took her first job as a pediatric staff nurse at Watts Hospital for the generous salary of $45 per month plus housing, meals and laundry service. (Eva's college education merited her a higher monthly salary than the average staff nurse.) Eva was soon promoted to night nursing supervisor. In addition to her nursing duties, she was expected to act as telephone operator, pharmacist and admitting officer! From this position she advanced to teaching "Nursing Arts" (basic nursing procedures) at the Watts Hospital School of Nursing. Almost all other classes were taught by physicians at that time. She soon advanced to Educational Director — a position she held until 1949. Ready for a "change", Eva took a job with the Durham City-County Health Department. It wasn't long before she realized that she was "low man on the totem pole" because of her lack of public health education. She had already received her MEd from Duke in 1950, so she entered UNC-Chapel Hill and obtained a MPH with a major in nursing in 1951. Eva enjoyed public health nursing, but her strong desire and innate talent for teaching led her back to Watts School of Nursing in 1955. She retained her position there as Educational Director until 1960 when she became the first dean of the School of Nursing at East Carolina College (later to become East Carolina University). She retired from her position as Dean in 1969, a role she describes as "the most

Eva Woosley Warren

satisfying of my professional life; the culmination of my life's goals."

Where has NCNA fit into Eva's plans and professional goals? From the very beginning! Long before her graduation from nursing school, her aunt "lectured" her about the importance of joining the state nurses' association and the Red Cross immediately after passing the state board exam. So she joined NCNA in 1934 and became truly involved in the association's activities because, for her, it was the natu-

ral thing to do. She was NCNA's treasurer (and on the Board of Directors) for twenty years; chairman of several committes, including education; and a past president of what is now District 11.

Of her experiences as an NCNA member in the last fifty years, which has made the greatest impression on her? "Being a board member for twenty years was an incredible experience," explains Eva. "I remember voting on the 'entry into practice' issue in 1965. It was a tremendous step. It was also one of the best things we did for nursing. We have not advanced with it as far as I would have hoped. It is still our biggest challenge."

During her retirement, Eva has enjoyed working in her flower and vegetable gardens and doing needlework. But she has also made time for community activities. She has taught nurses' aides for the local Home Extension Service and the Alamance County Council on Aging, and has taken histories at local Red Cross Bloodmobiles. She has been a member and past president of the local Business and Professional Women's organization; and has been active in her church, garden club and District 11. She has had the opportunity to travel and has visited all fifty states and central Europe. One of her pet projects has been to research the Woosley family in North Carolina and to have the results printed in book form. Copies have been placed in the Geneology Room of the North Carolina Archives and in the Moravian Archives in Salem.

ANA Delegates Meet to Discuss Titling and Licensure Report

On May 8, 1985, the NCNA delegates to ANA met with representatives of several NCNA structural groups and interested members to discuss the ANA Board of Directors "Titling and Licensure Report." This report was published in the April issue of the *American Nurse* and outlined six areas for which national consensus has been determined. The report concludes with a recommendation for the 1985 ANA House of Delegates to urge state nurses associations to direct efforts in four areas: Establish the baccalaureate degree with a major in nursing as minimum educational preparation for professional nursing and retain the title of "registered nurse;" establish the associate degree with a major in nursing for technical nursing; assure congruence of educational preparation and scope of practice; continue efforts to develop consensus on the legal title for technical nurse.

The discussion on May 8, 1985, focused on the areas of consensus and the

recommendations. The group agreed with the areas of consensus and the first three recommendations, but did not accept the idea of "continue efforts" in the last recommendation. The delegates were directed to work for retaining the title "R.N." for the professional nurse and be flexible in the title for the technical nurse. The group felt that the legal title for the technical nurse should be determined at the 1985 House of Delegates. In order for the NCNA delegates to decide their position on this title, the group urged the delegates to consider what is put forth at the House of Delegates; voice concern if the title "LPN" is suggested; and if the words "Registered Nurse" are suggested to be used in the title that another word be used to separate them, such as "Registered Technical Nurse."

The NCNA delegates to the ANA Convention will be housed and caucusing at the Hyatt Regency in Kansas City.

Focus on *Your* Practice

NCNA testified in Support of OSHA Standard Amendment

Judy Seamon presented testimony for NCNA on the OSHA Hazard Communication Standard on April 29, 1985. This testimony presented facts to illustrate NCNA's position in support of the proposed amendment to the OSHA Hazard Communication Standard. This amendment adds nurses to the definition of health professionals, thereby including nurses among those authorized for access to trade secret information in non-emergency situations.

Facts presented in the testimony included the acknowledgement that occupational health nurses provided 75% of the health care to the American work force, and in most situations the nurse is the only health professional in regular duty at the work site. At present, this OSHA standard defines health professonals entitled to trade secret information in non-emergency situations as physicians, industrial hygienists, toxicologists, and epidemiologists. None of these health professionals are commonly found on-site nor in daily contact with employees as is the occupational health nurse.

Mary Lou Moore, RNC, Ph.D, FAAN
Chairman, Commission on Practice

The North Carolina Humanities Committee awarded the NCNA Commission on Practice a planning grant of $500 to develop seminars which will focus on the use of the Code for Nurses in everyday practice. The planning committee will meet in early Fall to develop a proposal for these seminars. The development of this proposal has been a major project of the Commission on Practice this year. Mary Lou Moore, Commission Chairman, will chair the planning committee.

The Code for Nurses is one of three documents with which every practicing nurse should be very familiar. A booklet, *Perspectives on the Code*, is available from NCNA for $2. While the code is not a legal document, it has been cited at least once in court cases in North Carolina as an example of an expected standard of behavior.

Other documents which determine our practice are our North Carolina Nurse Practice Act (available from the Board of Nursing), the ANA Standards of Practice (available in both a generic form and for many nursing specialties from NCNA), and the policies of your practice setting. A number of nursing specialty organizations also have developed standards for specialty practices.

While no written document can provide the answer to every practice dilemma, having these four documents readily available and being highly familiar with their contents should ensure a high quality of nursing practice and protect you from decisions which may be harmful to patients/clients and to yourself.

Think Membership

Balloting Procedure Allows Absentee Voting in 85 Election

NCNA members may vote for officers and ANA delegates by absentee ballot. Voting also will take place at polls open during the 1985 October convention in Winston-Salem.

Members not able to attend the convention may request an absentee ballot and cast it by mail prior to the convention. The absentee ballots will be turned over to election tellers and counted along with the votes cast at convention.

Because of this voting procedure, nominations from the floor at the convention are no longer possible. However, any member can self-declare for any office for which the member is qualified. The Nominating Committee's slate will be published in the July-August *Tar Heel Nurse*, along with a consent-to-serve form for self-declaring. Members will then have until September 23rd to self-declare.

The following offices will be filled in the 1985 election: president-elect; vice-president; secretary; treasurer; two directors (for four-year terms); chairmen of commissions on education, health affairs, member services, and practice; nominating committee, collective bargaining representative; two ANA delegates-at-large and seven ANA delegates.

Following is the timetable and procedure governing absentee voting:

Nominating and absentee voting timetable and procedure

August 24, 1985—Deadline for publishing slate prepared by Nominating Committee.

Slate will be published in July-August Tar Heel Nurse, accompanied by a form for self-declaring for office and notice of deadline for self-declaring.

September 23, 1985—Deadline for self-declarations to reach Nominating Committee. NCNA consent form must be used.

September 26, 1958—Nominating Committee rules on qualifications of self-declared candidates. Ballot is printed.

October 3, 1985—Deadline for member to request absentee ballot. Request must be accompanied by stamped #10 (4"x9½") self-addressed envelope. The following will be mailed to each bona fide member requesting absentee ballot:

1. ballot
2. instructions for marking and mailing ballot
3. brief biographical data on self-declared candidates
4. unmarked inner envelope to be signed by voter
5. marked outer envelope to go to chairman of tellers

October 3, 1985—Absentee ballots mailed to members requesting.

October 11, 1985—Deadline for postmarking of voted absentee ballots to be returned to NCNA secretary.

Biographical information on self-declared candidates will be available at polls for members voting at polling place.

Voting day at convention—Absentee ballots delivered to tellers.

Legislative Update from page 1

covered by Article 3A of the bill (chiefly occupational licensing agencies) are to apply to the office of administrative hearings for designation of a hearing officer to preside at the hearing of a contested case if (a) a majority of the agency is unable to hear the case or (b) a majority elects not to hear the case. Other regulatory agencies are subject to the office of administrative hearings in all contested cases. NCNA will continue to monitor this bill.

■ HB 84, an act clarifying the HMO statute, was described in the March/April issue of the Tar Heel Nurse. The House did concur in the Senate Amendment sought by NCNA and other professional groups and the bill was ratified on March 26.

■ A committee substitute for SB 39, an act to mandate the use of seat belts for front seat occupants of motor vehicles, has faced many obstacles since its introduction on 2/18/85. The bill substitute received a favorable report from the Senate Judiciary I Committee and passed the full Senate on third reading on 4/17/85. The House Committee on Highway Safety then took several weeks to study the bill but finally gave it a favorable report. The bill spawned much debate on the House floor where it passed second reading by a 59-47 vote on Thursday, May 16. When the bill came up for third reading on Friday, May 17, yet another obstacle postponed action. The bill was amended to require that the issue be put to a statewide referendum in the fall. At that point, the bill was removed from the calendar. The bill was on the calendar again on Monday evening, May 20. Proponents were successful in removing the referendum amendment and the bill then narrowly passed third reading by a vote of 60-51. The Senate did concur in the House amendment and SB39 has been ratified.

■ An amended version of Rep. Richard Wright's bill to repeal the Pay Equity Study (HB 236) was ratified on April 30. Since that time, other bills have been introduced dealing with the pay equity issue. These include HB 802 (Rep. Anne Barnes, Chapel Hill) which creates a Pay Equity Commission and HB 1177 (Rep. Paul Pulley, Durham) which creates a state personnel classification study. Both bills were assigned to the House Appropriations Committee. NCNA supports a study of the pay equity issue and will continue to monitor all proposed legislation on this topic.

■ HB 836 would amend the Pharmacy Practice Act and allow RNs in public health departments, under certain conditions, to dispense prescription drugs and devices. Rep. Joe Hudson (D-Waxhaw) introduced HB836 on May 3 on behalf of a coalition of groups who have been working on the issue for approximately 18 months. The coalition included representatives of NCNA, local health directors, the

Association of County Commissioners, NC Pharmaceutical Association and Pharmacy Board, the State Health Director and Chief Nurse. Conditions prescribed in the bill include the following: (1) dispensing may occur only at the public health clinic; (2) clinic must obtain a pharmacy permit; (3) pharmacist-manager, or another pharmacist at his direction, must review dispensing records at least weekly and be responsible to Board of Pharmacy for all clinic dispensing activity; (4) the RN must complete a training program on labeling and packaging; and (5) only drugs and devices included in a formulary may be dispensed. The bill received a favorable report from the House Committee on Health on 5/14/85 and passed second and third readings in the House on May 15 and 16 respectively. The vote on second reading was 72-14 reflecting primarily Republican negative votes based on objections from Republican Rep. Brad Ligon who objected to "government intruding further into private enterprise." Third reading passage was by a 90-12 margin. The bill will now go to the Senate.

■ SB 286, introduced by Sen. Tony Rand (D-Fayetteville), would create a NC Medical Database Commission with a seven-member board with representatives of the business community, the insurance industry (both commercial and BCBS), one physician, one hospital administrator and one representative of state government. The bill sets out legislative intent and purpose to include the following: "maintain an acceptable quality of health care services in North Carolina and yet at the same time improve the cost efficiency and effectiveness of health care services." It further requires that information necessary for a review and comparison of cost, utilization, and quality of health services be supplied to the commission by all health care providers and third-party payors, to make compiled data available to interested persons to improve decision-making regarding purchase price and use of health care services, and to protect patient confidentiality. The bill awaits action in the Senate Judiciary IV Committee.

■ HB 348 (Rep. H. Payne, D-Wilmington), SB 335 (Sen. Harris, D-Kings Mountain), and SB 350 (Sen. Walker, D-Asheboro) all deal with workplace hazardous substances and the public's right to know of the presence of such substances. Both Senate bills were assigned to the Senate Human Resources Committee, and Rep. Payne's bill is in a subcommittee of the House Water and Air Resources Committee. NCNA will monitor these bills. One of our principal concerns is to assure that nurses are among the health professionals to whom specific chemical identity is made available when needed. Nurses, particularly in occupational health settings, are often the first line of defense in dealing with injuries/illnesses resulting from hazardous chemicals in the workplace.

■ HB 817 was introduced on May 2 by Rep. Marie Colton (D-Asheville). The bill provides for an appropriation of $80,000 during 1985-87 fiscal years to the Department of Human Resources, Division of Health Services. Monies will be used to conduct programs to train public health nurse supervisors, directors, public health staff and community health aides. HB 817 has been referred to the house Committee on Appropriations.

■ Rep. Caspter Holroyd (D-Raleigh), introduced HB 1021 on May 15, which would repeal Chapter 153A-77 of the General Statutes. This statute has allowed counties of 325,000 or greater to assume control of functions of all boards and commissions, including boards of health, social services and mental health. Thus far, only Mecklenburg County Commissioners have taken advantage of this provision. The NCNA House of Delegates passed a resolution at the 1984 convention in support of legislation to repeal the cited statute. HB 1021 has been referred to the House Committee on Health. NCNA will be visible in supporting Rep. Holroyd's efforts to repeal GS 153A-77.

While copies of all bills introduced just prior to the May 15 deadline were not yet available at the time of this writing, NCNA lobbyists are aware that some of the proposed legislation will deal with studies of health promotion, long term care insurance, elderly respite care, and professional liability. A Child Vaccine Injury Compensation bill (HB 1088) has been introduced amid a recent public flurry of controversy over DPT vaccines.

In addition, NCNA lobbyists are tracking more than 40 other bills.

Nurse-PAC Plans Celebrity Auction

Jo Franklin, Chairman of Nurse-PAC, reports that some big plans for the committee's convention activities are underway. Nurse-PAC will sponsor a "Celebrity Auction" on Friday evening, October 25, following the close of the Annual Banquet function at the NCNA Convention. Nurse-PAC members are busy contacting local, state and national celebrities of all kinds —political figures, movie stars, singers, etc. Personal items donated by these celebrities will be auctioned off to the highest bidder at the Nurse-PAC Celebrity Auction.

Items will be on display during a reception preceding the Friday evening Banquet. Convention participants will be able to enjoy a fun-filled evening with a professional auctioneer and bid on a personal treasure from their favorite celebrity.

Jo Franklin invites everyone to come to the event ready to enjoy the excitement of a rousing public auction ... and she reminds you to remember your checkbook!

Minimum Employment Standards for Registered Nurses

Philosophy

The North Carolina Nurses Association, the organization of professional nurses in North Carolina, believes that the quality of nursing practice is substantially influenced by and inseparable from the employment conditions of nurses. As professionals, nurses have the right and responsibility to influence their employment conditions to achieve the maximum in practice climate, and they have the responsibility and obligation to participate in determining standards of nursing practice and to implement and evaluate these standards in their work settings.

Minimum Responsibilities Of The Registered Nurse

The Registered Nurse is currently licensed to practice under the North Carolina Nursing Practice Act.

The Registered Nurse is a member of the professional organization for nurses.

The Registered Nurse adheres to the professional and ethical standards in the "Code for Nurses".

The Registered Nurse participates in the planning, establishment, and implementation of policies and procedures in the work setting.

The Registered Nurse shares responsibility with the employer for continuing professional growth and for maintaining knowledge of current nursing concepts and practices.

The Registered Nurse maintains adequate professional liability insurance coverage to provide protection to the patient and the nursing care provider. Financial responsibility for adequate individual coverage rests with the nurse but may be shared by or provided by the employer.

Professional Conditions of Employment

Nurse Executive

Nursing is represented at the executive level of management by a nurse who reports directly to the Chief Executive Officer. The nurse executive is educationally and experientially prepared for the position.

The nurse executive participates in decision-making that affects the organization as a whole, and is accountable for those functions directly pertaining to nursing.

The nurse executive assures that as a clinical practice discipline nursing has authority over its own practice.

Nursing Management

Nurse managers assure communication and participatory decision-making at all levels of practice in order to identify and manage those resources necessary to ensure safe and effective patient care.

Nurse managers assure that nurses at every level are involved in policy development and decision-making across the organization.

Nursing Practice

The employer respects the judgement of the nurse in accepting or rejecting an assignment. Factors to be taken into account by the nurse when making such a judgement are his or her level of fatigue, and the match between his or her competencies and preparation and the clinical assignment.

A Patient Classification System is used to establish appropriate hours of patient care, patient/staff ratios, and appropriate staff mix for the provision of safe, effective patient/client-centered care. Such a classification system includes time allotment for the following:

1. Assessing and planning, and implementing care to meet patients' identified bio/psycho/social/spiritual/cultural needs;
2. Evaluating the effectiveness of nursing measures;
3. Staff development activities;
4. Participation in decentralized decision-making.

Nursing personnel routinely participate in formal dialogue and collaborate with medical staff and other health care professionals in determining optimal approaches to patient care and resolving interpersonal conflicts.

Nursing Research

The employment setting provides an atmosphere which encourages and facilitates the identification of nursing problems and the systematic investigation of those problems by nurses.

Professional Development

Provisions are made for: a) a planned orientation program for each new employee; b) an organized, on-going training program to assure the acquisition of knowledge and skills necessary to perform in the individual's clinical area and to assist in the development of new skills as responsibilities change or increase; c) time off without loss of pay for participation in the activities of the professional organization (such time should be given on a fair and adequate basis determined by the needs of the individual and the institution or agency); d) time and financial aid for participating in educational institutes, workshops, or meetings which will improve the individual's on-the-job performance; e) time and/or financial assistance for participation in formal educational programs leading to baccalaureate or higher degrees in nursing.

Opportunities exist for career advancement in administration, education, and clinical practice.

General Conditions of Employment

Policies regarding conditions of employment are in writing and made available to the nurse prior to employment. Individual contracts should be negotiated for nursing administrators and middle management nursing positions.

Employment, assignment, promotion, and salary determination are based upon professional qualifications, including education and experience, irrespective of race, creed, color, sex, national origin, or other personal factors not pertinent to performance.

Standard procedures are established for pre-employment processing, such as, the posting of vacancies, procedures for interviewing, and criteria for determination of the best qualified applicant.

The title of the position reflects the responsibilities, duties and qualifications as elaborated in the job description. Each nursing position has a well-defined job description which includes line of accountability, minimum responsibilities, and necessary qualifications.

An appointment to a position in which a registered nurse has had previous experience is compensated above the beginning salary.

Promotion is based on performance, education, and experience. There is a cooperative job performance and salary review six months after employment and annually thereafter. Each nurse is entitled to an individual annual evaluation review with his/her immediate supervisor with an opportunity to have verbal input and a written response put on file.

The employment setting allocates adequate support space for storage of supplies, preparation for procedures, and documentation of care provided. Conference space is readily accessible.

Salary

For each position there is an established salary range to give recognition for previous satisfactory experience, additional responsibilities and additional educational qualifications.

Salaries are reviewed annually and adjusted to meet increases in cost-of-living. There should be, in addition, a plan for regular salary increases that reflect evidence of improved practice, continuing education, certification, and professional growth. Size of institutuion, complexity of patient care and administration, geographic location, and educational preparation and experience of the nurse are considered in determining the appropriate salary level of the nurse.

A nurse assigned temporarily to the full responsibilities of a higher position is compensated for such work at the rate of pay applicable to the higher position.

Part-Time Work

A nurse employed for less than the scheduled work week, but on a regular basis, receives not less than the hourly rate and benefits proportionate to those for full-time employees in the same positions.

Work Hours

A nurse is not required to work excessive amounts of overtime. When overtime is necessary it is compensated at not less than 1½ times the average hourly rate for that pay period.

No more than two different shifts are worked within a two week period. Differentials are paid for evening, night, and weekend shifts.

Rotation of shifts does not occur without adequate recovery time between shifts.

Holidays

At least eight holidays with pay are granted. If a holiday falls on the nurse's day off, or if the nurse is required to work on a holiday, one day off in lieu thereof is given within thirty days prior to or sixty days after the holiday. If a holiday falls during vacation time, one day is added to the vacation period.

Vacation

Annual paid vacation is at least 15 work days. Vacation time taken before the completion of one year is prorated.

Where employment is terminated, the nurse receives terminal vacation salary for the vacation days accumulated.

Sick Leave

One and one-fourth days of paid sick leave for each month on continuous employment, cumulative, are granted.

Leaves of Absence

Except in emergency situations, leaves of absence are requested in advance in writing. Leaves of absence are granted in writing, specifying the length of leave, the amount of salary to be continued and other benefits to be accrued. Leaves of absence do not affect accumulated sick leave, vacation, or tenure. When returning from a leave of absence, the nurse is reinstated in the same, comparable, or higher position at the earliest opportunity.

EMERGENCY LEAVE: When there is critical illness or death in the immediate family (as defined in the personnel policies), leave with pay is granted.

MATERNITY LEAVE: The nurse is granted up to six months of maternity leave without pay, beyond accrued benefits. Extension beyond six months is determined on an individual basis.

EDUCATIONAL LEAVE: After one year of continuous employment educational leave should be granted to further professional growth and development.

MILITARY LEAVE: Military leave is granted and shall not be considered part of earned vacation.

SABBATICAL LEAVE: Sabbatical leave should be established and appropriate compensation determined.

PERSONAL LEAVE: Requests for leaves of absence, other than for reasons stated above, are considered on an individual basis.

PROFESSIONAL AND CIVIC RESPONSIBILITIES: Time off with pay is granted to attend civic, educational and professional meetings, conventions, workshops and institutes which will contribute to the improvement of nursing practice.

JURY DUTY: The employer supplements jury duty compensation to equal the nurse's regular rate of pay.

Health Benefits

EMPLOYMENT HEALTH: Pre-employment and annual health examinations, including essential laboratory tests as indicated, are provided by the employer, without cost to the nurse.

Employee Health Services are available offering routine exams, prevention programs, treatment for work related illness/injury and screening and referral assistance for personal problems.

Adequate education about and protection against environmental and occupational hazards is provided. Should they be required for work-related illness or injury, appropriate diagnostic and therapeutic interventions are provided at no cost.

HEALTH INSURANCE: Employer-financed insurance (hospitalization, accident, and disability) are preferable; however, joint participation with the employee may be the initial step toward employer-financed plans.

Retirement

The employer makes available a retirement plan to supplement Social Security. The retirement fund provides an annual report to the employee of projected monthly income.

Grievance Procedure

A well-defined grievance procedure is established which also outlines the categories of employees covered. The steps to be followed are clearly stated and known to all involved.

Transportation

When a nurse is required to use his/her own vehicle to accomplish his/her job responsibilities a system of reimbursement is established and periodically reviewed to assure a fair return to the nurse.

(Continued on next page)

Minimum Employment Standards *from page 9*

Termination of Service

At least thirty (30) days written notice of resignation is given by the nurse. Reasons for resignation are given.

The nurse is not dismissed without cause. At least thirty (30) days written notice of dismissal or salary in lieu thereof are given by the employer. The employer states the reasons for dismissal.

Should it become necessary for an employer to immediately suspend a nurse for a suspected violation of the Nursing Practice Act or to terminate a nurse's employment for a violation, the employer informs the North Carolina Board of Nursing (the legal body empowered to prosecute violators) documenting the circumstances necessitating the suspension or dismissal.

> The North Carolina Nurses Association has developed Minimum Employment Standards for Registered Nurses and has promoted their implementation since 1947, as part of the Association's Economic and General Welfare Program. The Standards have been revised regularly since that time. This document is the 1985 revision, developed by the NCNA Commission on Member Services and approved by the Board of Directors. Additional copies are available from NCNA.

Commission on Member Services
CHAIRPERSON
Carolyn V. Billings, RN, MSN, CS

MEMBERS

Brenda Bessard, RN, BSN, MEd.	Kaye Helfrich, RN
Cynthia Cox Bussey, RN, C, BSN	Mary Mercer, RN, BSN
Carol Cox, RN, MPH, CSNP	Joyce H. Monk, RN, BSN
Davy F. Crockett, RN, BSN, MPA	Webra R. Price, RN, C, MSN
Jane Fox, RN, BSN	Elizabeth A. Trought, RN, MN

Sub-Committee on Minimum Employment Standards for Registered Nurses
CHAIRPERSON
Joyce H. Monk, RN, BSN

MEMBERS

Carolyn V. Billings, RN, MSN, CS   Elizabeth A. Trought, RN, MN
Miriam M. Quick, RN, MPh

NEWS BRIEFS

• *AJN* was one of this year's recipients of the Regional Media Award competition given by Sigma Theta Tau. The award was in recognition of the feature "Assessing the Democrats," which appeared in the February, 1984 issue.

• Sigma Theta Tau is accepting nominations for media awards to be given at the annual convention in November, 1985. Deadline for entries is August 15, 1985. Nominations are accepted as self-nomination, by any member of the communications or nursing field, and by members of Sigma Theta Tau. For information contact (317) 634-8171.

• The final report of the Nursing Competencies Study Group convened by the Program on Access to Health Care has been published. Copies have been disseminated to those who participated in the study. For copies call Mary Alice Sherrill at (919) 832-9550.

• Linda Crabtree publishes a newsletter for people with Charcot-Marie-Tooth Disease, also known as Peroneal Muscular Atrophy. Ms. Crabtree has lived with the disease for 41 years and would like to share her newsletter and remedy the frustrations that accompany this dease. For information write: Linda Crabtree, 34-B Bayview Drive, St. Catherines, Ontario, Canada, L2N4Y6.

• Professional Practice for Nurse Administrators/Directors of Nursing in Long Term Care (Phase I), authored by project co-director Mary P. Lodge, Ed.D., R.N., details the applied research effort of ANF which focused on improvement of quality of care of the aged through more definitive professional education and development

of the nurse administrator of long-term care settings for the present and future. To order call (800) 821-5834, Pub. No. Fo-27, cost $15.50.

• *Standards of Nursing Practice in Correctional Facilities.* Being in jail, prison, a juvenile detention facility, or a similar setting doesn't preclude an individual's need for—or the right to—health care. Incarcerated persons are entitled to health care that is equal to that provided in the community, and governed by the same regulations, according to a new publication from the American Nurses' Association. Being

employed in such a setting does not alter the scope of nursing practice for the practitioner. Nurses who provide care to persons in correctional facilities are guided by the same philosophy, ethics, responsibilities, functions, roles, skills, and legal authority as their counterparts in general nursing environments. To order call (800) 821-5834. Pub. No. CH-11, $4.00.

• The N.C. Hospital Association will hold their Summer meeting July 17-19, 1985, in Asheville, N.C., Grove Park Inn. Registration deadline is July 12, 1985. Call Barbara Tilton at (919) 832-9550 for details.

North Carolina Nurses Association
announces

MEMBERSHIP AWARD
REWARD AND RECOGNITION PROGRAM

Recognition of a registered nurse in North Carolina who has made a significant contribution to membership growth in NCNA.

AWARD:	Recognition for outstanding member who has individually done the most to increase membership.
GUIDELINES FOR ENTRIES:	Nominations are to be made by district executive boards. Nomination forms have been sent to each district.
DEADLINE FOR ENTRY:	September 1, 1985
SELECTION:	To be made by the Membership Committee, NCNA
	Award will be presented at the 1985 convention of the North Carolina Nurses Association, October 23-26, 1985 at the Winston-Salem Hyatt Hotel.
SUBMIT ENTRY TO:	Membership Committee North Carolina Nurses Association P.O. Box 12025 Raleigh, NC 27605

Focus \ on Districts

by Betty Godwin

Districts took a variety of approaches to inform the public that "nursing care makes the difference." This was the theme sponsored by ANA for National Nurses Day, May 6, 1985.

For most districts, May is the month for the last meeting before a summer break and the election of new officers, as well as the month to celebrate Nurses' Day. This allows districts to plan special meetings to celebrate those coincidental events, and honor these members who have made significant contributions to nursing and NCNA.

Members of District Ten have for several years contemplated some form of recognition that would be fitting for a loyal, supportive colleague who has devoted more than a half-century of her life to the nursing profession. The district voted to name Faye Simpson Alamance County's 1985 Nurse of the Year. The local news media were very cooperative in helping proclaim the announcement, which coincided with National Nurses's Week. District Ten sent flowers to Faye on Nurse's Day and invited her to be guest of honor at the May district dinner meeting at Tollner's Restaurant in Burlington. In responding to the District's tribute, presented by Vivian Scott, Faye spoke of her almost 60 years of continuous involvement in her district, state and national associations. She concluded by

saying: "And, I shall continue my membership so long as I have the presence of mind to sign a check in payment of my dues."

As districts have shared their many activities centered around Nurse's Day, it is evident that nurses are becoming more successful in their use of public media. Several districts sent the audio tape supplied by the NCNA Public Relations Committee to local radio stations. District Three produced their own tapes. District Twenty Two sponsored radio and television programs in several district towns, Wilmington, Kenansville and Whiteville.

Districts including Eight, Twenty Two and Thirty One sponsored public health education and assessment projects to communicate the theme, "Nursing care makes the difference." These projects included blood pressure checks in public shopping areas, distribution of health educational materials, and sponsoring community service educational seminars.

Through these efforts, nursing gains the visibility that is needed to promote nursing's image as a caring profession that has assumed a leadership role in health care. Activities such as these are not limited to Nurse's Day but must be a part of an ongoing statewide effort.

District 10 designated Fay Simpson Alamance County 1985 Nurse of the Year

Nurse employers celebrate nurses on Nurses' Day

Throughout North Carolina, hospitals, long term care agencies, health departments, and other employers of nurses acknowledged the contributions by nurses during the week of May 6, 1985. Many agencies presented nurses with flowers, receptions, special programs, and personalized expressions of "thank-you" to the agency. A number of these efforts to honor nurses were not limited to the agency, but were shared with the public, thus enhancing the public's awareness of nursing's role in health care.

Albemarle Hospital in Elizabeth City aggressively publicized Nurses' Day by distributing five exclusive feature articles on nurses to the local media. These articles focused on individuals and their practice areas. Moore Memorial Hospital in Pinehurst placed an ad in two local newspapers thanking the nurses for their care. Similarly, Medical Personnel Pool in Durham placed a large ad in the Durham Morning Harold and Raleigh News and Observer.

Sampson Memorial Hospital extended their efforts to publically acknowledge nurses by inviting other community employers to join them in sponsoring an ad in the local newspaper, the *Sampson Independent.* This type effort achieved several things: public awareness of nurses, nurses realizing they are appreciated, and development of good relations among the community health agencies that chose to participate.

This is but a mere sample of activities

(Continued on page 12)

Frankie Miller addressed District 20 meeting on May 14th.

NCNA announces new member benefit: Memberloan Program

ATTENTION, NCNA member—there is a new member benefit available for you— money!

NCNA is pleased to introduce The Memberloan Program as a service to its members. This program is a convenient and practical solution for those times when you need extra cash—and we all have those times!

The NCNA Memberloan Program includes these special features:

● **Money is available now**—For personal loans, no security is needed if you qualify—just your signature on a completed application.

● Your **decide how much** you want to borrow— up to $5000.00 for personal loans.

● **You decide how long** to take to repay your loan—from one to five years, depending on the size of your loan.

● **No prepayment penalties** are charged if you decide to pay off your loan early nor are any points or fees charged.

● **Flexible repayment loans** allow for smaller payments over a longer period of time.

● **Cash rebate** of 3% of all finance charges at the end of the loan if all monthly payments are paid when due.

● **Refinancing of loans** can occur if interest rates go down.

● **Total confidentiality** is assured to all members.

Just call the toll free number, 1-800-245-4486 for additional information or an application. When your application is approved, your check is mailed promptly. If you are a nurse with a good credit rating, you will probably qualify on your signature alone.

This special service is available only to nurses who are members of NCNA, a sponsoring association of the Memberloan program.

Watch for a mailing in June about this exciting new member benefit for all NCNA members!

NCNA committed to RN bargaining unit

The NCNA Board of Directors has renewed its commitment to the RN bargaining unit at Durham VA Medical Center in representing the unit in contract renegotiations. The NCNA Commission on Member Services, District 11 and VA Medical Center nurses have worked diligently for almost a year to revitalize and strengthen the bargaining unit and the unit has achieved the required 60% membership. The contract expiration date is June 22. NCNA will work diligently in bargaining for an acceptable contract.

ANA grants constituent membership on NCNA

The ANA Board of Directors has conferred continuing constituent membership on NCNA in accordance with Article V, Seciton 5(1) of the ANA Bylaws. This action was taken at the March 7, 1985 meeting of the board, based on the recommendation of the ANA Committee on Bylaws. A certificate of membership will be issued once constituent status is conferred upon all state nurses associations.

Nurse Employers Celebrate
from page 11

that centered around Nurses' Day. The Public Relations Committee of NCNA is pleased that these activities seem to increase each year and appreciate agencies sharing their ideas.

Think Membership

Health Vote '85 Results *from page 1*

better coverage for expensive catastrophic illness. (32.6%)

3. Spend less money on rare, expensive procedures such as transplants and more of our health care dollars on preventive medicine such as prenatal care for *all* women, and checkups and vaccinations for *every* child. (57.9%)

4. Have the government reimburse hospitals and doctors for treating patients without adequate insurance, but *only when* those hospitals and doctors demonstrate that they are holding costs down. (53.8%)

5. Require poor people whose medical care is paid by government to use only those doctors, hospitals, and other health care providers with a record of holding down costs. (53.5%)

6. Limit the use of very expensive technology for patients with almost no chance of recovery—that is, ration some type of medicine. (41.3%)

7. Change Medicare—the program that provides health insurance to everyone over 65—so that older people with higher incomes pay more of their own money before their insurance takes over. (50.6%)

8. Provide "at home" care instead of hospital or nursing home care for older people and those with long term illness. (75.4%)

9. Encourage people to use Health Maintenance Organizations (HMOs) where doctors try to hold down costs by emphasizing outpatient treatment and preventive medicine. (66.4%)

10. Develop statewide guidelines so that doctors caring for patients with little or no chance for recovery will know when to stop treatment. (57.1%)

11. Encourage patients with routine or minor illnesses to see nurses with special training or physicians' assistants who work in collaboration with doctors. (70.9%)

12. Have the government limit how much doctors and hospitals can charge for health care. (56.3%)

13. Change laws that seem to encourage doctors to order tests and procedures just to protect themselves from malpractice suits. (62.8%)

DISCHARGE PLANNING
Expanded Role for the Professional Nurse

Purpose and Concept ... This intensive one-day workshop is designed to provide specific strategies and tools for effective discharge planning which complies with current DRG demands. This is an "application" workshop to increase your skills in discharge planning.

Who should attend ... This workshop will benefit all registered nurses involved in discharge planning.

This is a practice workshop that focuses on the nurse's role and how nurses must consider ...

- DRG's
- JCAH Requirements
- Current situation - Decreased Length of Stays and Decreased Bed Utilization
- Locating Cost—Effective, Timely Patient Services
- Identifying Alternatives to Hospitalization
- Quality Assurance

Behavioral Objectives: Upon completion of the session each participant will be able to:

1. Explore the expanded role of nursing as it relates to discharge planning for a continuum of care.
2. Discuss the impact of continuity of care concepts on decreasing lengths of stay and increased readmission rates.
3. Correlate patient/family needs to specific criteria as evidenced by changes in health status.
4. Formulate a care plan which includes those needs identified or anticipated during the post-hospitalization or recovery period.
5. Utilize documentation techniques in compliance with quality assurance standards of the regulatory and accrediting bodies.
6. Develop practical methods within each specialty nursing unit to enhance the D/P team approach.
7. Identify common barriers, alternatives and resources for effective planning.
8. Analyze cost effective discharge planning versus minimal planning.

Agenda:

8:00 a.m.	All participants register
8:30 - 9:00 a.m.	I. Nursing Role
9:00 - 9:30 a.m.	II. Concepts and Standards
9:30 - 10:00 a.m.	III. Implications for D/P
10:30 - 10:45	BREAK
10:45 - 12:00 noon	IV. Care Plan Formulation
12:00 - 1:15	LUNCH
1:15 - 2:00 p.m.	V. Documentation Guidelines
2:00 - 2:45 p.m.	VI. Unit Development
2:45 - 3:00 p.m.	BREAK
3:00 - 3:30 p.m.	VII. Services Coordination
3:30 - 4:00 p.m.	VIII. Decreased Lengths of Stay
4:00 p.m.	EVALUATION

Workshop Faculty ... Meet and hear **Gail W. Hardy, RN, BS,** a nationally recognized Continuity of Care/Discharge Planning Consultant and Educator. Ms. Hardy's extensive hospital experience encompasses numerous management positions inlcuding Charge Nurse, Head Nurse, Nursing Supervisor, Discharge Planning Director, and Patient Management Services Coordinator. She currently serves as Case Manager of a Long Term Care Project developing community alternatives in care of the geriatric population. A person of enormous energy and dedication, Ms. Hardy also consults, develops educational materials and has been called upon to provide presentations to various health care organizations.

She is a member of both the A.N.A. and the N.L.N. Ms. Hardy is also founder of the North Carolina Association for Continuity of Care and Public Relations Chairman of the American Association for Continuity of Care. Her formidable depth of knowledge and experience combine dramatically in offering workshops with well-defined approaches and applications to effectively cope with the reality of the hospital environment.

Date and Location: August 8, 1985
Catawba Memorial Hospital (AHEC Building)
Hickory, NC

Directions to Location: From I-40, Exit #128 on to Fairgroves Church Road, continue north approximately 1/2 mile

---

Pre-Registration Form
Discharge Planning Workshop

Name _____

Address _____ Phone (H) _____

Employer _____ Phone (W) _____

Position _____

_____ Member $30 _____ Non-Member $40 _____ Full-Time Student $10 Amount Enclosed _____

MAKE CHECK PAYABLE TO NCNA AND MAIL TO: Attn: Registration, NCNA, P.O. Box 12025, Raleigh, N.C., 27605.

NURSE TO NURSE

By Carolyn Billings, Chairman
Commission on Member Services

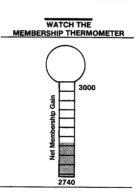

**WATCH THE
MEMBERSHIP THERMOMETER**

Net Membership Gain

3000

2740

The new minimum Employment Setting Standards are hot-off-the-press and appear in this issue of the *Tar Heel Nurse*. Revising these standards, first published in 1947, has been an important part of Commission activity over the last year. It is our hope that nurses all over North Carolina in a variety of work settings will find the standards useful in assessing and evaluating their employment opportunities. In updating the standards for 1985, the sub- committee assigned this task made use of the most recent research and nursing literature findings as well as industry standards. Your responses to the *N.C. Nurses Speak Out Survey* of last year helped us to determine which employment setting characteristics concerned *you* most.

Your feedback about this edition of the standards will assist us in future revisions. Let us know your reactions, won't you?

ACTIONS OF THE BOARD

The Board of Directors at a meeting on March 15, 1985, took the following actions:

- Adopted policies on reimbursement for presenters at NCNA conventions.
- Adopted policies on waiver of registration fees for members of committees planning workshops and programs.
- Expressed the Board's concern about the current issues and problems experienced by the Board of Nursing with the Joint Subcommittee and the NCNA Board's support of staff and leadership of NCNA to continue to work in a timely and effective manner with the Board of Nursing concerning issues related to those problems.
- Requested ANA to consider assisting SNAs in states where American Medical Association funds are being used to assist state medical societies to oppose reimbursement, independent practice, and expansion of roles of non-physician providers.
- Approved plans of the Commission on Practice to submit a planning grant proposal to the N.C. Humanities Committee for a project on using the ANA code in daily practice.
- Voted to support legislation mandating the use of seat belts, sponsored by the Coalition for Seat Belts for Safety. Appointed Sarah Pike Brown to the Coalition's Board of Directors.
- Voted to support SB 18, an act to establish a Missing Children's Center.
- Approved Minimum Employment Standards as revised by the Commission on Member Services and requested the Finance Committee to review the budget for funds to print the standards in brochure format.
- Received a report that nurses eligible for the bargaining unit at the Durham

VA Medical Center are working to reach the required 60% membership for renegotiating the contract due to expire in June.

- Responded to draft proposed amendments to ANA bylaws.
- Reviewed reports, at the end of the first year of the biennium, of progress toward priorities and identified needs for progress by October 1985.
- Voted that the legislative bulletin, *Nurses' Notes from the Capital,* be made available to students who are members of NCANS at the member price.

At a meeting on April 19, 1985, the Board took the following actions:

- Authorized convening of a group to evaluate the feasibility of developing a model nurse-managed service providing care for the elderly and directed that the group report back to the Board by September 1, 1985.
- Renewed the NCNA commitment to the RN bargaining unit at Durham VA Medical Center in representing the unit in contract renegotiation in view of the unit's achieving the required 60% membership.
- Commended the Commission on Member Services and District Eleven for their activities and support of the Durham VA bargaining unit.
- Approved the Membership Committee's video tape recruitment project and encouraged the Committee to proceed to completion of the project.
- Appointed Susan Bays to the Committee on Legislation.
- Approved Holiday Inn Four Seasons as 1988 convention site, October 26-29.

- Voted to appoint a representative of the Commission on Practice to the Ad Hoc Committee on Credentialing.
- Requested clarification of the liaison role on the Ad Hoc Committee on Credentialing of the clinical specialist in psychiatric-mental health nursing to the Conference Group of Clinical Specialists in Psychiatric-Mental Health Nursing.
- Directed that the report of the Ad Hoc Committee on Credentialing, when received, will be referred to the Commission on Practice for review and recommendations.
- Directed that the Finance Committee explore a three-phase approach to improving the NCNA financial projections: (1) a modest dues increase; (2) decrease in expenditures; (3) projections of effects of various percentage increases in membership.
- Directed that district presidents be notified, after the nomination deadline, when a member of a district is nominated for any NCNA award at the convention.

American Red Cross

We'll Help. Will You?

Gero division recommendations included in certification standards

by Margaret Keller

The Adult Day Health Services Standards for Certification were approved April 1, 1985 by the North Carolina Department of Human Resources. These standards apply to the operation of an Adult Day Health Center. Such centers are different from an Adult Day Care Center in that the Adult Day Health Center must include health care services; this is not required in Adult Day Care Centers.

It was necessary to establish these standards for Adult Day Health Services since this is one of the reimbursable services under the Medicaid Waiver that North Carolina applied for and received two years ago from the Department of Health and Human Services in Washington. DHHS/HICFA established these waivers as a package of nine services: (1) pre-screening before placement of client in a long-term care facility; (2) case management; (3) homemaker/home health aide service; (4) chore service; (5) respite care service; (6) home-delivered meals; (7) durable medical equipment; (8) home mobility aid; and (9) adult day health services. This is an effort to reduce the high cost of institutional care that was draining the Medicaid budget and provide more services in the home.

Most of these nine services are available in North Carolina but not all were reimbursable services from Medicaid prior to obtaining the waiver. There are Adult Day Care Centers in some counties but there were no operational Adult Day Health Care Centers available, thus standards had to be written and approved before claims could be submitted for Medicaid reimbursement.

A committee was formed in DHR of representatives from the Divisions of Social Services, Aging and Health Services. One nurse from the Division of Health Services and one nurse from the Division of Aging had input in preparing these standards.

In July 1984, the NCNA Division of Gerontological Nursing was asked to respond to the tentative final draft of these standards. At that time the standards stated that the "Health Care Coordinator" in an Adult Day Health Center have a minimum qualification of completed training as a licensed practical nurse. The proposed standards use the term "monitor" (not supervise) and the Health Care Coordinator was required to be available on the premises for a minimum of four hours.

Recommendations for changes submitted by NCNA's Gerontological group to the Division of Social Services (the Division of DHR responsible for certification) were as follows:

1. The Health Care Coordinator minimum qualifications be a registered nurse licensed to practice in North Carolina.

2. The terms "supervise and monitor" be used in list of responsibilities.

3. The minimum number of hours on the premises be changed from four to six hours.

The final approved standards include all the changes as recommended by NCNA's Gerontological Nursing Division except the minimum number of hours on the premises, which still remains at four hours. However, there is an additional qualifying statement, "the Coordinator must be on site additional hours per day if necessary to meet requirements for the provision of health care services."

It is anticipated that once these Adult Day Health Care Centers are established and certified, the major recipient of this service will be older clients with multiple health problems. Therefore, geriatric nurses have a vital interest and concern that nursing care services in these facilities are of high quality, and that a safe environment is provided.

This experience demonstrates that concerned nurses can influence the bureaucracy and hold out for standards of care that are safe, effective, and cost saving.

Calendar of Events

The following "Calendar of Events" will inform members of meetings of NCNA structural units and other related groups and agencies. All structural unit meetings will take place in headquarters unless otherwise indicated.

Meetings of the NCNA Board of Directors, committees and commissions are open to the membership. Members may attend to see the Association in action and to communicate with the elected and appointed officials. Members planning to attend should notify NCNA at least two days prior to the meeting, so that we can plan for adequate seating and plenty of coffee!

Date/Hour	Event
June 20, 10 a.m.	Peer Assistance Program Committee
June 20, 10 a.m.	Workshop Planning Committee
June 21, 9 a.m.	NCNA Board of Directors
June 24, 9 a.m.	"ABC's of Finance", Asheville, NC
June 24, 10 a.m.	Committee on Legislation
July 1, 10 a.m.	NCNA Executive Committee
July 4	HOLIDAY, NCNA Office Closed
July 8, 9 a.m.	ANA Delegate Meeting
July 18, 10 a.m.	Ad Hoc Committee RN Work Assignments
July 19, 9 a.m.	Commission on Education
July 23-25	ANA Convention, Kansas City, MO
July 27, 9:30 a.m.	Conference Group of Specialists in Psychiatric/Mental Health Nursing
July 29, 10 a.m.	Public Relations Committee
Aug. 1, 10 a.m.	Peer Assistance Program Committee
Aug. 2	NCNA Executive Committee
Aug. 8, 8:30 a.m.	Hickory D/C Planning Workshop
Aug. 9, 10 a.m.	Gero Executive Committee
Aug. 13, 9:30 a.m.	Commission on Practice
Aug. 13, 1 p.m.	Headquarters Committee
Aug. 14, 12 Noon	Med-Surg Executive Committee
Aug. 15, 12 Noon	Membership Committee
Aug. 16, 9 a.m.	NCNA Board of Directors
Aug. 28, 10 a.m.	Peer Assistance Program Committee
Aug. 29, 10 a.m.	Ad Hoc Committee on Structure
Sept. 18-21	NC Board of Nursing
Sept. 25, 10 a.m.	Peer Assistance Program Committee
Sept. 27, 9 a.m.	NCNA Board of Nursing
Sept. 28, 9:30 a.m.	Conference Group of Specialists in Psychiatric/Mental Health Nursing
Oct. 7	NCNA Executive Committee
Oct. 22	NCNA Board of Directors
Oct. 23-26	NCNA Convention

ABOUT PEOPLE

Virginia **Neelon**, Associate Professor of Nursing, was recently awarded the Nicholas Salvo Distinguished Teaching Award by UNC at Chapel Hill. The award recognizes "teaching excellence as evidenced by classroom effectiveness and ability to motivate and inspire students." ... **Mary Champagne**, Assistant Professor at UNC Chapel Hill School of Nursing was recently appointed to a 10 member panel to direct the American Association of Colleges of Nursing's project, "Essentials of College and University Education for Nursing." ... Cathy Hughes and **Ann Newman** are contributors for the book, *The Political Action Handbook for Nurses*, edited by Diana J. Mason and Susan W. Talbott and due to be published in the Fall of 1985 ... **Judith Seamon**, Morehead City, has been named to the UNC School of Public Health Board of Advisors.

NURSES
keep the Care
in Health Care!

Legislative session brings NCNA lobbyists to their knees!

News and Observer reporter, Seny Norasingh, caught Frankie Miller and Hazel Browning, NCNA lobbyists, looking over bills posted on the board in the Legislative Building and overflowing onto the floor on Wednesday, May 15. That date was the deadline for introducing bills in this session of the General Assembly and more than 130 were introduced to meet the deadline.

NORTH CAROLINA NURSES ASSOCIATION
P.O. Box 12025
Raleigh, North Carolina 27605

Non-Profit Org.
U. S. POSTAGE
PAID
Raleigh, N.C.
Permit No. 87

Vol. 47, No. 3   **May–June 1985**

Official Publication of the North Carolina Nurses Association, 103 Enterprise St., Raleigh, N.C. Tel. (919) 821-4250. Published 6 times a year. Subscription price $12 per year, included with membership dues indexed in *Cumulative Index to Nursing and Allied Health Literature* and available in MICROFORM, University Microfilms International.

JUDITH B. SEAMON .... President
HETTIE L. GARLAND .... President-Elect
GALE B. JOHNSTON .... Vice-President
SALLY S. TODD .... Secretary
CAROL A. OSMAN .... Treasurer

STAFF
FRANCES N. MILLER ..... Executive Director
HAZEL BROWNING .....Assoc. Exec. Director
BETTY GODWIN .... Asst. Exec. Director
PATRICIA W. BRYAN ..... Administrative Asst.
DOROTHY BENNETT .... Administrative Asst.

● 1985 NCNA

ISSN 0039-9620

TAR HEEL NURSE

Vol. 47, No. 4   OFFICIAL PUBLICATION OF THE NORTH CAROLINA NURSES ASSOCIATION   July-August 1985

You lose some, win some in General Assembly

By Hazel Browning

At press time, legislators and lobbyists were spending long days scurrying around in an effort to finalize the business of the 1985 session of the North Carolina General Assembly. The final gavel was expected to fall during the week of July 15.

More than 1420 House bills and 850 Senate bills were introduced during the 1985 session. NCNA lobbyists identified more than 110 of those bills as measures which would either directly or indirectly affect nursing practice and health care.

Just imagine tracking 110 bills originat-

ing in two different chambers, and assigned to two or more of 58 House and 29 Senate committees, each one being amended anywhere at anytime for any number of reasons, each one going through three readings in each chamber and many being assigned to heavy-weight conference committees for resolution of differences between the two chambers! No wonder lobbyists get gray!

● **SB 470**, NCNA's Third Party Reimbursement Bill, has traversed a treacherous and troubled route since the last legislative report in the *Tar Heel Nurse*. After being

assigned to a second Senate committee, the Committee on Insurance, public comment was heard on the bill on May 28. Proponents speaking in favor of the bill included the following: Michael Crowell, NCNA lobbyist and legal counsel; Judy Seamon, NCNA president; Cynthia Freund, member of NCNA and associate professor at UNC-Chapel Hill; and Al Adams, attorney lobbyist, representing the North Carolina Association of CRNAs. Strong statements citing the cost-effectiveness of qualified nurse specialists were made, and legislators were reminded that passage of this bill would in no way affect the professional or legal arrangements for clinical supervision as they presently exist between nurses and physicians.

Opponents of the bill filled their time with statements from insurers, the business community and opposing health care providers. Dr. Bill Demaria of Blue Cross Blue Shield stated that he could not endorse the bill since he has not yet seen a comprehensive study supporting the cost effectiveness of such legislation.

A representative of the North Carolina Citizens for Business and Industry group voiced concern that "mandating benefits" will further increase health care costs. A

(continued on page 9)

Board recommends dues increase

After more than three years of struggle to match NCNA's financial resources with program needs, the Board of Directors at its May 31, 1985, meeting voted to recommend a $35 dues increase to the House of Delegates in October.

After extensive investigation and discussion of the broad fiscal situation of NCNA, the Finance Committee submitted the recommendation for the increase to the Board in April. The Board deferred a decision at that time and met jointly with the Finance Committee to study every possible

option before deciding to recommend the increase.

An analysis of NCNA's financial experience for the past five years showed that the last dues increase of $15 in 1980 was quickly eaten up by the high inflation of the early '80's. Several events enabled the Association to avoid another dues increase until now. These were:

1. During the June 1982-June 1984 transition to a federation structure for ANA, the state associations paid a fixed

(continued on page 11)

Message from the President

Judith B. Seamon

NCNA Members! Do you know that each of us is approximately 2,250 pounds over-weight? Yes, we are—and this fact should shock us and move every one of us to immediate action, because it has adverse effects on the health of our profession. But rushing to the nearest weight control center or pulling out our favorite diets won't solve the problem.

The problem is that each NCNA member is carrying the weight of 18 other North Carolina nurses on his/her back—18 other nurses who should also be NCNA members. Not only is this unfair to each of us, it is also unfair to the health care system, consumers, and our profession.

Nurses as the largest group of health-care providers occupy a unique position in the health care system, especially in the current socioeconomic climate. We have enormous responsibilities and opportunities within the health care system that can benefit consumers and our own profession. The mechanism for focusing our energies and resources to meet these responsibilities and opportunities is our professional association.

You as a member are meeting an essen-tial part of your professional responsi-bility—as well as the responsibility of 18 other nurses. Each of us must convince some of our colleagues that they must assume their share of the responsibility to our profession.

When you talk with your colleagues, emphasize to them that this association is the group that protects their right and privi-lege to practice nursing by protecting the Nursing Practice Act. It is this Association that will be on the cutting edge for future issues regarding their practice. Basically, if nurses value their professional practice, they will insure it by membership in their professional organization.

Ask them to do their part in maintaining the health of our profession—and that part is belonging to their professional associa-tion. It works out to contributing about one-to-two hours per month of their salary to the protection of their professional prac-tice!

Let's see that the weight is evenly dis-tributed by getting other nurses to carry their share of the load, and thereby enhance the health of our profession.

OSHA right-to-know standard extended to include nurses

Commissioner of Labor John C. Brooks on July 3, 1985, announced the extension of the state OSHA hazard communication ("right-to-know") standard to cover virtu-ally all workplaces in North Carolina except those that handle only consumer products or that maintain only very small quantities of hazardous chemicals.

Previously the standard had applied only to manufacturing industries.

In addition to expanding the coverage of the standard, the department also added nurses to the four categories of medical professionals previously authorized for access to trade secret information when it is needed to treat an employee who has been exposed to a hazardous chemical. The department also has amended the standard to authorize an employee who has requested the identity of a chemical that he believes to be hazardous to refuse to work with that chemical if its identity is not provided within five working days.

Adding nurses to those groups of health professionals authorized for access to trade secret information was necessary because, according to Brooks, "Nurses can be the first providers of treatment to employees in industry. They ought to have access to whatever information they need to protect workers' health."

NCNA twice has provided testimony at Department of Labor hearings pressing for the amendment now in effect.

Think Membership

Nurses to elect new board members

Two registered nurses and two licen-sed practical nurses are to be elected to the Board of Nursing in balloting to be held soon. One community health RN and one RN educator will be elected.

Candidates for the RN community health position are (NCNA members indi-cated by asterisk):

Bobbie Ezzell Golec, New Bern, employed at Craven County Health Department;

Marilyn B. Overcash, Mooresville, Iredell County Health Department;

*Evelyn Schaffer, Salisbury, Rowan County Health Department;

Vashti F. Sugg, Greensboro, Guilford County Department of Public Health;

*Janet A Wagner, Fayetteville, Cape Fear Valley Medical Center.

Candidates for the RN educator posi-tion are:

*R. Leigh Andrews, Kitty Hawk, inde-pendent educator/consultant (seek-ing re-election);

*Loletta A. Faulkenberry, Burlington, fac-ulty member of Watts School of Nurs-ing;

Carolyn Moffett, New Bern, faculty mem-ber at Craven Community College;

*Sally S. Todd, Fayetteville, independent educator/consultant in nursing man-agement;

Clara B. Williams, Goldsboro, faculty mem-ber at Wayne Community College.

The terms for these positions are four years, beginning January 1, 1986.

Ballots will be mailed in August to all RN licensees to vote for the RN candi-dates and to all LPNs to vote for LPN can-didates.

NOTICE

Bring this issue of *Tar Heel Nurse* with you to the convention. It contains proposed bylaw amendments and pro-posed resolutions, as well as the report of the NCNA Nominating Committee, to be considered by the 1985 House of Delegates.

A special convention insert contains your registration form and hotel reser-vation form.

The next issue (September-October) will contain biennial reports of officers and structural units, ballots of structural units, and a discussion paper on struc-ture changes.

You will need to bring the Septem-ber-October 1985 issue with you also, along with your copy of NCNA Bylaws (from the November-December 1983 issue).

'ABC s of Finance' successfully presented by Joe and Sally Todd

by Betty Godwin and Sandra Randleman

On June 24, 1985, in Asheville and on July 8, 1985, in Raleigh, two dynamic individuals conducted a workshop entitled, "The ABC's of Finance for Nurse Managers". The workshop (expected to register 40 participants) more than doubled the expected registrations.

Co-Chairman of the Workshop Planning Committee Sandra Randleman and Assistant Executive Director of NCNA. Betty Godwin attributed this response to the topic and most importantly, the speakers — Sally Todd, MSN, RN, and Joe Todd, CPA. Because of their contribution to NCNA and nurses in the state of North Carolina, Betty and Sandra decided to conduct an impromptu interview with this unique couple. The interview proceeded as follows:

Betty and Sandra (hereafter referred to as B&S): What made you decide to focus your workshops on financial management for nurses?

.**Sally and Joe** (hereinafter referred to as S&J): We believe there is a need for this subject, particularly for nurses, and it is a subject that is not being conducted by others for nurses.

B&S: When you began today, you said that one was not allowed to justify budget on the basis that it "assured quality patient care". Could you elaborate on the reason(s) for this statement?

S&J: Quality implies a perception. Perception of "quality" will differ from person to person. If nurse managers discuss "needed" nursing care and what that costs, then nurses won't need to use the word "quality" because "needed" nursing care is a judgement that only nurses can make.

B&S: You affirm our belief that the catch phrase *used* to be "quality patient care". It seems this phrase is substituted with the phrase "cost effective patient care". What do you predict will be the future catch phrase?

S&J: We're not sure but nurses and nurse managers should believe "cost effectiveness" is here to stay.

B&S: Do you believe that nursing is cost effective?

S&J: We can't reliably answer that question until we collect more data, which brings us to a point of emphasis and that is, nursing lacks historical data, expecially as it relates to cost effective accomplishments. Nursing needs to focus attention on data collection now and in the future.

B&S: The health care environment is changing so rapidly. What nursing issues do you perceive as being critical for nursing to achieve professional autonomy (i.e., self governance and

Joe (left) and Sally Todd (center) listen as Sandra Randleman (right) explains how she intends to use new knowledge gained from the workshop "ABCs of Finance."

reimbursement) as other professionals have achieved.

Sally: That is a loaded question and I'd like to answer that question by reflecting on a quote from *Change Masters* — Rosabeth Moss Kanter, "Embrace change as an opportunity to test limits".

B&S: In your opinion, where does the concept of financial management need to begin and what role should NCNA play?

S&J: Financial management should begin in the undergraduate nursing curriculum; perhaps a basic accounting course as an elective with a follow-up project could prove very beneficial. For example, the undergraduate nursing student may develop a patient care plan and cost out the care provided for the patient. Because most of what happens relative to financial management occurs in the workplace, a very beneficial role of NCNA is to continue providing workshops on financial management for nurses because we believe financial management is a means of survival for nurses and nursing.

B&S: If "money talks", who do you suggest nurses should converse with?

S&J: We highly recommend that nurses establish a strong relationship with someone in the financial department to begin to understand and speak the language of finance.

B&S: Is there a common message to all nurse managers?

S&J: Yes. Collect statistical data to support or justify one's budget. This is a must for nurses.

B&S: Based on your experience, if you could make sure that each participant remembered one thing from the workshop, what would it be?

S&J: First, we must remember that we are all trained in the technical aspects of our field; nurses know their field and accountants know theirs. Therefore, nurses should not be intimidated to ask questions. Nurses *must* learn financial terminology to converse/communicate intelligently and nurses must not shy away from telling accountants to "speak English", if the need exists.

Many thanks to Joe and Sally for two most successful workshops.

Sally, being the secretary of NCNA, became aware of the financial needs of NCNA. Upon hearing this, Joe suggested they offer to conduct the workshops and donate their honorarium and any profits to NCNA. This is a particularly generous donation by Sally, as she is self-employed as an educator and consultant in health care management. Her service can be contracted by calling (919) 484-8797. Joe's contribution is equally generous, as a non-nurse who has a personal interest in nursing. Joe is a partner in the accounting firm, Todd & Rivenbark, in Fayetteville, North Carolina.

BEFORE YOU MOVE ...
... please let us know! To be sure you don't miss copies of TAR HEEL NURSE, send change of address to NCNA, P. O. Box 12025, Raleigh, NC 27605.

Living With Pain

October 22, 1985   9:00 A.M. - 4:00 P.M.

Hyatt Hotel
Winston-Salem, North Carolina

Purpose: To provide nurses with a comprehensive knowledge base for helping patients live with pain. This knowledge can be applied in any health care setting and in any age group. This would include caring for children and adults in both hospital and community settings.

Target Audience: All nurses involved in health care delivery. Content is applicable to numerous settings and all age groups.

Objectives: Upon completion of the workshop, you will be able to ....
1. Relate current literature and research findings to control of clinical pain.
2. Identify issues of chronic pain as it affects the quality of life.
3. State how pain treatment modalities in children differ from pain treatment modalities in adults.
4. Identify barriers that nurses must overcome to achieve effective pain control in the acute and critical care settings and the home health arena.

Benefits: This workshop will ....
1. Help nurses to recognize their own attitudes regarding pain and how these attitudes may impede pain control in their patients.
2. Help nurses to develop strategies to improve their clinical expertise in pain control.
3. Assist nurses in identifying the need to approach pain control from a multidisciplinary perspective.

Workshop Leaders:

Dr. Barbara Germino, RN, PhD.
Assistant Professor, School of Nursing
University of North Carolina
Chapel Hill, N.C.

Deborah Reed, RN, MSN
Clinical Nurse Specialist
John Umstead Hospital
Butner, N.C.

Pam Husain, RN, MSN
Head Nurse Neonatal ICU
North Carolina Memorial Hospital
Chapel Hill, N.C.

Alexandra Wright, RN, MSN
Clinical Nurse Specialist
Washington, D.C.

Jane Ray, RN, MSN
Assistant Professor, School of Nursing
University of North Carolina
Greensboro, N.C.

CERP: CERP and CEAP credit pending.

Agenda:

9:00 A.M. - 9:30 A.M.	Registration
9:30 A.M. - 10:30 A.M.	Round table discussion of research and current literature Barbara Germino
10:30 A.M. - 10:45 A.M.	Break
10:45 A.M. - 12:00 P.M.	Pain in the Pediatric Setting — Pam Husain
12:00 P.M. - 1:00 P.M.	Lunch
1:00 P.M. - 2:30 P.M.	Overcoming stumbling blocks to pain control Alexandra Wright, Deborah Reed, Jane Ray
2:30 P.M. - 2:45 P.M.	Break
2:45 P.M. - 3:30 P.M.	Pain problems
3:30 P.M. - 4:00 P.M.	Evaluation

Registration Information: Members $40   Non members $60

Registration deadline is October 1, 1985. No refunds or cancellations after October 18. Registration includes cost of breaks, lunch and workshop materials. If a minimum of 30 persons are not registered by October 1, this workshop will be cancelled.

Accommodations: A block of rooms has been reserved through September 22 at the Hyatt Winston-Salem at a flat rate of $55 per room. Please specify that you are an NCNA Workshop participant. Make reservations directly to the hotel: (919) 725-1234.

PRE-REGISTRATION FORM

Living With Pain
October 22, 1985

Name_____

Address _____

Amount enclosed (   ) Member $40   Phone   (H) _____

(   ) Non-member $60

(W) _____

Make check payable to and mail to NCNA, P.O. Box 12025, Raleigh, NC 27605

Focus on Districts

by Betty Godwin

Leadership Orientation Day . . .
'A Guided Tour of Skills and Strategies'

Members give their individual attention to the "financial forecast" during the Leadership Orientation Day.

On June 28, 1985, 32 members representing 16 districts boarded a cruise vessel that took them on a guided tour of leadership skills and strategies. Before departure, Captain Judy Seamon plotted the course, noting the pathways between ANA, NCNA, and the districts. From there we listened attentively to a financial status report and forecast from the NCNA Treasurer Carol Osman. Her forecast began with a tracing of events that led NCNA through a past period of financial growth that is now counterbalanced with unmet financial need. She explained how the transition into the Federation structure gave NCNA a short-term financial advantage by keeping NCNA's dues assessment to ANA at the membership level of July 1982. All membership revenue in excess of that number was retained by NCNA. As of July 1984, NCNA must pay ANA according to actual membership—which has increased since 1982. This growth is good and needed; nonetheless, NCNA must share a greater percentage of membership dues collected in this state with ANA. Coupled with this situation, NCNA has felt the effects of inflation and program expansion which adds to our costs. Even though membership recruitment is the best alternative, it simply has not kept up with the pace of financial need. The other alternative course chosen by the

NCNA Board of Directors is to propose a $35 dues increase at the 1985 NCNA House of Delegates.

Once the forecast was completed the cruise ship set sail for the legislative connection. Once the connection was made the group divided. The Council of District Presidents met to discuss items such as a proposed NCNA structure revision that will be shared in the next issue of the *Tar Heel Nurse*. The other district leaders had the opportunity to enjoy the cuisine of the local area. The group reconvened in the afternoon and, together, entered the gateway to success, an archway of marketing strategies to increase membership. They perused new brochures and viewed the new video recruitment tool available to all districts. Once inside the gateway the group chose optional tours of skills and strategies to help them fulfill their leadership roles at the district level. Optional tours included the Presidential Palace, District Theatre, Market Place, Capitol Hill, and the Museum of Records and Reports.

This concluded a long day with an agenda that allowed no waste of time. If the evaluations reflect the truth, all left with a wealth of souvenirs that included information, skills and strategies to assist in district leadership.

Volunteers sought for FAS project

The comprehensive Fetal Alcohol Prevention Program at Bowman Gray School of Medicine plans to conduct regional workshops on the Fetal Alcohol Syndrome (FAS) and is attempting to identify health professionals with an interest in this topic.

The purpose of the workshops is to educate these health professionals about FAS so that they may then return to their local communities and volunteer their time to increase the public's awareness of FAS. This "grass roots" effort will be an attempt to reach previously untapped segments of society, and will require the volunteers to become very involved with community groups.

Workshops are tentatively planned for January, 1986. Interested individuals please contact the Fetal Alcohol Syndrome Prevention Program at Bowman Gray School of Medicine at (919) 748-2213, or use the toll-free hotline at 1-800-532-6302, by November 15, 1985.

Conference to aid RNs with professional pressures

"Intervention for Nursing Practice Problems" will provide a unique sharing experience for nurses. This conference will give RN's the opportunity to share professional experiences and expand their knowledge of strategies to deal with pressures that confront them in daily practice.

The conference is presented in memory of Beth Haltiwanger, RN, BSN, in cooperation with Nursing Staff I Development of North Carolina Baptist Hospitals, Inc., and Wake Forest University. Dr. Al Haltiwanger, Beth's father, spearheaded the effort to organize this conference, which will explore effective prevention and problem solving strategies for nurses to use in their professional lives.

The faculty includes Sally Todd, Carolyn Billings, Hettie Garland, and Alice Roye. The conference will be held at Graylyn Conference Center of Wake Forest University, in Winston-Salem, on November 12-13, 1985. A conference fee of $99 includes workshop materials, three meals, lodging at Graylyn Conference Center and a social hour. Further information can be obtained by contacting Nursing Staff Development, North Carolina Baptist Hospitals, Inc., 300 S. Hawthorne Road, Winston-Salem 27103.

Annual Checkup on Laws Affecting N. C. Nurses, 1985

Dates/Locations:

October 3, 1985
Hickory
Catawba Memorial Hospital —
AHEC Building
Directions: From I-40, Exit #128
onto Fairgrove Church Road,
continue North approximately
½ mile.

October 4, 1985
Greensboro AHEC — Auditorium
Rm. 30
Moses H. Cone Hospital
Directions: From Wendover Ave.,
No. 220, exit onto N. Elm Street.
Park in front of Education
Center.

November 15, 1985
Greenville
Willis Building
Directions: Located near downtown
Greenville on the corner of First
and Reade Streets overlooking
the Tar River.

Produced in association with Northwest, Greensboro and Eastern AHECs.

Faculty: Wade Smith, Michael Crowell, and Kim Wetherill are practicing attorneys with the law firm of Tharrington, Smith and Hargrove of Raleigh. Mr. Smith and Mr. Crowell served as registered lobbyists for NCNA during the 1985 General Assembly session. The Tharrington, Smith and Hargrove law firm has represented NCNA as corporate legal counsel since 1983.

This workshop is designed for registered nurses, licensed practical nurses, and other health professionals.

Course Description: This six-hour workshop will acquaint the health care provider with recent developments in the courts and state legislature concerning health law. This series is a refinement and update of the series done in 1984. Evaluations from 1984 were excellent and participant responses will be used to plan this 1985 series.

This workshop will cover issues of: ● Malpractice ● Negligence ● Liability in rejecting and accepting assignments ● Documentation

Course objectives: Upon completion of this workshop, the participant will be able to:
1. Discuss the nurse's responsibility to identify parameters for safe nursing practice.
2. Identify how nurses' notes can be used in law suits.
3. Define malpractice in North Carolina.
4. Discuss negligence.
5. Discuss actions from the 1985 N.C. General Assembly that affect nursing.

Workshop Schedule: 8:30 a.m. — Registration   9:00 a.m. - 4:00 p.m. — Program

Registration Information: The registration fee is reduced from last year! Members — $35; Non-Members — $50; Full-time students — $10 (space available basis)

Fee covers cost of breaks and limited handouts, including updates to the 1984 Law Manuals.

Please pre-register at least two weeks in advance of the workshop selected. No refund for cancellation within 48 hours of the workshop but substitutions are encouraged. Fifty participants are needed per location for workshop production.

Law Manuals will be available upon request for a cost of $6.50. Many nurses and institutions bought manuals following the 1984 workshop series. If you have a 1984 manual, updates will be provided at no additional charge.

Credit: CEAP and CERP credit pending.

PRE—REGISTRATION FORM
Annual Checkup on Laws Affecting North Carolina Nurses 1985
PLEASE REGISTER AT LEAST TWO WEEKS IN ADVANCE OF WORKSHOP SELECTED.

Name _____ Position/Employer _____

Address _____

Telephone (work) _____ (home) _____

Fee: $35 Members $50 Non-Members $10 Full-time students (space available basis)
Please check: ( ) RN   ( ) LPN   ( ) Full-time student   ( ) Other
Check workshop attending: ( ) Hickory, Oct. 3   ( ) Greensboro, Oct. 4   ( ) Greenville, Nov. 15

Please identify health related questions you wish to hear addressed during a one hour question/answer period at the close of the workshop:

_____

_____

Make check payable to NCNA and mail to: Amount Enclosed: Registration Fee _____
NCNA, P. O. Box 12025, Raleigh, NC 27605   Law Manual ($6.50) _____

                                                    Total _____

NEWS BRIEFS

- The AJN Educational Services Division is now accepting entries for its fifth biennial media festival. Competition will culminate in June 1986 when the winners will be shown at the ANA Convention in Anaheim, California. Entry fee is $75. Deadline is January 31, 1986. Contact AJN Educational Services Division, 555 West 57th St., New York, NY 10019.
- NAACOG is seeking papers and poster displays for a research conference to be held August 8-10, 1986 in Minneapolis, Minnesota. Deadline for abstract submission is December 15, 1985. Contact Denise Savage, Department of Education and Research, NAACOG, 600 Maryland Avenue, S.W., Suite 200 East, Washington, D.C. 20024.
- Laurie N. Sherwen, R.N., Ph.D., has been named director of a project entitled, "Core Competencies for Preparation of Graduates of Baccalaureate Schools for Beginning Maternal/Infant Nursing Positions," under a grant awarded to the March of Dimes. Participating in the three year project are ANA, AACN, and NAACOG.

Publications

- The Nursing Index will be added by ANJ to the *International Nursing Index* (INI) beginning in 1986. The annual subscription rate will be $250. Contact ANJ Company, International Nursing Index, 555 West 57th St., New York, NY 10019.
- *Building Community Support for Health Promotion Programs: A Model*, new from the American Nurses' Foundation, tracts a small pilot school project through its progression to a full-fledged community health promotion program. Cost is $16.50. Contact Publications Orders, ANA, 2420 Pershing Rd., Kansas City, Missouri 64108.
- "Nutrition For Special Needs", and "Nutrition For Everyone" are slide/tape programs released by AJN Company. Contact AJN Company Educational Services Division, 555 West 57th Street, New York, NY 10019.
- *Directions for Nursing Research: Toward the Twenty-First Century*, available from ANA. Cost is $2.75. (Pub. No. D-79) Contact Publications Orders, ANA, 2420 Pershing Rd., Kansas City, Missouri 64108.
- "Writing for Publications", a new audiocassette course developed by Signe S. Cooper is available from University of Wisconsin-Extention, Continuing Education in Nursing, 528 Lowell Hall, 610 Langdon St., Madison, Wisconsin 53703. Telephone: (608) 262-0566.
- *Weight Control for Better Health*, a patient education booklet is available

from Krames Communications, Dept. WCH 53, 312 90th St., Daly City, California 94105.
- National Easter Seal Society announces three new publications: *Rehabilitation: 25 Years of Concepts, Principles, Perspectives* (Pub. No. G-20, $9.95); special issue of *Rehabilitation Literature*, "Aging and Disability" (Vol. 46, No. 5-6, $6.00); new edition of *Disabling Myths about Disability* (Pub. No. A-207, $1.50). Contact National Easter Seal Society, 2023 W. Ogden Ave., Chicago, Illinois 60612.

Professional Development Opportunities

- AJN Company launches a new division, the Professional Seminars Division, to

meet nurses' multi-faceted educational needs. The first series will be the AJN Company Computer Software Lab, to be held October 31, November 1-2, 1985, at the Chicago Hilton and Towers.
- "Potlatch '85", a continuing education seminar sponsored by the Washington State Nurses Association is scheduled September 17-20, 1985. Contact WSNA at (206) 622-3613.
- "Nursing as a Force for Social Change" will be sponsored by the University of Pennsylvania School of Nursing 50th Anniversary Committee, September 20-21, 1985. Contact Diane O. McGivern, Ph.D., FAAN, Associate Dean, Univer-

(continued on page 20)

Calendar of Events

The following "Calendar of Events" will inform members of meetings of NCNA structural units and other related groups and agencies. All structural unit meetings will take place in headquarters unless otherwise indicated.

Meetings of the NCNA Board of Directors, committees and commissions are open to the membership. Members may attend to see the Association in action and to communicate with the elected and appointed officials. Members planning to attend should notify NCNA at least two days prior to the meeting, so that we can plan for adequate seating and plenty of coffee!

Date/Hour	Event
Aug. 21, 10 a.m.	Nurse PAC
Aug. 26, 10 a.m.	Workshop Planning Committee
Aug. 29, 10 a.m.	Ad Hoc Committee on Structure
Sept. 2	HOLIDAY, NCNA Office Closed
Sept. 4-7	North Carolina Board of Nursing, (Marriott, Charlotte)
Sept. 6, 10 a.m.	NCNA Executive Committee
Sept. 6, 10 a.m.	MCH Executive Committee
Sept. 14, 9:30 a.m.	N.C. Federation of Nursing Organizations
Sept. 21, 10 a.m.	Planning Meeting, Humanities Grant
Sept. 25, 10 a.m.	Peer Assistance Program Committee
Sept. 26, 10 a.m.	Workshop Planning Committee
Sept. 26, 10:30 a.m.	Nominating Committee
Sept. 27, 9 a.m.	NCNA Board of Directors
Sept. 28, 9:30 a.m.	Conference Group of Specialists in Psychiatric/Mental Health Nursing
Oct. 3	"Laws Affecting North Carolina Nurses—1985" — Catawba Memorial Hospital, AHEC, Hickory
Oct. 4	"Laws Affecting North Carolina Nurses—1985"— Greensboro AHEC
Oct. 7, 10 a.m.	NCNA Executive Committee
Oct. 10, 1:30 p.m.	Joint Practice Committee
Oct. 22, 9 a.m.	NCNA Board of Directors
Oct. 22	"Living with Pain" workshop — Hyatt, Winston-Salem
Oct. 23-26	NCNA Convention
Nov. 15	"Laws Affecting North Carolina Nurses—1985"— Greenville
Nov. 28	HOLIDAY, NCNA Office Closed

NURSE TO NURSE

By Carolyn Billings, Chairman
Commission on Member Services

PROFESSION. We toss the word around a lot in nursing. We have been asserting for some time now that nursing is a profession, not an occupation, and that nurses are "professionals". We're hard at work defining the difference between technical and professional nursing practice. Entry into the profession is a hot topic with titling, grandfathering, and educational implications.

There are countless definitions and criteria about what characterizes a profession, but the one I like best is stated by Eliot Freidson, a sociologist who studies professions. Freidson argues that the crucial attribute to distinguish a profession is the "power to control the terms, conditions, and content of (the) work". I think that's where nursing is most vulnerable.

As nurses, most of us are employees of agencies in which the terms, conditions, and content of our work is structured (and controlled) by the employer. Nursing judgements, however sound, however in compliance with the Nursing Practice Act, or however patient-centered they may be, are subject to review and to overrule by the economics, politics, or simple whim of the employing agency. It's as basic as this: nurses must routinely choose between their legal, ethical, professional, and humanistic awareness and their need to protect themselves. In North Carolina the "at will" doctrine in state law makes it possible for a private employer to fire any employee without cause. When that employee is a nurse and that employer is a private health care facility, that circumstance severely limits the nurse's freedom to practice professional nursing independent of unreasonable consequence. The nurse's awareness that (s)he stood ground in compliance with the Nursing Practic Act or for the safety and well-being of patients is small comfort when (s)he is out looking for a new job in a tight market.

Nursing history includes a long and difficult struggle for identity and recognition for political influence and social reform. Our claim to the role of patient advocate and our commitment to the public welfare has long been our "reason for being". We've come a long way, Baby—and we have a long way to go.

We must now be alert to every new opportunity to form PARTNERSHIPS with health care factions ... partnerships based on egalitarian principles rather than paternalistic hierarchical relationships. We must stand behind professionalism and take professional stands. In doing this, some of us will suffer painful consequences, but all of us will gain ..among those the health-care consumer for whom we are pledged to care!

State Senator Wilma Woodard, right, met with representatives of N-CAP in Washington on May 20 to explore strategies for her future campaign for the Fourth District Congressional seat now held by Republican Bill Cobey. Shown with Senator Woodard is Pat Ford-Roegner of the Nurse PAC staff.

ABOUT PEOPLE

Susan Kennerly, Charlotte, has been elected to her second term as chairman of the Board of Nursing. **Leigh Andrews,**Kitty Hawk, is vice chairman ... **Joyce Smyrski** and **Maude Speckman,** in June assumed new positions as educational consultants for the Board on Nursing. . .**Becky Knight** has been named deputy director of Greensboro AHEC where she has been serving as assistant nursing education director.

WATCH THE MEMBERSHIP THERMOMETER

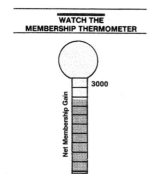

Net Membership Gain

3000

2740

General Assembly from page 1

representative of Health Insurance Association of America, also described how "mandating benefits" will further escalate health care costs.

Although SB 470 did NOT mandate benefits, the opponents, strategy was effective as legislators voiced real concern about this effort.

As a result, the Senate Insurance Committee took action on June 4 to send SB 470 to a subcommittee. The subcommittee was chaired by Senator Tony Rand; other members included Senators H. Hardison, W. Staton, and C. Ballenger. Because of substantial opposition in the full Insurance Committee to the original bill, NCNA lobbyists developed a committee substitute which we hoped would fare better. One argument against the original bill was that it mandated reimbursement to nurses; the committee substitute made reimbursement *permissible* if the insurer and the subscriber agreed on it. The substitute bill gave the Commissioner of Insurance authority to refuse approval of insurance companies' policies if they arbitrarily refused subscriber requests for inclusion of nurse reimbursement in their plans.

NCNA lobbyists had an extremely difficult time in persuading Senator Rand to convene the subcommittee to take action on the bill. The subcommittee finally met on July 5, four and one-half weeks after being assigned to the subcommittee. Opponents (insurers and the medical community) had planted seeds of doubt in the minds of at least two Senators as to whether or not the substitute language was, in fact, *permissive* to the subscriber. Although legal counsel for NCNA, counsel representing the North Carolina Association of Nurse Anesthetists, and a representative from the Office of the Insurance Commissioner attempted to eradicate the smoke screen generated by opponents, Senator H. Hardison (D-Deep Run) stood firm in his opposition to the proposed committee substitute. A motion by Senator W. Staton (D-Sanford) to adopt the proposed committee substitute failed by a vote of 1 to 2 with Senator Cass Ballenger joining Senator Hardison in the negative vote.

Back to square ONE! Lobbyists and legal counsel were not, however, going to be dispelled without using every available option. During the following weekend, a second proposed committee substitute was drafted ... a much simpler, one page bill that simply clarified a statement in current statutes that reads, "Nothing herein shall be construed to *authorize* contracting with or making payments directly to a nurse not otherwise permitted". Basically, the second substitute proposal to change this language read, "Nothing herein shall be construed to *require or prohibit* contracting with or making payments directly to a nurse".

This second proposed committee substitute was distributed on July 9 to the four subcommittee members and to opponents in an effort to secure some agreement on the issue. The lobbyists for Blue Cross Blue Shield and for Pilot Life Insurance Company agreed that they would not oppose this draft. To no one's surprise, the medical community, i.e., lobbyists representing the North Carolina Medical Society and North Carolina Association of Anesthesiologists, remained rigid in their opposition to any change in current statutes.

As a result, NCNA lobbyists were never able to secure support for the second proposed committee substitute from Senators Rand, Hardison, and Ballenger. The short version of a long story is that no action has been taken on Senate Bill 470 and none is expected in this legislative session.

The records of several political figures are worth reviewing. Senator Ted Kaplan (D-Winston-Salem), as primary sponsor of the bill, was willing to take on what he knew would be a "hot" issue. He worked behind the scenes on several occasions to encourage Senator Rand to convene the subcommittee and deal with the issue. Senator Bill Staton (D-Sanford) signed the original bill before it was filed in the Senate and never swayed in his support for the concepts in the bill. He was willing to support either of the two proposed committee substitutes to facilitate our efforts to reach a compromise on the issue. Insurance Commissioner Jim Long and two members of his staff, Alan Feezor and Bill Hale, were very supportive in developing both of the two proposed committee substitutes, and they were visible in their support for these committee substitutes. These people deserve a few notes of thanks for their efforts on our behalf!

● **HB 52** has been reviewed in past issues of the *Tar Heel Nurse* as an act to rewrite the Administrative Procedures Act. It is virtually impossible to tell you what came out in the end. The bill was ratified on July 12, at about 8:00 p.m. This bill, too, had been a very controversial one, as versions passed by the House and the Senate were drastically different. A conference committee finally hashed out the differences between the two bodies but not many people know the end result yet. Copies of the massive finalized bill are not yet available to the public but rumors about the compromise do not sound good. We will try to have an update on this issue in the next *Tar Heel Nurse* after more information becomes available.

● **HB 836** (reviewed in May/June *Tar Heel Nurse*) amends the Pharmacy Practice Act to allow RNs in public health departments, under certain conditions, to dispense prescription drugs and devices. Having passed the House on May 15, the bill was considered by the Senate Human Resources Committee on June 5, and was given a unanimous favorable report. When the bill surfaced on the Senate calendar on

June 6, no opposition was voiced. Second reading roll call vote revealed a 45 to 1 landslide victory for the bill, which then easily passed third and final reading on a voice vote. It was ratified on June 6.

● **SB 286**, described in the May/June *Tar Heel Nurse*, would have created a North Carolina Medical Database Commission. A committee substitute for the bill was given a favorable report in the Senate Judiciary IV Commitee and then sent to the Appropriations Committee, since it required funding. SB 182, a major bill appropriating funds for various statewide projects, was released on Thursday, July 11. The bill contained provisions creating the Medical Database Commission (SB 286). NCNA lobbyists had sought Senator Tony Rand's support to add a nurse as a member of the Commission, since he was the sponsor of SB 286; Senator Rand agreed. However, when the bill came out, a nurse was not specified on the Commission. The Senate passed the bill without amendments. But, Senator Wilma Woodard was helpful in convincing Representative Billy Watkins to introduce an amendment for NCNA, which the House adopted, specifying that a nurse be a member of this Commission.

Since this was one of some 17 amendments to the bill adopted in the House, a conference committee was appointed to resolve the differences between the two chambers. Representative Watkins was a member of that conference committee, and he assured NCNA lobbyists that "the nurse will remain!" And the nurse did remain! That appointment on the Medical Database Commission is a very important accomplishment for nursing. A note of thanks to Senator Woodard and Representative Watkins would be appropriate.

● **HB 1021** is summarized in the May/-June issue of the *Tar Heel Nurse*. The bill as introduced would have reinstated a requirement that all counties or districts have appointed boards of health, social services and mental health. The bill received a favorable report from the House Committee on Health on June 4. Rebecca Mitchell presented NCNA's statement of support for the bill at the committee hearing. When HB 1021 was discussed on the House floor on June 11, some members of the Mecklenburg delegation attempted to amend the bill by leaving in language that would repeal the statute that enables county commissioners to take over the power and authority of these boards but adding language to provide an exception, namely those county commissioner groups who have already assumed the powers of these boards could continue to hold those powers. That exception in fact would apply only to Mecklenburg County. Some legislators began to question the constitutionality of such an amendment and the bill was re-referred to the Judiciary I Committee, where it was considered on June 27. Gwendolyn Jones of Durham presented *(continued on page 10)*

(continued on page 10)

Come and see Winston-Salem

by Kay Jackson
and
Dee Anderson
District Three Members

Distric Three is looking forward to being your hosts for the 1985 NCNA convention. Our city has much to offer, and we can't wait to share it with you!

For those of you who enjoy sightseeing, there are quite a few interesting attractions. Old Salem is a restored Moravian congregation town that has been a popular tourist attraction for many years. Tours are available 9:30 a.m. to 4:30 p.m. weekdays, which take you through Old Salem's restored buildings, including Winkler Bakery, home of Moravian Sugar Cake and Moravian Sugar Cookies.

Reynolda House, former home of Richard J. Reynolds, is a museum of American Art. Reynolda House offers the visitor the unique experience of enjoying the highlights of American painting in the warm, comfortable setting of a house that preserves the taste of a southern industrialist in the early part of the twentieth century. Visiting hours are Tuesday through Saturday, 9:30 a.m. to 4:30 p.m. Another popular art museum is the Southeastern Center for Contemporary Art, which is located in the former home of James G. Hanes. Visiting hours are 10 a.m. to 5 p.m., Tuesday through Saturday. Interesting exhibits can also be found at The Sawtooth Center for Visual Design in downtown Winston-Salem.

Industrial tours are also of interest. R.J. Reynolds Tobacco Company offers tours from 8 a.m. to 10 p.m., Monday through Friday. Exhibits depict all aspects of the tobacco industry along with memorabilia and artifacts. The Stroh Brewery Company offers a unique opportunity to view each step of brewing and packaging beer. After touring, guests are invited to enjoy a glass of beer or a soft drink in The Brown Bottle hospitality room. Tours are conducted Monday through Friday from 9 a.m. to 4 p.m.

For the majority of you who love to shop, Winston-Salem offers many opportunities to do just that. Hanes Mall offers over 75 different stores with a variety of fine merchandise. Bargain hunters will love The Marketplace, a new off-price center. Fine specialty shops can be found at Reynolda, Brookstown, and Old Salem. There are many other shopping centers throughout the city that you might find of interest.

For those of you who would like to get out and enjoy our lovely fall weather there are many parks and recreation facilities throughout the city. Indoor sports can also be found at several bowling alleys and skating rinks. Winston-Salem also boasts 12 indoor movie theatres.

The Barn Dinner Theater is also a great place to spend an evening in nearby Greensboro. During the week of convention, the theater will be playing "Deathtrap". Reservations can be made by calling (919) 292-2211.

District Three members will be on hand during the convention at designated times to provide specific information about local entertainment and dining. You will also receive a packet of information about Winston-Salem at the convention registration desk.

We're looking forward to seeing you in the fall!

Let's not judge disabled people by what they can't do but by what they can do.

President's Committee on Employment of the Handicapped
Washington, D.C. 20210

General Assembly from page 9

NCNA's statement of support for the bill.

Committee members also were scheduled to consider HB 604 on June 27. HB 604 would *further expand* the power and authority of Mecklenburg's county commissioners (remember, Mecklenburg County is also the only county that has taken over the power and authority of local boards of health, social services and mental health).

Obviously, discussion about HB 1021 brought on discussion about HB 604, since HB 1021 would make Mecklenburg County return to a system like all other 99 North Carolina counties, while HB 604 would allow Mecklenburg County Commissioners to further depart from the laws governing other counties and expand their power base over county services.

The end result was that a committee substitute for HB 1021 was adopted. The substitute cited the statute that allows county commissioners to take over the named boards and increased the population limit in that statute to 400,000, thereby assuring that no additional counties would make similar changes for quite some time, since they would be unlikely to meet the population limit. In addition, Representative Casper Holroyd (D-Wake) introduced a bill—HB 1405—to provide for a study of this issue, and that has been referred to the Committee on Appropriations. Meanwhile, an amended version of HB 604 received a favorable report.

When HB 1021 returned to the House floor on July 2, it passed second reading by a vote of 59 to 42 and then was again amended. This time, a sunset provision was added to the bill making it revert to the present population limit (325,000), on June 30, 1987. The House then passed the bill by a vote of 80 to 20 on third reading.

Since that time, HB 1021 has passed through the full Senate with a minor technical amendment. The House is expected to concur in the Senate amendment, and then the bill will be ratified. This action will at least maintain "status quo" for a while, since counties other than Mecklenburg are not expected to reach the 400,000 population limit that would allow their county commissioners to take over the power and authority of these boards.

In related action the House re-referred HB 604 (which would have further expanded the power and authority of Mecklenburg's county commissioners) to the House Judiciary I Committee. This committee has taken no further action on HB 604.

● **HB 348, SB 335, SB 350, SB 421, and SB 699** contain a variety of provisions about the "right to know" about hazardous substances. It has been interesting to watch the progress—or lack thereof—on these bills, since the House and Senate members have some divergent ideas on the issue. A conference committee is currently working frantically to come to some consensus. We will try to follow up on this story when we know the end result.

● **Another issue whose story is yet to be determined is that of pay equity.** At least six bills were introduced dealing with the issue in a variety of ways. *Something* is expected to emerge in one of the "money" bills yet to be released. More later.

● **SB 417** would create an Indigent Health Care Study Comission. Senator Tony Rand introduced the measure on April 25. NCNA lobbyists have spoken to Senator Rand regarding the need for nurse representation on this study commission. He has agreed to amend the bill to include a nurse. NCNA lobbyists have drawn up the necessary amendment forms and delivered them to Senator Rand. The provisions of SB 417 are expected to be included in a major bill appropriating funds to conduct studies during the next two years. We will watch closely to determine that a nurse has, in fact, been included in the membership of this important study commission.

In a few weeks, we should know more about the actions of the 1985 session of the General Assembly. The rapidity of action on a volume of proposed bills in the final hours of the session makes it extremely difficult to keep all the plates spinning! Watch for the final legislative report in the next issue of the *Tar Heel Nurse* after the dust has settled. In the meantime, a few prayers probably wouldn't hurt!

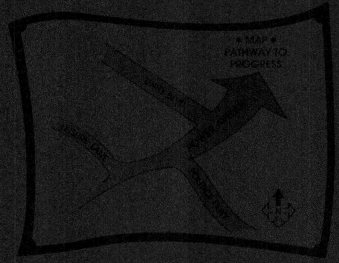

1985 CONVENTION

North Carolina
Nurses Association

* MAP *
PATHWAY TO
PROGRESS

October 23 - 26, 1985

Hyatt Winston-Salem
and
Benton Convention Center

Winston-Salem, NC

An Invitation from NCNA

Convention Purposes

Experience the NCNA Convention!

Faculty

Dues Increase from page 1

monthly assessment based on the SNA's membership as of July 1, 1982. NCNA's membership increased moderately after July 1, 1982, and we were able to retain all the dues money generated by that growth.

2. During the transition period, ANA also returned to states over a six-month period all ANA dues pre-paid up to July 1, 1982.

   NCNA did not use this "windfall" money in its budget at the time but earmarked it as operating reserve for foreseen financially critical times.

3. Throughout 1984, NCNA practiced severe economies — such as greater use of volunteer "labor" and volunteer consultation, streamlined office functioning to postpone adding clerical staff, decreased staff travel, and dropped membership in several organizations.

   These measures kept the Association from dipping into the "windfall" money — UNTIL NOW. To maintain current operating levels, since early 1985 NCNA has been dipping into the "windfall" money at a rate that will use up the money by early 1986.

Our current need for more resources — increased legislative activity, communication to members and the public, involvement in ANA at national level, liaison with a variety of groups — was foreseen months before the 1984 ANA convention. NCNA believes other SNA's face the same challenges and the same need for more financial resources. That is a major reason NCNA led an effort at the 1984 ANA convention to reduce ANA's share of dues resources to allow more dues money to go to states. We were not successful — ANA's share remained the same and the SNA's share was not increased.

The Board and Finance Committee made an in-depth analysis of membership experience and dues income over the past five years. It revealed that without the "windfall" money NCNA would have experienced a deficit as early as 1983. They examined various alternatives based on the following assumptions:

- 2800 membership level;
- 10% membership loss if there is a dues increase (history indicates this loss can be expected);
- income and expenditures based on

1985 budget figures (a "bare bones" budget reflecting priorities and needs the membership has said are essential).

This projection of the effect of various alternatives on our financial status produced the following scenarios:

1. **No Dues Increase,** with a 5% membership increase and 1985 budget figures — a deficit of $39,844 (with 5% inflation factor, deficit of $48,632). To meet the "bare bones" current budget, we would have to maintain a membership level of 4300 full-pay members.

2. **$25 dues increase,** assuming 10% membership loss and current budget needs — receipts over disbursements, $4,338 (with 5% inflation factor, deficit of $4,450).

3. **$35 dues increase,** assuming 10% membership loss and current budget needs — receipts over disbursements, $29,328 (with 5% inflation factor, $20,540).

4. **$45 dues increase,** assuming 10% membership loss and current budget needs — receipts over disbursements, $55,995 (with 5% inflation factor, $37,207).

All of this data has been shared with the Council of District Presidents. Additional information will be disseminated prior to the convention. Board members are available to their "personal districts," as well as to individual members, to discuss the recommended dues increase.

Members of the Finance Committee are: Carol Osman, NCNA treasurer and chairman; Judi Allen, Margaret Keller, Angie Hemingway, Frances Hayes, Sandra Wilkes, and Lou Brewer.

Sally Todd provided assistance in budget analysis and projections.

Letters to the Editor

As an officer for a private duty registry, I would like to respond to a statement made by Fay Harris in her letter published in the March-April issue of *Tar Heel Nurse*. I agree that a private duty nurse should be accountable for the care she gives, but let's not categorize ALL private duty nurses as being neglectful. Private duty nurses can be registered nurses, licensed practical nurses, nurses aides or sitters. In our city, RN's and LPNs are required to take medicine-math tests at hospitals before being allowed to give medications. If the specific case to which Ms. Harris refers involved an RN or LPN, we agree that benefits should be denied, but we can't understand a hospital allowing such an unqualified person to do private duty nursing in the first place.

Our agency provides the hospitals with a statement to be given to a patient when private duty nurses are ordered. It contains information regarding the duties of a private duty nurse, responsibilities of the patient to the private duty nurse and general information regarding payment of fees and insurance requirements for coverage of private duty services. Many patients mistakenly believe that Medicare will pay for these services, so that is made specifically clear in our statement that under no circumstances will it pay.

Barbara Willard, RN

North Carolina Nurses Association
announces

MEMBERSHIP AWARD
REWARD AND RECOGNITION PROGRAM

Recognition of a registered nurse in North Carolina who has made a significant contribution to membership growth in NCNA.

AWARD:	Recognition for outstanding member who has individually done the most to increase membership.
GUIDELINES FOR ENTRIES:	Nominations are to be made by district executive boards. Nomination forms have been sent to each district.
DEADLINE FOR ENTRY:	September 1, 1985
SELECTION:	To be made by the Membership Committee, NCNA
	Award will be presented at the 1985 convention of the North Carolina Nurses Association, October 23-26, 1985 at the Winston-Salem Hyatt Hotel.
SUBMIT ENTRY TO:	Membership Committee North Carolina Nurses Association P.O. Box 12025 Raleigh, NC 27605

NURSES
keep the <u>Care</u>
in Health Care!

Message from the Nominating Committee

The Nominating Committee is presenting this slate to the membership at least 60 days prior to the 1985 convention in compliance with requirements in the Bylaws.

Bylaws also assure the right of any member to self-declare for any office for which the member is qualified. On the facing page is an official form for self-declaring for any office listed on the slate. The deadline for self-declarations to reach the Nominating Committee is September 23, 1985. The official form must be used.

Immediately after September 23, the Nominating Committee will rule on qualifications of self-declared candidates, and the official ballot will be printed, with the names added of those determined to be qualified who have self-declared.

Members desiring to vote by absentee ballot in the 1985 election of NCNA officers may send a written request for an absentee ballot. This request must reach NCNA headquarters no later than October 3, 1985, and must be accompanied by a stamped #10 (4" x 9½") self-addressed envelope. On October 3 the absentee ballot will be mailed to current members requesting it.

Voting by absentee ballot is an option. The other option is to appear at the polls during scheduled voting hours at the convention and cast your ballot in person.

Candidates for NCNA Office
1985 Elections

President-Elect
Sarah P. Brown, Raleigh
Jo Franklin, Salisbury

Vice-President
Davy Crockett, Kernersville
Johnea Kelley, Durham

Secretary
Joyce Monk, Farmville

Treasurer
Sheila Englebardt, Greensboro
Angie Hemingway, Chapel Hill

Board of Directors (two to be elected)
Betty Baxter, Greensboro
Joan Bounds, Durham
Lou Brewer, Raleigh
Sandra Randleman, Lewisville
Evelyn Wicker, Durham

Chairman, Commission on Education
Frances Eason, Rocky Mount
Bettie Gordon, Charlotte
Linda Wright, Morganton

Chairman, Commission on Health Affairs
Rachel Stevens, Hillsborough

Chairman, Commission on Member Services
Carolyn Billings, Raleigh
Cynthia Luke, Wilmington

Chairman, Commission on Practice
Mary Lou Moore, Winston-Salem
Judith Roberts, Raleigh

Collective Bargaining Representative
John Chetney, Jr., Durham
Diane Horton, Durham

ANA Delegates-At-Large (two to be elected)
R. Leigh Andrews, Kitty Hawk
Margaret Bye, Raleigh
Judith Seamon, Morehead City
Edward (Mac) Stroupe, Greensboro

ANA Delegates (seven to be elected)
Carolyn Billings, Raleigh
Sarah Brown, Raleigh
Rebecca Carnes, Chapel Hill
Davy Crockett, Kernersville
Sheila Englebardt, Greensboro
Jo Franklin, Salisbury
Estelle Fulp, Raleigh
Betty Garrison, Charlotte
Vida Kay Jackson, Winston-Salem
Sue Modlin James, Jamestown
Johnea Kelley, Durham
Therese Lawler, Greenville
Barbara Jo McGrath, Lumberton
Rebecca Pitts, Asheville
Webra Price, Winston-Salem
Sandra Randleman, Winston-Salem
Russell Eugene Tranbarger, Greensboro
Connie Wolfe, Shallotte

Nominating Committee (five to be elected)
Patrick Ausband, Morehead City
Wanda Boyette, Clinton
Debbie Craver, Lexington
Loletta Faulkenberry, Burlington
Rachel Funderburk, Morganton
Joan Martin Jones, Greensboro
Marlene Rosenkoetter, Wilmington
Eris Russell, Black Mountain
Gwendolyn Waddell, Chapel Hill
Rebecca Wilson, Rocky Mount

1985 NCNA NOMINATION FORM

PRESIDENT-ELECT, VICE-PRESIDENT, SECRETARY, TREASURER, 2 DIRECTORS AT LARGE, NOMINATING COMMITTEE, COMMISSION CHAIRMEN, ANA DELEGATES & ALTERNATIVES

I wish to run for the office of: _____

NAME _____

ADDRESS _____ CITY _____ ZIP _____

TELEPHONE NUMBER (Home)_____ (Business)_____

Specific Area of Practice _____

EDUCATION: (Please indicate those levels which you have completed.)

_____ Diploma   _____ Associate Degree   _____ Baccalaureate (specify BA, BS, BSN, etc.)

     _____ Master's (specify MA, MS, MEd, etc.)   _____ Doctorate (specify PhD, EdD, etc.)

PRESENT EMPLOYMENT POSITION: _____

FORMER POSITIONS HELD: _____

PROFESSIONAL ACTIVITIES: (Please list professional organizations or activities in which you have participated in the last 5 years, on the district/local, state, or national level. *Please do not include present offices in this section.*)

District/Local: _____

State: _____

National: _____

PRESENT OFFICES:

District/Local: _____

State: _____

National: _____

I will serve if elected.

(Signed) _____

THIS FORM MUST BE RECEIVED NO LATER THAN SEPTEMBER 23, 1985. MAIL TO: NOMINATING COMMITTEE, NCNA, P.O. BOX 12025, RALEIGH, N.C. 27605.

Proposed amendments to NCNA bylaws — 1985

CURRENT BYLAWS	PROPOSED AMENDMENTS	RATIONALE
ARTICLE IX. COMMISSION ON EDUCATION	**ARTICLE IX. COMMISSION ON EDUCATION**	
Section 2. Functions	Section 2. Functions	
The Commission on Education shall:	The Commission on Education shall:	
A. Recommend establishment of forums for each of the major educational programs in nursing to identify, study, and advise on the concerns of educational programs in this state.	A. No change	
B. Assist district associations and special interest groups of members in identifying and meeting needs for continuing education.	B. Develop policies and criteria to be implemented by the Continuing Education Approval Unit and the Continuing Education Provider Unit.	This additional function is proposed for the Commission on Education to meet ANA accreditation standards as a continuing education approver and provider.
C. Evaluate relevant scientific and educational developments and changes in health needs and practices, with reference to their implications for nursing education.	Old subsections b, c, d, e, f, g, and h unchanged but renumbered	
D. Encourage and stimulate study and innovation in all areas of nursing education.		
E. Work with the committee on legislation to recommend action concerning federal, state, and local legislation in the field of education.		
F. Disseminate information about education programs.		
G. Act as liaison with the Board of Nursing, Board of Governors, the State Board of Education and other groups concerned with the preparation of health workers.		
H. Work jointly with the Commission on Practice to assist health care facilities in the creation and improvements of staff development through inservice programs.		
	Section 3. Continuing Education Approval Unit	Relocated from Article XII.
	The Continuing Education Approval Unit shall consist of not fewer than eleven members. One member shall be elected by each division on practice and at least six members, including the chairman, shall be appointed by the Board of Directors upon recommendation of the forums or subunits of the association. If more than eleven members are deemed necessary by the Continuing Education Approval Unit, the Board shall appoint additional members. Unexpired terms shall be filled by appointment of the Board of Directors upon recommendation of the unit. Ex-officio members (without vote) and/or consultants may be added by the unit. A majority of the members of the unit shall hold a minimum of a master's degree. This unit shall:	Changes name of the CERP committee to accurately reflect NCNA's role as a C.E. approver. To meet ANA accreditation standards as an approver, a majority of the unit's members must be master's prepared.
	A. Implement a continuing education approval process, utilizing criteria adopted by the Commission on Education and ANA guidelines.	Functions of unit are restated to meet ANA accreditation standards.
	B. Supply consultation to providers and learners as needed.	

Section 4.   Continuing Education Provider Unit

The Continuing Education Provider Unit shall consist of no fewer than seven members, including the chairman, to be appointed by the Board of Directors. The chairman of the unit shall hold a minimum of a master's degree. This unit shall:

    A.   Provide continuing education activities, utilizing criteria adopted by the Commission on Education and ANA guidelines.

    B.   Work collaboratively with other structural units in providing continuing education activities.

    C.   Evaluate the effectiveness of the association's role and involvement in providing continuing education for nurses.

Old sections 3 and 4 unchanged but renumbered.

ARTICLE XII.   STANDING COMMITTEES

Delete Section 4.

Renumber subsequent sections

Changes name of special Workshop Planning Committee to accurately describe NCNA's role as C.E. provider.

Functions are stated to meet ANA accreditation standards as C.E. provider.

Content relocated to Article IX. Places C.E. approval functions under Commission on Education to meet ANA accreditation standards.

ARTICLE XII.   STANDING COMMITTEES

Section 4.   Continuing Education Review Program Committee

The ___ __g ___ E__n ___w Program ___ __e shall consist of not ___ f__ __n eleven ___es, one ___ __r elected by __h division on ___ p__e and at ___ __t six ___es, __dg the ___n, ___ p__d by the Board of Di ___ __es upon ___ __n of the ___ f__s or ___ b__ts of the ___ __n, __d such) ___ __io ___ __rs (without __te) and/or ___ __ds as ___ __d by the ___ __e. If ___ __e ___tn eleven ___rs __e ___d ___ __ry by the Continuing E__n Review ___ __m ___ __e, the ___ B__d shall ___ __nt __ditional ___ __rs. Absence __m ___ __e ___tn two t__e regularly ___ __d ___ __s without notification and explanation ___ __d ___ __te to the ___ __e b__l ___te ___gn ___m the ___ __e. Unexpired ___ts shall be filled by ___ __nt of the Board of Di ___ __es, upon ___ __n of the CERP ___ __te. This ___ __te shall:

    A.   Review applications for approval of continuing education offerings for credit for registered nurses, to assure high quality and protect reciprocity with other states.

    B.   Establish and maintain a record-keeping system.

    C.   Supply consultation to providers and learners as needed.

ACTIONS OF THE BOARD

At a meeting on May 31, the Board of Directors took the following actions:

● Heard a request that NCNA file an amicus brief in a case involving alleged wrongful discharge of a nurse; requested NCNA legal counsel to review the case as to the appropriateness of NCNA filing an amicus brief in support of two specific issues: (1) right of the nurse to adhere to the legal requirements of the Nursing Practice Act without penalty, and (2) right of the nurse to protect the life and safety of patients without penalty.

● Considered a request from the National Federation of Licensed Practical Nurses for a position on titling for licensure and voted to respond to NFLPN citing conclusions of the Board of Directors and ANA delegates.

● Approved registration fees for the 1985 convention.

● Approved voting hours for 1985 elections.

● Nominated Cynthia Luke for appointment to the ANA Committee on Ethics.

● Asked for input for ANA national awards for nurses from appropriate structural units and districts.

● Approved a request from North Carolina Association of Nursing Students that the NCANS president give an update report to the NCNA Board at least twice yearly.

● Appointed Bettie Gordon to the Human Rights Committee.

● Voted to present a proposal to the 1985 House of Delegates for a $35 dues increase and made plans for submitting appropriate data to members and delegates concerning the necessity for a dues increase.

At a meeting on June 21, 1985, the Board took the following actions:

● Reviewed and accepted the auditor's report for 1984.

● Received a report on a joint meeting of the Board and Finance Committee and accepted plans for further presentation of data in support of a proposed dues increase.

● Approved dissemination to the membership of the proposal for structure changes.

● Directed the Committee on Bylaws to draft bylaw language to present to the 1985 House of Delegates to realign the CERP Committee to report to the Commission on Education and designating this committee as the NCNA C.E. approval unit, making changes in the composition and functions of the committee to meet ANA accreditation criteria.

● Identified the Workshop Planning Committee as the NCNA C.E. provider unit; directed the Bylaws Committee to draft bylaw language to realign this committee to report to the Commission on Education and to clarify the committee's functions to meet ANA accreditation standards.

● Directed the Executive Committee to plan for meeting other recommendations outlined in the ANA site visitors' report to be consistent with ANA C.E. accreditation standards.

● Voted not to file amicus brief in the case of alleged wrongful discharge of a nurse and requested that additional information, including the briefs, be made available to NCNA legal counsel; requested NCNA legal counsel to study this additional material and meet with the Executive Committee on July 1; authorized the Executive Committee to take action on the most appropriate mechanism to support the plaintiff nurse in this situation; directed that whatever action is taken in this case be supported with funds from voluntary contributions.

● Selected members for recognition at the 1985 convention Awards Banquet.

● Extended the deadline for a report from an Ad Hoc Committee on the Development of a Model Nurse-Managed Gerontological Facility.

● Recommended Ernestine Small, Cindy Freund, and Terri Lawler for appointment to fill a vacancy on the ANA Cabinet on Nursing Education.

● Made recommendations of Mallie Penry, Ruth Ouimette, Ellie McConnell, and Martha Henderson for appointment to the Governor's Council on Aging.

The Executive Committee reported to the Board it had taken the following actions at meetings on June 7 and June 20:

● Approved a loan from the Memorial Education Fund to Rebecca Ward Carnes for a continuing education course at the Kennedy Institute of Ethics.

● Voted to review and revise the criteria and application process for educational loans.

● Authorized the Headquarters Committee to proceed with refurbishing the building.

● Clarified the charge to the Ad Hoc Committee on the Development of a Model Nurse-Managed Gerontological Facility.

● Reappointed Hettie Garland as a consultant to the N.C. Medical Society's Health Care Professionals Committee;

● Appointed Hazel Browning as interim executive director during the current absence of the executive director.

● Reinstituted a temporary policy that Board of Directors members, who are members of committees, staff those committees and report any committee actions to the staff for information and feedback.

● Supported recommendations of the Third-Party Reimbursement Subcommittee on legislative strategies.

● Directed the Headquarters Committee to make recommendations regarding staff compensatory time and overtime.

Thanks, districts!

Commission and Committee Appointments 1985-87

North Carolina Nurses Association
Biographical Data and Consent-To-Serve

NAME _____

ADDRESS _____ CITY _____ ZIP _____

DISTRICT _____ AREA OF PRACTICE_____

SCHOOL OF NURSING _____

ADDITIONAL PROFESSIONAL EDUCATION _____

PRESENT POSITION _____ PLACE OF EMPLOYMENT_____

PROFESSIONAL ORGANIZATION ACTIVITIES (List offices and committees on national, state, or district level, for last five years.)

District _____

State _____

National _____

PRESENT OFFICE(S) _____

Check committee appointment desired (you may check more than one)

_____ Commission on Education
_____ Commission on Health Affairs
_____ Commission on Member Services
_____ Commission on Practice

Committees:
_____ Legislation
_____ Membership
_____ Workshop Planning

Committees (cont.)
_____ Bylaws
_____ Convention Program
_____ Continuing Education Review Program
_____ Headquarters
_____ Finance
_____ Human Rights

Committees (cont.)
_____ Public Relations
_____ Resolutions
_____ Peer Assistance Program Committee
_____ Nurse PAC

I would be willing to serve as a resource person in the following areas: _____

Committees are appointed after each election to carry out the duties assigned by the Board of Directors and/or the Bylaws. Terms are for the biennium.

The present policy of the Board of Directors does not allow travel reimbursement for meetings of NCNA structural units. January 9, 1986, is the date of orientation for commission and committee members. All commission and committee members are expected to attend.

If appointed, I agree to fulfill to the best of my ability the duties and responsibilities of the committee for which I am submitting my name.

Telephone (work) _____

(home) _____   _____
Signature

Please return to NCNA Headquarters, P.O. Box 12025, Raleigh, NC 27605, by October 1, 1985.

Policies and Guidelines
for Commission and Committee Chairmen
and Members

A. **Establishment of Committees**
1. Elected and appointed commission and committee members will be notified of appointment or election by written notice, and consent to serve will be requested. Term of appointment will be stated.
2. Chairmen will be notified of names and addresses of members of the respective commission or committee.
3. Chairmen of special or ad hoc committees will be notified at the time of appointment of the specific charge to the committee.

B. **Responsibilities of the Chairman**
1. Schedule meetings and clear meeting dates with headquarters.
2. Prepare agenda prior to each meeting and send to headquarters for mailing to members. .
3. Notify staff for materials and information needed prior to meeting.
4. Conduct meeting according to *Robert's Rules of Order*.
5. Submit goals and plans annually to the Board and/or responsible structural unit.
6. Report to Board and/or responsible structural unit prior to or during their regularly scheduled meetings.
7. Designate recorder for each meeting if there is no elected secretary.
8. Review minutes for accuracy prior to their being submitted to headquarters (using recommended format for minutes), and see that approved minutes reach headquarters within 72 hours of meeting.
9. Minutes received in unusable form will be returned to the chairman and secretary for correction.
10. See that all members complete travel vouchers and prepare travel summary before leaving the meeting.
11. Prepare a written interim report for the Board and/or responsible structural unit to be submitted September 1 of the even year of the biennium.
12. Prepare written biennial report for Board and/or responsible structural unit to be submitted by August 1 of odd year of the biennium.
13. Monitor attendance at meetings and notify Board and/or responsible structural unit if more than two consecutive meetings are missed.
14. Obtain authorization from the Executive Director for expenditure of any NCNA funds and transmit promptly to headquarters any funds collected in the name of the Association.

C. **Responsibilities of Committee and Commission Members**
1. Respond promptly to communications regarding meetings and committee business.
2. Attend scheduled meetings. Absence from two consecutive meetings may mean deletion from committee roster.
3. Notify chairman or headquarters if unable to attend meetings.
4. Participate in discussion of committee business and share responsibility in any activity.
5. Follow *Robert's Rules of Order* during committee discussions.
6. Prepare for meetings for informed discussion.
7. Resign if no longer able to attend.

D. **Responsibilities of Staff to Committees**
1. Assist chairman and committee as necessary.
   Provide materials and information requested by chairman and committee.
   Assist committee with implementation of decisions.
   Perform secretarial work of committee.
   See that minutes received in proper form are distributed to members within one week.
   Maintain in headquarters the official file of the committee/commission.

E. **Responsibilities of Special Appointeees**
1. Attend scheduled meetings.
2. Provide regularly a report to the Board.
3. Prepare a written report by September 1 of the even year of the biennium.
4. Prepare a written report by August 1 of the odd year of the biennium.

Proposed resolutions

Resolution I: SMOKING

(Submitted by District Eleven)

WHEREAS, The 1984 ANA House of Delegates adopted a resolution calling on ANA to recognize the intensity of the problem of smoking among nurses and the need for nurses to be actively involved in smoking cessation; and

WHEREAS, research has shown that the prevalence of smoking is higher among nurses than among women in general, and that proportionally fewer nurses than physicians, dentists, and pharmacists have stopped smoking; and

WHEREAS, nurses, as the largest group of health care providers, serve as role models in health maintenance and are in a position to encourage and support smoking cessation as a service to themselves, their clients and the public; and

WHEREAS, tobacco smoking is one avoidable cause of disease and premature death in our society and one of the most important public health issues of our time; and

WHEREAS, there is evidence of increased prevalence of smoking and tobacco-related diseases such as lung cancer in women; therefore, be it

RESOLVED, that NCNA promote increased awareness among nurses and nursing students of smoking as a health threat and the difficulties of reducing the tobacco habit; and be it further

RESOLVED, that NCNA encourage nurses and nursing students to stop smoking;

RESOLVED, that NCNA promote non-smoking policies at NCNA meetings and conventions; and be it further

RESOLVED, that NCNA encourage and assist nurses to appropriately counsel patients as to the risks of smoking, and assist or refer those who desire to stop smoking; and be it further

RESOLVED, that NCNA urge other nursing organizations to join this position of discouraging smoking; and be it further

RESOLVED, that NCNA send copies of this resolution to health professions organizations and groups concerned with smoking or the public health.

Resolution 2. GRADUATE STUDY ON NURSING
(Submitted by Commission on Education)

WHEREAS, The promotion and protection of high standards of nursing practice and education is one of the six priorities established by the NCNA Board of Directors for this biennium; and

WHEREAS, nursing practice in the 1980's is more complex and demanding than at any previous time in the history of nursing; and

WHEREAS, the degree of specialization in nursing education and practice is developing at an unparalleled pace; and

WHEREAS, graduate study in nursing in North Carolina "*is more readily available?*" with a good selection of areas of concentration — clinical specialties, education, administration; and

WHEREAS, graduate study in nursing at the master's level is only attained in schools of nursing; therefore, be it

RESOLVED, that NCNA inform the public as well as the profession that preparation for advanced nursing practice is gained through graduate study in nursing; and be it further

RESOLVED, that NCNA advise members and other qualified, interested candidates to pursue graduate study in nursing in programs offered by NLN approved schools of nursing which will prepare them for positions in advanced nursing practice and education.

ANA site visitors conclude members NCNA's top resource

Irene Morelli of Maryland and Edith Pence of Ohio visited NCNA June 17-18, 1985, to verify NCNA's qualifications to be accredited by ANA as a Continuing Education provider and approver. Ms. Morelli was the team leader and will represent NCNA at the Eastern Regional Accrediting Committee in August, when the final decision will be made.

Overall, the visit was very positive, and constructive recommendations were made. On the top of the list of NCNA's strengths was the "obvious commitment," "loyalty," "enthusiasm," and "qualifications" on the part of our member volunteers. There were several suggestions made about the structure of our association as you will note in the proposed bylaw changes explained in this issue.

Keep all fingers and toes crossed in hopes that we are approved. Accreditation by ANA will verify that NCNA's continuing education efforts meet nationally recognized standards. This is particularly important for nurses who need to maintain certification and nurses who need to acquire or maintain licensure in states where continuing education is mandatory.

Irene Morelli (left) and Edith Pence (right) complete an intense two-day ANA site visit on a positive note of good humor.

NCNA testifies on proposed ALS regulations

Sarah Pike Brown represented NCNA by presenting testimony on Advanced Life Support regulations at a hearing held on July 17 by the North Carolina Board of Medical Examiners. Ms. Brown's comments focused on the proposed rule changes regarding the practice and educational requirements of the Mobile Intensive Care Nurse.

Testimony clearly addressed NCNA's opposition to the proposed rule changes which, in effect, strip MICNs of their field skills and their educational program and remand nurses to radio communcations.

Ms. Brown concluded her testimony by drawing the hearing officers' attention to the Board of Medical Examiners' violation of the Administrative Procedures Act by not notifying all parties known to have an interest in the proposed rule changes about the hearing. With that she officially requested that no further action be taken on the proposed changes until a subsequent hearing is held with proper notice to all interested parties.

Celebrity Auction promises to be fun-filled evening at convention

Nurse PAC Chairman Jo Franklin reports that her home computer is ablaze with activity as plans for the Nurse PAC Celebrity Auction accelerate. The auction will be held on Friday, October 25, following the NCNA Awards Banquet at the 1985 Convention in the Hyatt Winston-Salem.

A professional autioneer will make the evening lots of fun, and Nurse PAC members promise many *special* items to bid on. Celebrities invited to contribute include Nancy Reagan, Elizabeth Dole, Jane Fonda, Jim Valvano, Dean Smith, Carol Burnett, Cindy Lauper and America's best-loved sex symbol, Tom Selleck! And that's just the beginning.

Items to be sold at auction will be displayed for participants' viewing at an Oktoberfest reception prior to the Awards Banquet and auction. Come and look over the goods, choose your favorite celebrity's contribution, and be ready to make your bid! Oh! By the way, don't forget your checkbook!

PLANNING FOR TOMORROW.
SECURING NURSING'S FUTURE

American Nurses' Association
1986 Convention / June 13-19 / Anaheim, California

News Briefs from page 7

sity of Pennsylvania School of Nursing, Philadelphia, PA 19104 (215-898-8285).
• "Nurses: Charging for Caring" sponsored by the Hawaii Nurses Association October 11, 1985. Contact Ganong Seminar, HNA, 677 Ala Moana Suite 601, Honolulu, Hawaii 96813.
• "National Conference On Health Policy and Quality of Care for Older Americans" co-sponsored by the ANA, will be held November 12-13, 1985 in Alexandria, Virginia. Contact Department of Health Care Resources, American Medical Association, 535 N. Dearborn St., Chicago, Illinois 60610.
• "Nursing Research: Integration into the Social Structure", sponsored by the

ANA Council of Nurse Researchers, will be held December 4-7, 1985 at the Hotel Inter-Continental in San Diego. Contact Marketing, ANA, 2420 Pershing Rd., Kansas City, Missouri 64108.
• Third annual "National Symposium on Physiological Placing", sponsored by Cordis Corporation, will be held February 12-15, 1986 in Miami. Contact Susan Catania, Cordis Corporation, Department of Educational Services, PO Box 025700, Miami, Fla. 33102-5700 or call 1-800-327-2490.
• "Aging: A Celebration of Life? The Paradox of Living Longer", the 32nd annual meeting of the American Society on Aging, will be held March 23-26, 1986 in San Francisco. Submit an abstract for presentation. Contact American Society on Aging, 833 Market St.,

Suite 516, San Francisco, CA 94103 or call (415) 543-2617.
• ANA Minority Fellowship Programs received a Kellogg Grant to conduct leadership and management seminars for selected participants, primarily minority women from a pool of post-doctoral candidates who have received educational support through the Minority Fellowship Programs. The first seminar will occur in April 1986.

Take stock in America.

NORTH CAROLINA NURSES ASSOCIATION
P.O. Box 12025
Raleigh, North Carolina 27605

Vol. 47, No. 4   July-August 1985

Official publication of the North Carolina Nurses Association, 103 Enterprise St., Raleigh, N.C. Tel. (919) 821-4250. Published 6 times a year. Subscription price $12 per year, included with membership dues. Indexed in *Cumulative Index to Nursing and Allied Health Literature* and available in MICROFORM, University Microfilms International.

JUDITH B. SEAMON.............. President
HETTIE L. GARLAND .... President-Elect
GALE B. JOHNSTON .... Vice-President
SALLY S. TODD .... Secretary
CAROL A. OSMAN .... Treasurer

STAFF
FRANCES N. MILLER ..... Executive Director
HAZEL BROWNING .....Assoc. Exec. Director
BETTY GODWIN .... Asst. Exec. Director
PATRICIA W. BRYAN ..... Administrative Asst.
DOROTHY BENNETT .... Administrative Asst.

UNIVERSITY of NORTH CAROLINA

AUG 23 1985

HEALTH SCIENCES LIBRARY

ISSN 0039-9620

TAR HEEL NURSE

Vol. 47, No. 5   OFFICIAL PUBLICATION OF THE NORTH CAROLINA NURSES ASSOCIATION   September-October 1985

ANA delegates act on titling issue

Ten NCNA delegates represented North Carolina nurses at the 1985 ANA House of Delegates in Kansas City in July—the first such meeting to be held outside ANA's biennial convention.

The 698-member House is ANA's top policy-making body.

The NCNA delegation: (forefront) Judy Seamon (left) and Sheila Englebardt; (seated left to right) Carol Osman, Hettie Garland, Connie Wolfe, Estelle Fulp; (back row standing left to right) Wanda Boyette, Barbara Jo McGrath, Cathy Hughes, Eris Russell.

Following are major actions of the 1985 House:

■ Reaffirmed its support for two levels of nursing practice, a professional level and a technical level.

■ **Urged state nurses associations to:**

• Establish the baccalaureate with a major in nursing as the minimum educational requirement for licensure to practice professional nursing;
• retain the legal title "Registered Nurse" for the baccalaureate prepared nurse;
• establish the associate degree with a major in nursing as the educational requirement for licensure to practice technical nursing, with the provision that such degrees be awarded by state chartered institutions of higher learning, such as community or junior colleges;
• establish "Associate Nurse" as the legal title for the person licensed to practice technical nursing; and
• assure that the educational preparation and scope of practice of those licensed to practice technical nursing are congruent.

■ Charged the Cabinets on Nursing Education, Practice and Services to define the scopes of practice for both the professional and the technical level, to be reported to the 1986 House of Delegates.

■ Called for development of an action plan to implement its decisions on education and titling, in cooperation with SNAs, the National Council of State Boards of Nursing, state boards of nursing, and the two national organizations that represent LPNs. The action plan also is to be reported to the 1986 House.

The most vigorous discussion centered

(continued on page 19)

NCNA accredited as approver, provider of continuing education in nursing

by Betty Godwin

Hard work and patient waiting have ended in a success story! NCNA has been accredited for four years, August 1985-1989, as a C.E. approver and provider. The notification came in September from the Eastern Regional Accrediting Committee of the ANA.

Two major changes that will affect providers of continuing education will be the new fee structure and new deadlines for submitting applications. One recommendation was to develop a more realistic budget for the approval program. It was evident that the current review fees fall far short of covering the cost of the service. A criteria for ANA approval is that one must have the resources to implement the program. The CERP committee is "costing out" the approval process and will have a proposal for the next meeting of the Board of Directors.

Another change that will affect the pro-

(continued on page 2)

Bring to Convention

Bring this issue with you to the convention. It contains proposed goals, priorities, and legislative platform that will be voted on by the House of Delegates, and a proposal for structure changes that will be the subject of discussion at a special forum.

Message from the President

Judith B. Seamon

"Pathway to Progress"—the theme of our upcoming convention—could not be more relevent to the current needs of the nursing profession to secure its rightful place within the health care system and within contemporary and future society.

Consideration of "Power Avenue" is especially important because of our reticence as nurses to deal with the concept of power—frequently believing that power is a negative concept. Just as a boat without power is dead in the water, a car without power is dead on the road, our homes without power are almost nonfunctional, so are we as nurses without power useless as a viable force within the health care system and society.

Synonyms for power include force, energy, strength, might, authority, jurisdiction, control, command and several others. Among the expected definitions given by Webster is one which is quite unexpected, i.e., "an angel of the fourth lowest rank." At first, that held no meaning for me in regard to anything, especially nursing, until I began to reflect on some comments made at a meeting of the North Carolina Hospital Association last winter. At this meeting, which also included representatives from the North Carolina Medical Society and NCNA, governance in hospitals was being discussed. The "three-legged stool" theory of hospital management was noted—

namely, the management of a hospital is supported by the three "legs" of administration, the medical staff, and the trustees. At that time, I commented during my presentation on that program that the problem was clear—because everyone knew a three-legged stool was very unstable, and the fourth leg which would provide stability was very accessible and essential to hospital governance—namely, nursing! Yet, why wasn't nursing being perceived as a stabilizing force to these decision-makers. More importantly, why hasn't nursing taken the responsibility or been able to achieve that position of stability? Perhaps it is because, without realizing it, we have been accepting the definition of our power as the "angel of the fourth lowest rank," and have believed that we should maintain the "fourth lowest rank." It is time to assess and perhaps change many of our perceptions about power and begin to increase our proactive stance as the largest group of health care professionals. Join us at convention as we explore the "Pathway to Progress" and "Power Avenue"!

This is my last opportunity to address you through the *Tar Heel Nurse* as your president. The experience has been challenging, rewarding, and exciting, and I thank you for the opportunity and urge your continued support of the new administration for the 1985-87 biennium.

NCNA accredited *(from page 1)*

viders is the new deadline for submitting applications for credit. In the past the CERP committee encouraged providers to submit programs six weeks prior to the first offering date but would review offerings as long as they were received before the program was offered. The site visitors stated that offerings must be submitted with enough time before the first offering date to have been reviewed and a decision made regarding credit. The CERP committee has decided to continue to encourage six weeks but will accept programs four weeks in advance of the program.

The advantages of being ANA accredited will outweigh the difficulties felt in adjusting to these changes. Having ANA approval will eliminate the need many nurses experience in having to go outside North Carolina to receive credits to maintain certification or licensure in states where continuing education is mandatory. Ultimately all nurses will benefit by know-

ing that programs provided or approved by NCNA meet national standards, which reflects quality.

Biennial Report

The NCNA 1983-85 Biennial Report, traditionally printed in this pre-convention issue of *Tar Heel Nurse*, is not included in this issue this year. The reason is cost containment.

The report—a compilation of biennial reports of all officers, structural units, and special representatives—will be distributed to each convention registrant. Other members may receive the report on request from headquarters following the convention.

NEWS BRIEFS

● The AJN Company's Educational Services Division is now accepting entries for its fifth biennial media festival. The competition will culminate in June, 1986. For details write AJN Company, Educational Services Division, 555 West 57th Street, New York, NY 10019.

● The 37th edition of the most comprehensive statistical portrait of nurses and nursing in the United States, *Facts About Nursing 84-85*, is now available from ANA. Pub. No. D-84, $22.50. Publications Orders, ANA, 2420 Pershing Road, Kansas City, Missouri 64108. For charge orders call 1-800-821-5834.

● The following videotapes are now available from AJN: "Preparing Children for the Hospital Experience," "The Early Years," "The Middle Years," "The High School Years," "My CAT Scan." Write AJN Company, Educational Services Division, 555 W. 57th Street, New York, NY 10019 or call 1-800-223-2282.

Professional Development Opportunities

● "The AJN Company Computer Software Lab," October 31, November 1, 2, 1985 in Chicago. Call 1-800-223-2282 to register.

● "Association of Rehabilitation Nurses 11th Annual Educational Conference to be held November 13-17, 1985 in Atlanta. Write RNI Conference, 2506 Gross Point Road, Evanston, Illinois 60201.

● "Setting the Agenda for the Year 2000," the 13th Annual Scientific Session of the American Academy of Nursing to be held December 3, 1985, San Diego, California. Register by November 1, 1985, American Academy of Nursing, ANA Fiscal Affairs, 2420 Pershing Road, Kansas City, Missouri 64108.

● "Nursing Research Integration into the Social Structure," sponsored by the ANA Council of Nurse Researchers, December 4-7, 1985 in San Diego, California. For information write ANA Fiscal Affairs, ANA, 2420 Pershing Road, Kansas City, Missouri 64108.

● "Translating Commitment into Reality," the third in a series of annual symposia presented by the American Academy of Nursing, will be held January 23-25, 1986 in Clearwater Beach, Florida. For information call 1-800-821-5834.

NURSES
keep the <u>Care</u> in Health Care!

Why NCNA needs a dues increase —

The Board of Directors and Finance Committee are sharing with the membership some of the data that led to the decision to propose a $35 dues increase.

1. Alternatives for dues at the state level
   - assumptions: (a) 2800 membership level
     (b) 10% membership loss (estimate based on literature review)
     (c) Income and expenditures based on 1985 budget figures — which is a "bare bones" budget and is based on input from membership regarding priorities and needs.

   A. **No dues increase,** 5% membership increase, and 1985 budget figures.

   RESULTS: Receipts over disbursements=deficit of $39,844 (with 5% inflation factor deficit of $48,632)

   Note: In order to meet the projected "bare bones" expenditures of the budget and have no dues increase, we would have to maintain a membership level of 4300 full-pay members.

   B. **$25 dues increase,** plus all three assumptions

   RESULTS: Receipts over disbursements=$4,338 (with 5% inflation factor deficit of $4,450)

   C. **$35 dues increase,** plus all three assumptions

   RESULTS: Receipts over disbursements=$29,328 (with 5% inflation factor=$20,540)

   D. **$45 dues increase,** plus all three assumptions

   RESULTS: Receipts over disbursements=$55,995 (with 5% inflation factor=$37,207)

2. Last dues increase approved in October 1980 and effective January 1981 was for $15.

3. Financial Status for 1980 through 1985.

	1980	1981	1982	1983	1984
Receipts	188,482	226,747	203,595	267,381	241,053
Disburse.	183,750	205,487	195,786	242,432	254,004
CR/CD (under)	4,732	21,260	7,809	24,949*	(12,951)

4. The programs, services, and visibility of NCNA have increased (i.e., legislative activities; CERP program; liaison with numerous agencies; impact on health planning and decision-making bodies; resource to a wide variety of agencies/groups/public on nursing data and position statements; more efficient and effective communication; national recognition and respect with resulting national involvement and benefits).

5. Cost-containment measures already implemented: streamlining of NCNA functioning by word processing/computer, volunteer consultants, decreased staff travel for structural meetings, increased use of volunteer "labor", volunteer negotiator for V.A., use of student help for staffing of the office, decreased mileage allowance, cancellation of subscriptions.

BANK DRAFT
If **you pay dues by bank draft**—

Current	Proposed
Annual dues — $115	**Annual dues — $150**
Monthly bank draft — $9.58	Monthly bank draft — $12.50
	difference — **$2.92**/month
	less than 10¢/day

The dues bank draft system is a convenient way to assure that your NCNA membership remains current. The bank draft option is explained on the membership application form.

Dues are automatically deducted from your checking account each month. This system avoids the problems some members might have with either paying one larger check per year for annual dues or three installment payments per year. No fuss, no mess, no bother!

How we compare with other SNAs

Only eight other SNAs have SNA dues less than $55. These vary in membership from 172 in the Virgin Islands to 2,976 in North Carolina.

SNA	Membership	SNA Dues
Alabama	2763	$ 50
Arkansas	765	52
Georgia	2659	51
Louisiana	1711	50
North Carolina	2976	50
South Carolina	1109	50
Tennessee	2153	54
Virgin Islands	172	35
Wyoming	354	50

Other SNAs with membership comparable to NCNA:

Maryland	3313	$ 65
Missouri	3083	90

How we compare with other SNAs

ORGANIZATION	ANNUAL DUES	BENEFITS
Physical Therapist Association	$245 (state & national)	national journal state newsletter discounted registration fees optional association-sponsored insurance programs
American Medical Records Association	$105 national $20 state (rebate from national)	national journal national office maintains individual c.e. records discounted registration fees
Pharmaceutical Association	$90 national $60 state	national journal state journal discounted registration fees
Society of Hospital Pharmacists	$15 national $80 state	newsletter
Respiratory Therapists	$75 national ($10 rebated to state)	scientific journal magazine discounted registration fees optional group insurance programs
NCAE	$135 national and state plus local (varies)	national publication state publication liability insurance
Medical Society	$190 state & local $330 national	state journal national journal
Dental Society	$345 national and state plus local (varies)	national journal state newsletter no registration fee at state convention
Psychologists Association	$100 national $65-$75 state (based on income)	national magazine and newsletter discounted registration fee optional group insurance programs state newsletter
NCNA	$115 national, state and local	national newsletter state newsletter district newsletter discounted registration fees optional group insurance program member loan program

needs, costs grow faster than income

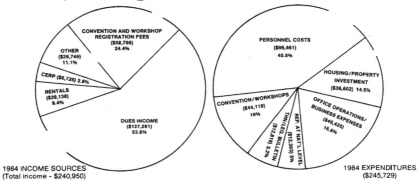

1984 INCOME SOURCES
(Total income - $240,950)

- CONVENTION AND WORKSHOP REGISTRATION FEES ($58,786) 24.4%
- OTHER ($26,749) 11.1%
- CERP ($6,725) 2.8%
- RENTALS ($20,138) 8.4%
- DUES INCOME ($127,261) 53.8%

1984 EXPENDITURES
($245,729)

- PERSONNEL COSTS ($99,461) 40.5%
- HOUSING/PROPERTY INVESTMENT ($36,602) 14.5%
- OFFICE OPERATIONS/BUSINESS EXPENSES ($40,425) 16.8%
- CONVENTION/WORKSHOPS ($44,119) 18%
- REP. AT NAT'L LEVEL ($12,303) 5%
- TN/LEG. BULLETIN ($12,819) 5.2%

Comparison of typical fixed costs* of NCNA
1980 and 1985

		1980		1985
Tar Heel Nurse				
printing, one issue	(Av. 6 pgs.)	$ 472.16	(Av. 16 pgs.)	$1,780.68
postage, one issue		110.76		203.64
Utilities (monthly average)		442.25		900.86
Real Estate taxes (annual)		2,981.21		4,048.73
Telephone (one month's service)		246.48		486.47
Post office box rent (annual)		40.00		53.00
Auditing fee		1,850.00		2,700.00
Service contract, one typewriter		81.50		118.00
Postage meter rental (one quarter)		46.80		114.43
Legislative Bulletin Service (reg. session)		368.16		901.25
Janitor service (one month)		306.00		323.00
Postage, one first class letter		.15		.22
Property owner insurance (annual)		873.00		1,086.00
Water service (monthly average)		27.43		62.18
Paper (one ream)		3.21		3.90
Association Professional Liability Insurance		-0-		1,173.00
FICA taxes (employer share per month)		394.09		598.17

Personnel Costs	1980	1984
Salaries	$ 76,601	$ 87,596
Payroll Taxes	4,861	6,633
Insurance	278	1,795
Retirement	5,004	3,290
Adv	-0-	147
	$ 86,744	$ 99,461

*Data from invoices on file at NCNA

How your dues dollar is distributed

ANA's share - 48% ($55)   NCNA share - 43.5% ($50)   District share -8.5% ($10)

Community
BULLETIN BOARD

Guest tickets may be purchased for the three meal functions planned for the 1985 NCNA Convention. These tickets are priced as follows:

October 23—Keynote Dinner Session (6:45 p.m.—9:30 p.m.) $20.00;

October 24—Luncheon Session (12:30 p.m.—2:30 p.m.) $18.00;

October 25—Awards Banquet (6:00 p.m.—8:30 p.m.) $25.00.

If you are interested in purchasing a guest ticket, please notify NCNA, (919) 821-4250, immediately to assure available space. Only a few meal tickets will be available for on-site purchase due to hotel requirements for meal guarantees.

■ Several alumni groups will use the convention as an opportunity to meet and catch up on old friendships. These include the following:

● The Alumni Association of Presbyterian Hospital School of Nursing will host a coffee on Friday, October 25, from 7:30 a.m.—9:00 a.m., in the Lee Room, Hyatt Hotel, for Presbyterian School of Nursing Alumni and friends.

● The UNC-Chapel Hill School of Nursing Alumni Association will hold a coffee and dessert reception for alumni and friends on Wednesday, October 23, from 9:30 p.m.—10:30 p.m., in the Granville Suite of the Hyatt Hotel.

■ A program, "Managing More With Less: Between the Rocks and the Ranks," will be presented at the convention by the Nursing Practice Administrators Section. The speaker will be Sally Todd, R.N., M.S.N., president of a private consultant firm, editor of a nursing management newsletter and an adjunct professor for UNC-Chapel Hill.

This program will assist the participant in developing such strategies as: (a) thinking like an entrepreneur, (b) releasing creativity in self and others, (c) using power tools and (d) tying rewards to performance.

The program will be held during the Nursing Practice Administrators meeting from 12 Noon—1:50 p.m. on October 23, 1985. Please note that this **is not** a luncheon meeting.

■ Tours have been arranged for October 24 as a part of Thursday afternoon's "Leisure Living" activities. Reservations

can be made by completing the form below and sending the form and appropriate check to Margaret Glenn Tours by October 18 or by calling (919) 724-6547. If a sufficient number of persons do not register for both tours, only one tour may be offered. If desired, a full refund will be given if the tour conducted is not the one of your choice. Please note: Submit fees for the **bus rates**. If an insufficient number register for bus rates, you may pay the additional fee for van transportation on the day of the tour.

■ Nurse PAC will sponsor a "Celebrity Auction" at the convention. Chairman Jo Franklin reports that celebrity items are coming in daily and they expect to have as many as 100 items to auction away. Some of the items received so far include:

• an autographed basketball from Duke University,
• an autographed photograph of Coach Jim Valvano, NCSU Head Coach,
• a fun "family cookbook" from Fritz and Joan Mondale, autographed by both,
• a shawl and perfume from France donated by N.C. Rep. Bea Holt,
• tee shirts from Insurance Commissioner Jim Long,
• tee shirts and baseball caps from "Gillys".
• admission to one day workshops sponsored by UNC Department of Nursing,
• an autographed photograph of Michael Jackson,
• a David Hartman "Good Morning, America" coffee mug,
• lots of luncheons with legislators,
• lunch with Lieutenant Governor Bob Jordan,
• lunch in Washington with Congressman Bill Hefner and
• a Cabbage Patch preemie!

The auction will be held at 8:30 p.m. following the October 25 Awards Banquet. Plan to come and don't forget your checkbook!

■ Nurse PAC will have several items available for purchase at their convention booth. Don't buy your 1986 calendars yet because Nurse Calendars will be available at the Nurse PAC booth. In addition, Nurse PAC members plan to sell copies of the "Political Action Handbook for Nurses" at a special rate. Don't forget to drop by the booth and see all of these exciting materials.

Emergency Resolutions

Emergency resolutions may be submitted to the Resolutions Committee by 5 p.m. on Wednesday, October 23. Emergency resolutions are those whose significance could not have been apparent by the deadline date and which, because of timeliness, require immediate action.

Emergency resolutions may be turned in at the convention registration desk or to Resolutions Committee Chairman, Eunice Paul.

Voting Reminder

Any current member of NCNA may vote for NCNA officers in the 1985 election—by absentee ballot or at the polls during the convention.

Those who missed the October 3 deadline for requesting an absentee ballot may vote at the convention, whether or not the member is registered for the convention. The polling place will be in the Davis Room of the Hyatt Hotel, Winston-Salem. Voting hours are 9 a.m.—4 p.m. and 7 p.m. - 9 p.m. on Thursday, October 24, and 7:30 a.m. - 10:30 a.m. on Friday, October 25. At the polling place the member must present a current membership card to receive a ballot.

Proposed goals, priorities, legislative platform

These proposed goals, priorities, and legislative platform have been approved by the Board of Directors for presentation to the 1985 House of Delegates.

NCNA GOALS:

1. Sustain and strengthen NCNA's role as spokesman for nursing in all arenas, including the legislative arena, that affect health care, and provide guidance in the framing of the legal base for the practice of nursing.
2. Increase the number of nurses who participate in the shaping of the nursing profession.
3. Promote and protect high standards of nursing practice and education.
4. Advance the professional status of nursing in the workplace and the economic position of nurses commensurate with professional responsibility.
5. Strengthen district/state communications and relationships to build a stronger organization of better informed members.
6. Participate actively in shaping health policy and setting trends that improve the standards and availability of health care services for all people.

Priorities for the 1985-87 Biennium:

1. Increase membership by recruitment and retention.
2. Stabilize the financial base of NCNA.
3. Increase services to facilitate leadership development and district growth.
4. Bring together concerned groups of both nurses and non-nurses to develop an action plan for implementing two levels of nursing practice in North Carolina.

5. Increase the visibility of NCNA as a political force.
6. Protect all arenas of nursing practice, including specialty practice, through a strong legislative program, monitoring of regulatory agencies and support of appropriate legal action in litigation.
7. Support the advancement of the professional and economic status of nurses commensurate with their professional responsibility.
8. Evaluate nursing's current and potential role and contribution to safe and effective health care for special populations, especially the elderly.

1986-87 Legislative Platform

The North Carolina Nurses Association endorses legislation and regulatory authority to:

* Protect the public through maintenance of a strong Nursing Practice Act and through authority for the Board of Nursing to regulate the practice of nursing and all of its specialties and to set standards for nursing education programs.
* Protect the rights of patients and their families to safe, affordable, and accessible health care.
* Allow consumers direct access to the qualified health care provider of their choice by removing barriers restricting consumer choice.
* Provide for adequate health care to populations with recognized, special needs, especially the growing number of older citizens.
* Protect the right of citizens to a safe, health environment.
* Improve the work environment, the economic base, and the professional and legal status of nurses.
* Strengthen opportunities for individuals to achieve the educational preparation essential for competent nursing practice.
* Provide expertise on health care issues by inclusion of qualified registered nurses on advisory and policy-making bodies.

Update on final actions of 1985 General Assembly

By Hazel Browning

The dust has finally settled at the Legislative Building after the 1985 session of the North Carolina General Assembly adjourned on Thursday, July 18. At press time for the July/August issue of the *Tar Heel Nurse*, some issues of interest to nursing were still unsettled. This report is a follow-up on those issues.

• SB 417 creates an Indigent Health Care Study Commission as described in the July/August issue of this newsletter. The contents of this bill were incorporated into SB 344, "The Independent Study Commissions and Committees Act of 1985". With the help of Senator Wilma Woodard (D-Wake), final language specifies that a nurse be appointed by the President of the Senate to serve on the study commission. This commission will consider issues of access to and financing of health care services for North Carolinians who are unable to pay for their medical care. The nursing perspective will add a very valuable element to the work of this group.

• The "right to know" about hazardous substances issue was a hot one in the 1985 session. Several bills were introduced identifying many different ways to deal with this item. Our primary concern as it related to nursing practice was to assure

that a nurse provider had access to specific chemical identity of a hazardous substance in both emergency and non-emergency situations. With support of the North Carolina Department of Labor, Labor Commissioner John Brooks and the bill sponsor, Representative Harry Payne (D-Wilmington), these specific requirements were included in the final version of the bill. This action will affect directly the nurse functioning in occupational health settings.

• HB 52 was ratified on July 12. The 33-page bill makes major revisions in the Administrative Procedures Act which governs the administrative rule making and adjudicatory procedures for state agencies, including the Board of Nursing. A special article of the bill deals with administrative hearings of occupational licensing agencies.

A majority of the Board of Nursing may elect to conduct administrative hearings and will designate the location of those hearings. Normally, these cases would be conducted in the county where the agency maintains its principal office—in this case, Wake County. When a majority of the board members are unable or elect not to hear the case, the board may apply to the Office of Administrative Hearings for designation of a hearing officer to preside. These cases will be heard in the county of

residence of the licensee unless designated otherwise by the hearing officer to better promote the ends of justice or better serve the convenience of witnesses.

At one point, HB 52 specified fees for services from the Office of Administrative Hearings, which could have presented a very costly proposition for the Board of Nursing. The final version of the bill does not specify any fee for those services.

ABOUT PEOPLE

Ruth E. Long of Durham has been appointed to the Durham County Mental Health Board for a term expiring in July, 1989. The appointment was made by the County Commissioners ... **Maida Dundon**, Winston-Salem, on behalf of the NCNA Commission on Practice, provided comments on the draft revisions of the ANA *Code for Nurses with Interpretive Statements*, a project of the ANA Committee on Ethics ... **Cathy Hughes** of Charlotte received one of the 1984/85 Outstanding Service Awards given in the summer by the North Carolina Black Leadership Caucus. The Caucus is composed of black elected and appointed officials and community leaders. Cathy now holds the position of utilization review coordinator for the CAREolina Health Plan, a health maintenance organization recently formed in Concord ... **Sarah Hitchcock**, director of nursing at Rex Hospital in Raleigh since 1961, is retiring effective October 1.

ACTIONS OF THE BOARD

The Board of Directors took the following actions at a meeting on August 16, 1985:

• Ratified a referendum vote approving proposed amendments to the bylaws.

• Approved contingency plans recommended by the Executive Committee to meet expenses for the remainder of 1985.

• Directed the Executive Committee to develop a plan, based on options identified by that Committee, for reducing NCNA's activities and services beyond 1985 in the event additional dues resources are not available.

• Accepted a program proposed by the Peer Assistance Program Committee, contingent upon the Committee's adoption of suggestions from legal counsel; directed that the program be resubmitted to the Board for final approval.

• Adopted a contingency plan developed by the Executive Committee for operation of the Association in the event of extended absence of the executive director.

• Revised and adopted a policy statement developed by the Executive Commit-

tee establishing criteria for NCNA's participation in legal action involving issues critical to nursing practice.

• Designated the Commission on Member Services as the fund-raising agent for the NCNA Legal Fund and appointed Joyce Monk as the chairman of the 1985 fund-raising drive.

• Requested that a fact sheet be developed on the titling issue for early dissemination.

• Requested that information on policies and expectations of officers, ANA delegates, and alternate delegates be included on the consent-to-serve form.

• Approved a legislative platform for 1986-87, as recommended by the Committee on Legislation, for presentation to the 1985 House of Delegates.

• Received a report from the Ad Hoc Committee on Credentials and referred it to the Commission on Practice.

• Received a report from the Ad Hoc Committee on Statewide Planning for Nursing Education and referred it to the Commission on Education.

• Developed proposed goals and priori-

ties to be submitted to the 1985 House of Delegates.

• Selected individuals to receive awards and citations at the 1985 convention.

• Appointed Jane Roberts to the Peer Assistance Program Committee.

The Executive Committee reported to the Board that it took the following actions at a meeting on July 1, 1985:

• Directed that an amicus brief be filed in a pending legal case, when and if the time is appropriate, in support of the issue of wrongful discharge related to upholding the Nursing Practice Act.

• Reaffirmed the actions of the Board of Directors taken on June 21, 1985, that any legal action taken in this case be supported by outside funds.

• Referred recommendations from ANA C.E. accreditations site visitors to various structural units for follow-up action.

• Developed a plan to recognize nursing leaders at the 1985 NCNA convention.

The Executive Committee also reported to the Board the following actions taken at a meeting on August 2, 1985:

(continued on page 20)

Proposal
for
New Organizational Structure

The Ad Hoc Committee on Structure is presenting the work it has completed thus far on the revision of the NCNA organizational structure. The NCNA Board of Directors has approved the dissemination of this structure proposal for additional input from the membership prior to and during the 1985 NCNA Convention. This proposed structure has been designed based upon information received from the Council of District Presidents, the membership, present NCNA structural units, the NCNA Board of Directors, and current information available on association structure from the literature. In addition, the committee convened with the purposes and functions of NCNA as stated in the bylaws. All of the information has been correlated subcommittees for specialized input for each of the major proposed structural units. The proposed structure chart represents the committee's visualization of a new structure based upon all of the above-named factors.

The committee will be present at the 1985 NCNA Convention Forum scheduled Friday, October 25, 1985, from 2:30 p.m. until 4:15 p.m. Members present at the Forum will be given a response form to complete.

This issue of Tar Heel Nurse has a detailed explanation for each of the proposed structural units, defining composition and functions of each.

The committee welcomes comments and recommendations written on the response form so that all may be considered. To prevent duplication of responses, the committee request that members planning to attend the convention Forum wait to complete the response form after participating in the Forum discussion.

The proposed structure chart shows seven "cabinets" rather than the current four commissions. This reflects the addition of three new structural units at this organizational level and the renaming and revision of four commissions found in the present NCNA structure.

You will also note that many of the current permanent subgroups appear in an optional format. This change is based on current association literature recommending minimal permanent structure and the generous use of ad hoc groups or committees in order to address changing needs and issues in a timely fashion without having to effect bylaws changes. Therefore, it is proposed that any of the cabinets could form as few or as many interest groups as deemed appropriate and useful in order to respond effectively to the needs of the membership and the Association.

The committee structure has been altered by combining and/or relocating various committees. Several committees remain unchanged.

As chairman of this ad hoc committee, I express my appreciation for the tireless, enthusiastic and thoughtful work of the committee in carrying out its charge. The committee members have worked well together.

We will appreciate your consideration and input regarding each proposed structural unit.

Ad Hoc Committee on Structure

Judy Seamon, Chairman
LaVonne Beach
Lottie Daw
Jean Gosnell
Vicky Rosan Hutter
Jan Leggett
Katherine Smith

Proposed NCNA Organizational Chart

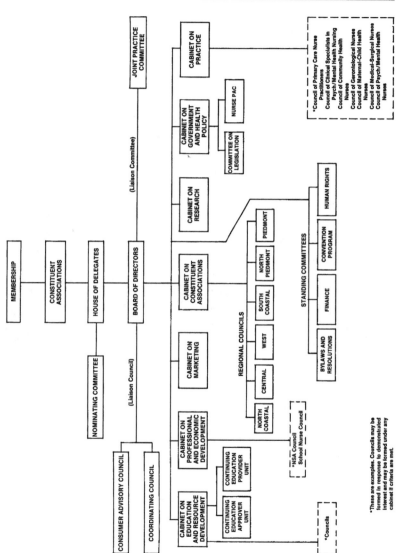

Proposed Structure

CURRENT STRUCTURE

Committee on Membership (Standing Committee)

Composition: Chairman is the NCNA Vice-President. No fewer than five members appointed by the Board of Directors.

Functions: Relate to membership recruitment.

Public Relations Committee (Special Committee)

Composition: Chairman and members appointed by the Board of Directors.

Functions: Relate to publicity for NCNA.

Commission on Member Services

Composition: Chairman elected. Eleven members including chairman of sections and the collective bargaining representative.

Functions: Coordinate and evaluate the Association's direct services to individual members as these relate to economic and general welfare of nurses.

NO CURRENT STRUCTURAL UNIT IS RESPONSIBLE FOR RESEARCH.

Commission on Practice

Composition: Chairman elected. Eleven members including chairman of each Division on Practice and conference groups.

Functions: Relate to practice standards, needs of special clinical interest groups, etc.

PROPOSED STRUCTURE TO NCNA

Cabinet on Marketing

I. A. *Composition:* 11. Chairman to be elected by NCNA membership. Ten members appointed by the NCNA Board of Directors.

B. *Functions:* Combines functions of current Committees on Membership and Public Relations and those of Commission on Member Services that relate to recruitment/retention of members and direct services/benefits to individual members.

II. **Cabinet on Research**

A. *Composition:* 11. Chairman to be elected by NCNA membership. Ten members appointed by the NCNA Board of Directors. A majority of the membership shall be doctorally, masters, and baccalaureate prepared nurses.

B. *Functions:* Promote nursing research, serve as clearinghouse for research activities; seek funding for research projects.

III. **Cabinet on Practice**

A. *Composition:* 11. Chairman to be elected by NCNA membership. Ten members appointed by the NCNA Board of Directors according to current policies with representation from various areas of practice.

Suggested representation is as follows:

```
3  Acute Care Setting
     —Maternal Child Health
     —Adult
     —Psychiatric/Mental Health
1  Extended Care
1  Independent Practice
2  Advanced Practice
1  Community Health
1  Education
1  Administration
```

RATIONALE FOR CHANGE

Combines membership recruitment and retention and public relations activities of NCNA as functions of one organizational unit as opposed to having functions distributed among three organizational units.

Elevates status of membership committee to a cabinet to reflect importance of functions.

Chairman will be elected and participate as a member of the Board of Directors without having to fulfill duties as a major NCNA officer. (Currently, chairman of Membership Committee is Vice-President.)

Nursing research is an essential function of profession, and NCNA should have a mechanism to promote and support this function.

Composition combines practicing nurses from various areas of practice, nurse administrators, and educators.

CURRENT STRUCTURE

Commission on Health Affairs

Composition: Chairman elected. Ten members appointed by Board of Directors.

Functions: Relate to interpreting nursing to the public (allied health groups, community service groups, governmental agencies, etc.); promote nursing participation in health planning, etc.

Committee on Legislation (Standing Committee)

Composition: Chairman and at least five members appointed by Board of Directors.

Functions: Relate to legislative efforts of NCNA.

Nurse PAC (Special Committee)

Composition: Chairman and members appointed by Board of Directors.

Functions: Political action committee of NCNA.

Commission on Education

Composition: Chairman elected. Eleven members including chairmen of Forums and CERP Committee.

Functions: Relate to NCNA's role in addressing educational issues.

PROPOSED STRUCTURE TO NCNA

B. *Functions:* Essentially same as current Commission on Practice and remain clinically focused.

IV. Cabinet on Government and Health Policy

A. *Composition:* 11. Chairman to be elected by NCNA membership. Members include the chairman of the Legislative Committee, chairman of Nurse PAC, and 8 at-large members to be appointed by NCNA Board of Directors.

B. *Functions:* Combines functions of (1) current Committee on Legislation that relate to development of legislative priorities and objectives; (2) current Commission on Health Affairs that relate to nursing input into health policy. Serves as "umbrella" for Nurse PAC.

C. Subgroups of Cabinet on Government and Health Policy

1. *Legislative Committee*

   a. *Composition:* 11. NCNA Board of Directors appoints the chairman and 10 members representing various interests of the association and geographic areas of the state.

   b. *Functions:* Translate the Cabinet on Government Health Policy's recommendations into action plans of strategies to accomplish identified legislative goals in a timely and effective manner.

2. *Nurse PAC*

   a. *Composition:* NCNA Board of Directors appoints the chairman and at least 10 members.

   b. *Functions:* Same as current functions of Nurse PAC (special committee)—raising funds and making contributions to state and local candidates; educating nurses about the political process.

V. Cabinet on Education and Resource Development

A. *Composition:* 11. Chairman to be elected by NCNA membership. The chairman shall hold a minimum of a master's degree. Members include the chairman of the Continuing Education Approval Unit, chairman of the Continuing Education Provider Unit, and eight members at-large appointed by the NCNA Board of Directors according to current policies with representation from different groups.

Suggested representation for at-large members is as follows:

4   Educators:
2   Chief officers from schools of nursing
    —Professional
    —Technical
2   Faculty
    —Professional
    —Technical
1   Chief nursing officer from hospitals
1   Chief nursing officer from community health agencies
2   Middle management (any practice setting)

RATIONALE FOR CHANGE

Coordinates NCNA efforts related to influencing health care by involvement in:
- the political and legislative process;
- the interface with governmental and regulatory agencies;
- the voluntary and private sectors involved in health care planning and policy.

Combines nurses from practice and education settings to address educational and nurse manpower resource development issues. Representation of educators on Cabinet based on level of preparation in which school is engaged.

Meets ANA criteria for being accredited as a continuing education provider and approval unit.

Recommend that an appointment policy be developed that would provide for at least one-half the Cabinet to continue each biennium to assure continuity for long-range and strategic planning.

B. *Functions:* Promote strong linkage between nursing education and practice; relate trends in the health care delivery system and nursing manpower needs to nursing education; develop policies and criteria for NCNA C.E. approver and provider units.

Functions reflect a pro-active approach to nursing education to meet future nursing needs by consumers.

C. Subgroups of Cabinet on Education and Resource Development

1. Continuing Education Approval Unit

A. *Composition:* Not fewer than 11 members appointed by the Board of Directors. The chairman and a majority of members must be masters prepared. Members must have experience in developing, implementing and/or evaluating continuing education programs.

B. *Function:* Serve as C. E. Approval Unit of NCNA

Meets ANA C. E. accreditation criteria.

2. Continuing Education Provider Unit

A. *Composition:* Not fewer than seven members, including the chairman, to be appointed by the Board of Directors. The chairman of the unit shall hold a minimum of a master's degree.

B. *Functions:* Serve as C.E. Provider Unit of NCNA.

Meets ANA C.E. accreditation criteria.

VI. Cabinet on Professional and Economic Development

A. *Composition:* 11. Chairman to be elected by NCNA membership. Ten members appointed by the NCNA Board of Directors, according to current policies with representation from various groups, including one representative each from any bargaining unit represented by NCNA. A majority of members shall be staff nurses.

Suggested representation for at-large members:
—Acute Care (include nurses from secondary and tertiary care settings)
—Community Health
—Independent Practice
—Education

Composition strengthens the voice of staff level nurses in a variety of work settings.

B. *Functions:* Essentially same as functions of current Commission on Member Services that relate to professional and economic issues and status of nurses in the workplace.

Functions strengthen NCNA's role in addressing issues related to economic and general welfare of nurses.

VII. Cabinet on Constituent Associations

A. *Composition of Cabinet:* 11

6 Regional chairs — Change yearly (each regional council elects a chairman and a chairman-elect)

4 Board Appointees — Appointed every 2 years (must be active at district level)

Enhances the leadership role of district presidents by decentralizing the Council of District Presidents into regional councils.

Chairmanship of regional councils and the cabinet rotate in such a way as to provide continuity but minimize the amount of responsibility of any one person over an extended period of time.

Cabinet will provide a structural unit that can address district needs more readily and consistently than the former Council of District Presidents.

CERP Committee (Standing Committee)

Composition: Chairman appointed by Board of Directors. Other members appointed or elected by selected structural units.

Functions: Implements the continuing education approval program.

Workshop Planning Committee (Special Committee)

Composition: Chairman and members appointed by Board of Directors.

Functions: Relate to sponsoring workshops that meet needs not specifically addressed by any other single structural unit, or that are believed to have potential for fund raising for NCNA.

Commission on Member Services

Composition: Chairman elected. Eleven members including chairman of sections and the collective bargaining representative.

Functions: Relate to addressing issues related to economic and general welfare of nurses.

Council of District Presidents

Composition: All presidents of district associations. Elects two representatives to the NCNA Board of Directors.

Functions: Provides a link between NCNA and members.

CURRENT STRUCTURE

PROPOSED STRUCTURE TO NCNA

Chairman elected by NCNA membership — Elected every 2 years (must be active at district level); will chair cabinet and sit on Board of Directors

B. *Functions:* Resources for identifying and developing services needed by the membership; assist and guide district associations and regional councils; strengthen communication among NCNA Board of Directors, regional councils, and district associations.

C. **Suggested Regional Councils and Suggested Central Meeting Locations:**

North Coastal	17,18,19,20,24,30,32	Greenville
South Coastal	14,15,16,21,22,27	Duplin County-Kenansville
West	1,2,23,26,28,29,34	Asheville
North Piedmont	3,7,8,9,31	Winston-Salem or Greensboro
Central	10,11,13,33	Durham
Piedmont	4,5,6,12,25	Statesville or Salisbury

D. **Regional Council Composition:** District Presidents and Presidents-Elect. Regional Councils will elect chair from presidents and will elect chair-elect from presidents-elect. This allows continuity of leadership even though the chairman serves a one year term.

E. *Functions:* Interpret to district membership purposes and functions of NCNA; promote district activities that enhance these purposes and functions; provide linkage between district associations and Cabinet of Constituent Associations.

VIII. **Councils**

A. *Definition* — A council is an organizational unit through which members participate in the improvement or advancement of the profession in an area of nursing practice or interest. Councils are accountable to the Board of Directors through the appropriate Cabinet.

B. *Designation* The Board of Directors may establish councils upon the recommendation of a Cabinet.

C. *Composition* — Each member of a constituent association may affiliate with one or more councils upon meeting each council's eligibility requirements.

D. *Responsibilities* — Provide a community of peers and a principal source of expertise in areas of interest and serve as a forum for discussion of relevant issues and concerns; develop positions and policies for recommendation to the cabinets and promote implementation of professional standards.

E. *Executive Committee* — A council would elect a five-member executive committee to conduct Council business.

RATIONALE FOR CHANGE

NCNA Board of Directors would establish regional boundaries, based on input form constituent associations.

Encourages constituent associations to adopt president-elect system.

Allows formation of special interest groups without having to change bylaws as needs and interests change.

Committee on Bylaws
Standing committee that responded to bylaws changes.

Committee on Resolutions
Standing committee that responded to resolutions.

Committee on Finance
Composition: Chairman is treasurer of NCNA. At least three members appointed.
Functions: Relate to NCNA budget, expenditure and investment of all NCNA funds.

Convention Program Committee
Composition: No fewer than six persons, appointed by Board of Directors.
Functions: Develop focus, select topics and speakers, formulate convention schedule.

Human Rights Committee
Composition: No fewer than five members representative of both sexes and various ethnic groups; appointed by Board of Directors.
Functions: Devise strategies to achieve equity within NCNA; support equal employment opportunities for minority nurses; promote accessibility to quality health care for underserved populations.

Headquarters Committee (Standing Committee)
Composition: Chairman is NCNA President-Elect; at least five members appointed by Board of Directors.
Functions: Relate to property management and personnel policies of NCNA.

NO CURRENT STRUCTURAL UNIT IS RESPONSIBLE FOR THIS FUNCTION.

F. *Dissolution* — A council could be dissolved by the Board of Directors, on recommendation of appropriate cabinet, when the council fails to carry out its responsibilities or need/interest are no longer demonstrated.

IX. **Committees**
A. **Bylaws/Resolutions:**
   1. *Composition:* At least 7 members appointed by the NCNA Board of Directors.
   2. *Functions:* Retain current functions of both committees as specified in Bylaws.

B. **Finance Committee:**
   1. *Composition:* The Finance Committee shall consist of at least five persons including the treasurer of this association, who shall be chairman of the committee. One member shall be a member of the Cabinet on Marketing.
   2. *Functions:* Same as current bylaws

C. **Convention Program Committee:** Retain composition and functions as specified in current Bylaws.

D. **Human Rights Committee:** Retain composition and functions as specified in current Bylaws.

E. **Headquarters Committee:** DELETE. Shift assigned functions to the NCNA Executive Committee.

F. **Peer Assistance Program Committee:** Leave as special committee.

G. **Consumer Advisory Council:**
   1. *Composition:* Number not to exceed 25; appointed by the Board.
   2. *Functions:* Serve as an advisory group to the Board of Directors on consumer health issues.

Combines functions of two committees into one. Streamlines committee activity.

Increases number of members responsible for NCNA budget. Provides communication between Finance Committee and the Cabinet on Marketing.

Functions appropriate for Executive Committee ... streamlines committee activities.

Provides input by consumers.

CURRENT STRUCTURE

Coordinating Council:

Composition: Joint committee composed of Boards of Directors of NCNA and N.C. League of Nursing.

Functions: Coordination of those programs of common concern.

NCNA Board of Directors

Composition: Five officers, four commission chairmen, four directors-at-large, two directors elected by Council of District Presidents.

Functions: Implements actions and directives of the NCNA House of Delegates. Transacts general business between NCNA House of Delegates.

Executive Committee

Composition: Elected officers.

Functions: Has full powers of Board of Directors to transact business between Board meetings.

PROPOSED STRUCTURE TO NCNA

H. **Coordinating Council:** Leave as joint committee.

X. **NCNA Board of Directors**

   A. *Composition:* 15
      —President
      —President-Elect
      —Vice President
      —Secretary
      —Treasurer
      —7 Cabinet chairmen
      —3 Directors-at-Large

   B. *Functions:* Same as current bylaws.

   Duties of the Board of Directors and Board members remain the same as in current Bylaws with the exceptions of (1) President-Elect will no longer chair the Headquarters Committee; and (2) the Vice-President will no longer chair the Membership Committee.

C. **Executive Committee**

   1. *Composition:* Remains same.

   2. *Functions:* Same as current functions with addition of functions of current Headquarters Committee.

RATIONALE FOR CHANGE

Composition reflects revised structure (seven cabinet chairmen) but maintains officers and elected directors to equal a membership of fifteen.

Structure Proposal Response Form

Instructions:

Please complete the following response form reflecting your opinions regarding the structure proposal. This same proposal will be discussed at the 1985 convention where the *same* response form will be disseminated to those in attendance. *If you plan to attend this convention forum, please wait and complete the questionnaire following forum discussion.* The Ad Hoc Committee on Structure regards your input as critical, but would like to minimize duplication.

Structural Unit	Composition				Functions				Comments
	Representation adequate		Method of selection satisfactory		Clear		Appropriate		
	Yes	No	Yes	No	Yes	No	Yes	No	
Cabinet on Marketing									
Cabinet on Research									
Cabinet on Practice									
Cabinet on Government and Health Policy									
Subgroups: Committee on Legislation									
Nurse PAC									
Cabinet on Education and Resource Development									
Subgroups: C.E. Approver Unit C.E. Provider Unit									
Cabinet on Professional and Economic Development									
Cabinet on Constituent Associations									
Six Regional Councils									
Committee on Bylaws and Resolutions									
Committee on Finance									
Committee on Convention Program									
Committee on Human Rights									
Consumer Advisory Council									
Board of Directors									
Executive Committee									

Headquarters Committee: Do you agree with deletion of their committee and assigning functions to the Executive Committee?
___ Yes ___ No
Comments

PAP Committee: Do you agree that this committee should remain a special committee?   ___ Yes   ___ No
Comments

OVERALL EVALUATION OF PROPOSAL

1. To what extend do you feel the proposed structural units will address your current and future needs in your professional practice?
___ All units address my needs

___ Some units (please list those that *will not* address your needs)

___ No units will address my needs (please explain below)

2. Do you feel this structure provides you with adequate representation at the state level?   ___ Yes   ___ No (please explain)

3. Do you feel the Cabinet on Constituent Associations and Regional Councils will strengthen the "grassroots" level of NCNA?
___ Yes   ___ No (please explain)

Signature _____ (date) _____
(optional)

Return to: NCNA, P.O. Box 12025, Raleigh, N.C. 27605

NCNA to establish fund for legal action

The Board of Directors has authorized the establishment of a special fund to support legal action by the Association in cases involving critical legal issues affecting the nursing profession. The Fund is to be generated from voluntary contributions.

The Board has designated the Commission on Member Services to spearhead an initial fund-raising effort and has appointed Joyce Monk, member of the Commission, as chairman of the drive.

Recognition of the impact of court decisions on the practice of nursing is the impetus for establishing the Legal Fund as a long-term strategy to enable NCNA to respond appropriately through the court system on critical nursing practice issues.

Requests for legal action by the association are to be evaluated by the Board of Directors on a case-by-case basis utilizing the following criteria:
· NCNA's involvement in the case is consistent with the purpose and functions expressed in the bylaws.
· The case has statewide implications.
· The case has substantial implications for the nursing profession.

The following regional coordinators have been appointed:

Northern Coastal—Sue Sutcliffe of Ahoskie; Southern Coastal—Charlotte Hoelzel, Wilmington; West—Rebecca Pitts, Asheville; North Piedmont—Davy Crockett, Kernersville; Central—Gwen Waddell, Chapel Hill; — Betsy McLean, Charlotte.

The Commission's theme for the current drive is "Summon Your Support," and the initial goal is to raise $3,500 by the end of October. Contributions can be made payable to the NCNA Legal Fund and mailed to headquarters.

Name _____ Address_____

Telephone: (H)_____ (W)_____

NCNA Member ____ Yes ____ No District _____

Amount Contributed $_____

Make checks payable to "NCNA Legal Fund" and mail to:
NCNA, P.O. Box 12025, Raleigh, NC 27605

Contributions

Since the last *Tar Heel Nurse*, three districts have contributed an additional $400 to the 1985 ANA Delegate Fund. They are Districts Eight, Twenty-Eight, and Thirty-One.

The contributions have made possible additional checks of $44.44 to the nine delegates who shared in the Fund.

WATCH THE MEMBERSHIP THERMOMETER

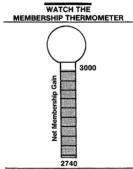

3000

Net Membership Gain

2740

We're only 23 short of our goal of 3,000 members. Help us get to the top by convention time!

Calendar of Events

The following "Calendar of Events" will inform members of meetings of NCNA structural units and other related groups and agencies. All structural unit meetings will take place in headquarters unless otherwise indicated.

Meetings of the NCNA Board of Directors, committees and commissions are open to the membership. Members may attend to see the Association in action and to communicate with the elected and appointed officials. Members planning to attend should notify NCNA at least two days prior to the meeting, so that we can plan for adequate seating and plenty of coffee!

Date/Hour	Event
Oct. 3	"Laws Affecting North Carolina Nurses — 1985" - Catawba Memorial Hospital, AHEC, Hickory
Oct. 4	"Laws Affecting North Carolina Nurses — 1985" - Greensboro AHEC
Oct. 7, 10:00 a.m.	NCNA Executive Committee
Oct. 10, 1:30 p.m.	Joint Practice Committee
Oct. 11, 10:00 a.m.	Commission on Member Services
Oct. 14, 9:30 a.m.	Ad Hoc Committee on Foundation
Oct. 22, 9:00 a.m.	NCNA Board of Directors
Oct. 23-26	NCNA Convention
Nov. 23, 9:30	N. C. Federaton of Nursing Organizations
Nov. 14-15	Orientation Retreat, new Board of Directors (tentative)
Nov. 15	"Laws Affecting North Carolina Nurses — 1985" - Greenville
Nov. 28	HOLIDAY, NCNA Office Closed
Dec. 2	Joint Midwifery Committee - Raleigh Hilton
Dec. 25	HOLIDAY, NCNA Office Closed

Candidates for office in NCNA organizational units

COMMUNITY HEALTH DIVISION
Chairman
Shirley Mozingo, Selma
Vice-Chairman
Joanne Corson, Raleigh
Secretary
Margaret Brake, Cary
Nominating Committee
Lou Brewer, Raleigh
Diane Crouse, Lexington
Jackie Harrell, Four Oaks
Donna Jackson, Selma
Hilda Newton, Gastonia
CERP Committee
Annie Hayes, Whiteville
Sue Hunter, Wilson

GERONTOLOGICAL NURSING DIVISION
Chairman
Sharon Sells, Stanfield
Su Modlin James, Jamestown
Vice-Chairman
Mary Eplee, Whiteville
Betty Mauney, Charlotte
Secretary
Marilyn Rowland, Winston-Salem
Linda Howard, Matthews
Nominating Committee
Pamela McAllister, Matthews
Mary McIntyre, Nashville
Voneva Nunn, Charlotte
Marilyn Wood, High Point
CERP Committee
Marge Bye, Raleigh

MATERNAL-CHILD HEALTH DIVISION
Chairman
Judy Barnes, Kinston
Vice-Chairman
Cynthia Luke, Wilmington
Hope Smith, Durham
Secretary
Kathryn Harmon, Durham
Elaine Hunkins, Greensboro
Nominating Committee
Ruth Bowers, Durham
Maida Dundon, Clemmons
Martha Eakes, Greensboro
Janice Leggett, Greenville
Susan Ridgeway, Durham
CERP Committee
Martha Ballard, Cary
Vickie Healey, Chapel Hill

MEDICAL-SURGICAL DIVISION
Chairman
Jane Ray, High Point
Vice-Chairman
Deborah Reed, Cary
Secretary
Shirley Jenkins, Apex
Nominating Committee
James Brown, Wilmington

Vercie Hardee, Raleigh
Mary James, Fayetteville
Theresa Tranbarger, Greensboro
CERP Committee
Karen Gallimore, Archdale
Ginger Sandlin, Chapel Hill
Reba Walters, Oxford

PSYCHIATRIC-MENTAL HEALTH DIVISION
Chairman
Rosemary Strickland, Durham
Vice-Chairman
Mable Carlyle, Black Mountain
Secretary
Nancy Quinn, Burlington
Nominating Committee
Dorothy Honeycutt, Raleigh
Sandra Wilkes, Raleigh
Jeannie Yount, Washington
CERP Committee
Patricia Hayes, Madison
Margaret Raynor, Garner

BACCALAUREATE AND HIGHER DEGREE FORUM
Chairman
Carolyn Jones, Charlotte
Vice-Chairman
Paul Allen Gray, Jr., Wilmington
Margaret Hargett, Greensboro
Secretary
Sherry Laurent, Charlotte
Elizabeth Cooper, Greensboro
Nominating Committee
Martha Engelke, Greenville
Mary Field, Chapel Hill
Patricia Lawrence, Durham

DIPLOMA FORUM
Chairman
Loletta Faulkenberry, Burlington
Vice-Chairman
Gail Pruett, Durham
Secretary
David Williams, Durham
Nominating Committee
Rosalind McDonald, Kinston
Estelle O'Brien, Browns Summit
Donna White, Clayton

ASSOCIATE DEGREE FORUM
Chairman
Donnye Rooks, Smithfield
Nancy Sumner, Rockingham
Vice-Chairman
Linda Phillips, Shelby
Secretary
Donnie Greene, Raleigh
Nominating Committee
Rhonda Ferrell, Warsaw
Wilma Harris, Elizabeth City
Sue Morgan, Waynesville

CONTINUING EDUCATION FORUM
(no ballot)

SPECIALISTS IN PSYCHIATRIC-MENTAL HEALTH NURSING
Chairman
Libba Wells, Hillsborough
Vice-Chairman
Marilyn Earle, Raleigh
Barbara Rynerson, Chapel Hill
Secretary
Margaret Raynor, Garner
Nominating Committee
Jo Ann Adams, Cary
Carolyn Billings, Raleigh
Elizabeth Munsat, Chapel Hill

PRIMARY CARE NURSE PRACTITIONERS CONFERENCE GROUP
Chairman
Joyce Nixon, Gastonia
Sophie Szwagiel, Durham
Vice-Chairman
Mary Lyn Field, Chapel Hill
Janet Wolfe, Hillsborough
Linda Tull, Weaverville
Secretary
Paula Sumner, Raleigh
Judith Zentner, Hickory
Nominating Committee
Jo Ann Adams, Cary
Amanda Greene, Carrboro
Marie Shirey, Raleigh
Cynthia Van Deusen, Asheville

SCHOOL NURSE SECTION
Chairman
Christine Fisher, Garner
Vice-Chairman
Gayle Brown, Hamptonville
Secretary
Carol Cox, Greenville
Nominating Committee
Elizabeth Best, Winston-Salem
Maida Dundon, Clemmons
Eddie Grubbs, Winston-Salem

NURSING PRACTICE ADMINISTRATORS SECTION
Chairman
Kathy Madry, Greensboro
Vice-Chairman
Margaret Whittington, Raleigh
Secretary
Johanna Winchester, Greensboro
Nominating Committee
Brenda Bessard, Raleigh
Avis Duncan, Greensboro
Linda Ellington, Chapel Hill

ANA convention highlights *(from page 1)*

on the title for technical nursing practice. During the debate 17 titles were proposed, and delegates also considered the option of not selecting a title at this time. There was strong support for the title, "Licensed Practical Nurse," but the title "Associate Nurse" was adopted by a majority vote of 405 of the 678 delegates voting.

In making recommendations regarding titling of two levels of nursing practice, the ANA Cabinet on Nursing Education considered many factors, such as the changing needs of consumers of nursing services, the increasing employment marketplace for nurses with baccalaureate in nursing backgrounds, and the increase in enrollments of nursing students in nursing programs granting baccalaureate degrees in nursing.

- There is decline in length of patient stay in community hospitals, and acuity of patients' conditions is increasing.
- There is a shift toward a greater use of RNs versus other nursing staff and toward employing a greater percentage of RNs with baccalaureate degrees.
- Projected nursing personnel requirements indicate that by 1990 even larger numbers of RNs with baccalaureate degrees will be needed.

The House adopted eight bylaw changes, referred two, and rejected 29 other proposed changes. Five of the changes "fine-tuned" the federation structure adopted three years ago. A sixth change clarifies the ANA cabinets' responsibility in adopting standards. Another change calls on the Nominating Committee to offer at least two nominees for each office. Another change related to responsibilities of the Committee on Bylaws to review SNA bylaws for conformity with ANA bylaws.

Delegates rejected proposals for: creating the office of president-elect; reducing the size of the House; limiting bylaw changes to special meetings or meetings in odd-numbered years; and geographic presentation on the board of directors.

Several other rejected changes related to election rather than appointment of certain committees.

The House also took action on other matters:

- encouraged the involvement of nurses in the organ and tissue donation and transplantation process;
- voiced unanimous support for the Vietnam Women's Memorial Project and collected over $5,000 in individual contributions to the project;
- urged support of legislative initiatives that address the problem of hunger and malnutrition in the U.S.;
- added as a 1986 legislative priority the reducing of barriers to quality, accessible prenatal and perinatal care for all women;
- charged ANA to publicize the long-range implications of inadequate funding for social and health programs for women and children;
- asked ANA to support federal legislation banning the use of sulfiting agents on foods and in drugs;

- adopted a procedure for N-CAP, ANA's political action committee, to determine the endorsement of a candidate for President of the U.S.;
- changed the name of N-CAP to ANA-PAC;
- in a 15-minute "challenge" collected over $33,000 for ANA-PAC's campaign fund;
- charged ANA to initiate introduction of legislation or regulatory changes in the Medicare and Medicaid programs to provide: (1) direct reimbursement for services of all registered nurses or organized nursing services, and (2) nursing control over the nursing care of long-term care clients;
- urged increased ANA support and assistance to state nurses associations in monitoring and opposing legislation that would restrict nursing practice and in supporting mechanisms for recognizing and expanding nursing practice;
- urged steps to ensure affordable professional liability insurance coverage for certified nurse midwives and for all registered nurses.

The 1986 ANA convention will be held June 13-19 in Anaheim, California.

NCNA President Judy Seamon at a floor mike speaks to the issue under discussion.

The delegation celebrated Gene Tranbarger's election to the ANA Cabinet on Nursing Services. Congratulating Gene are Eris Russell, Estelle Fulp, and Sheila Englebardt, his campaign manager.

Tar Heel nurses take the podium! Left, Judy Seamon as chairman, presides over the Constituent Forum, which met prior to the convening of the House of Delegates. Right, Barbara Jo McGrath, as chairman of the ANA Nominating Committee, reports to the House.

Nursing leaders appointed to two study commissions

Nurses will be represented on at least two commissions authorized by legislation passed in the 1985 session of the North Carolina General Assembly. NCNA members and lobbyists worked diligently to procure a seat for nursing on the two bodies and were pleased to hear recently of the fruits of their labor.

Lieutenant Governor Bob Jordan has announced the appointment of Russell E. Tranbarger, R.N., to the Indigent Health Care Study Commission. This group will study issues of access to and financing of health care services for North Carolinians who are unable to pay for their medical care. This issue is becoming a critical one in North Carolina, and the findings of the study commission could effect much needed change in the health care system.

Tranbarger is administrator for nursing at Moses H. Cone Memorial Hospital in Greensboro. He is currently enrolled in a doctoral program at North Carolina State University and was recently elected as a member on the ANA Cabinet on Nursing Services. Gene's history of service to NCNA and the nursing profession in general is lengthy and impressive, including a term as NCNA president during 1977-79. The study commission will certainly benefit from the talents Gene Tranbarger has to offer.

Speaker of the House Liston Ramsey has announced his recommendation of Dr. Cynthia M. Freund as a nurse member of the newly created North Carolina Medical

Tranbarger   Freund

Database Commission. This recommendation is subject to Governor Martin's approval.

The North Carolina Database Commission was created to establish an information base to be used to improve the appropriate and efficient usage of medical care services. The commission will develop a system for compiling a uniform set of data and disseminating aggregate data and will make recommendations to the General Assembly for changes needed in the North Carolina General Statutes to further the purposes of the commission.

Dr. Freund is chairman of the Department of Core Studies at UNC-Chapel Hill School of Nursing. Cynthia's vitae is replete with notable accomplishments and contributions to the nursing profession. Her experience at the Wharton School of Business related to health care and administration and her vast array of experiences in the health care field combine to create an insight that will greatly facilitate the work of this commission.

District Three honored Ms. Tennille at a recent meeting for her work in the General Assembly as a proponent of health care legislation.

Board actions *(from page 7)*

• Developed proposals for both short term and long term contingency plans related to NCNA's financial status. These proposals will be presented to the NCNA Board of Directors on August 16, 1985.

• Approved the purchase of a telephone system to be installed by Jarvis Corporation.

• Reviewed a proposal from the PAP Committee for presentation to the Board on August 16, 1985.

• Recommended to the NCNA Board of Directors a policy statement regarding NCNA involvement in legal action.

NORTH CAROLINA NURSES ASSOCIATION
P.O. Box 12025
Raleigh, North Carolina 27605

Vol. 47, No. 5   September-October 1985
Official publication of the North Carolina Nurses Association, 103 Enterprise St., Raleigh, N.C. Tel. (919) 821-4250. Published 6 times a year. Subscription price $12 per year, included with membership dues. Indexed in *Cumulative Index to Nursing and Allied Health Literature* and available in MICROFORM, University Microfilms International.

JUDITH B. SEAMON . . . . President
HETTIE L. GARLAND . . . . President-Elect
GALE B. JOHNSTON . . . . Vice-President
SALLY S. TODD . . . . Secretary
CAROL A. OSMAN . . . . Treasurer
                STAFF
FRANCES N. MILLER . . . . . Executive Director
HAZEL BROWNING . . . . . Assoc. Exec. Director
BETTY GODWIN . . . . Asst. Exec. Director
PATRICIA W. BRYAN . . . . . Administrative Asst.
DOROTHY BENNETT . . . . Administrative Asst.

HEALTH SCIENCES LIBRARY

OCT 10 1985

UNC Health Affairs Division
Health Sciences Library
Chapel Hill, NC 27514

Non-Profit Org.
U.S. POSTAGE
PAID
Raleigh, N.C.
Permit No. 87

● 1985 NCNA

ISSN 0039-9620

HEALTH SCIENCES

TAR HEEL NURSE

Vol. 47, No. 6   OFFICIAL PUBLICATION OF THE NORTH CAROLINA NURSES ASSOCIATION   November-December 1985

'85 convention stresses unity in nursing

By Hazel Browning

The Winston-Salem Hyatt Hotel and Benton Convention Center provided the setting for the 1985 NCNA Convention on October 23-26. The agenda was packed, the speakers were dynamic, the candidates were campaigning and the House of Delegates was intent on issues facing NCNA and the nursing profession—all elements of another very successful and exciting convention.

During the four days of programming, 430 North Carolina nurses and guests attended. Barbara Brown, a doctoral student in Health Services Administration at the Medical College of Virginia, Virginia Commonwealth University, kicked off the convention theme, "Professional Power: Pathway to Progress" at the keynote session on October 23. That theme was further developed by Willis Goldbeck, president of the Washington Business Group on Health, in a session titled, "Politics Parkway: Route to Influence", and by Cynthia Freund, chairman of the Department of Core Studies at UNC-Chapel Hill School of

Nursing, in a Friday session, "Unity Boulevard: Expressway to Power".

This was election year for the Association, and candidates for statewide offices were very visible. Buttons, posters and printed materials spilled over easels and convention registrants' upper torsos. Results of the statewide elections are included elsewhere in this edition of the *Tar Heel Nurse*.

The House of Delegates met for a total of seven hours over the latter two days of the convention. A major issue facing the delegates was a recommendation from the Board of Directors for a $35 increase in membership dues. An understanding of the current financial situation and the need for the increase in dues had been facilitated through communications with the Council of District Presidents, inclusion of financial information in the *Tar Heel Nurse*, finance-fact sheets and a Finance Forum held on October 23.

During House of Delegates debate, NCNA members clearly voiced their concern for fellow nurses currently facing economic difficulties. Another major concern reiterated in discussion was the need to maintain a financially stable professional association, ready and able to speak out on issues of concern to nurses, including the economic difficulties currently facing many nurses.

Final action of the House approved the recommended $35 dues increase effective with December renewals. In subsequent main motions adopted by the House, delegates directed structural units of the Association to follow up on concerns raised about the economic dilemma facing nurses (see main motions of the House of Delegates listed in this issue of the *Tar Heel Nurse*).

In preparation for the 1985-87 biennium, the House of Delegates approved the *(continued on page 2)*

(continued on page 2)

Orientation set for NCNA leaders

The N.C. State Faculty Club—in the heart of Wolfpack territory—will be the scene for NCNA's 1986 Leadership Orientation on January 9, 10:00 a.m.-4:00 p.m. Registration starts at 9:15 a.m.

NCNA "Leaders of the Pack" will have a vigorous warm-up for the challenges of the 1985-87 biennium. All commission and committee members and officers of divisions, forums, sections, and conference groups are expected to attend. District leaders and interested members also will be welcome.

Persons attending will be expected to pay for their own lunch at $7.70. NCNA will absorb costs of meeting materials. Those who have not returned a response form and who plan to attend should notify NCNA immediately.

Outgoing President Judy Seamon was the "victim" of a surprise roast at the 1985 Convention Awards Banquet. Shown here are two of the interesting mementos she received: a T-shirt emblazoned with "NO! I am not the den mother!" and the world's largest briefcase.

Convention stresses unity in nursing — from page 1

NCNA goals, priorities and legislative platform to give direction to future activities of the association. Five resolutions and several proposed bylaw changes were approved by the delegates. The resolutions are included in this issue. Bylaw revisions were adopted to bring NCNA structure into compliance with ANA accreditation standards as a result of NCNA's approval as an ANA accredited continuing education approver and provider.

Several special events planned during convention were well received by attendees. The NCNA Peer Assistance Program (PAP) Committee hosted a "Sharing Time" on Wednesday afternoon where the committee spent time with interested members reviewing the recently approved PAP program. Those who attended this session also had an opportunity to view a slide show produced by the Pennsylvania Nurses Association, "The First Step".

A 63-booth trade show was a focal point on Thursday. Exhibits representing hospitals, state agencies and private enterprise were open throughout most of the day.

The Committee on Human Rights hosted a continental breakfast on Thursday morning. Ralph Debois Mitchell, a motivational speaker lived up to his billing and motivated a lot of folks over coffee and croissants!

Convention registrants had an opportunity in forums to provide input to the Ad Hoc Committee on Guidelines for RN Work Assignments and the NCNA Ad Hoc Committee on Structure. These two committees will continue their work into the next biennium.

Jo Franklin, Chairman of Nurse-PAC reported that Friday evening's Celebrity Auction added almost $3,000 to the Nurse-PAC coffers. Not only was that event profitable, it was also FUN! Al Braye, a professional auctioneer, really knew how to open pocketbooks and pull out pens and checkbooks. Some especially coveted items included an autographed M.A.S.H. script and Executive Director Frances Miller's walking cane.

Friday evening's award banquet was a highlight. NCNA recognized excellence in

Board of Directors Awards: Wanda Boyette, left, receives the award from Gale Johnston; Gale Johnston, center photo, receives the award from Sally Todd; Judy Seamon, photo at right, receives the award from Hettie Garland.

a variety of nursing practice arenas and acknowledged those who have made outstanding strides in membership promotion activities.

Maida Dundon, Clemmons, received the 1985 NCNA-March of Dimes Nurse of the Year Award for contributions to maternal/child nursing practice. She is a maternal and child health nursing consultant with the North Carolina Division of Health Services.

Laura Coker, Winston-Salem, received the Medical-Surgical Nurse of the Year Award. She is a nurse specialist and coordinator of clinical trials in the Department of Neurology at Bowman Gray School of Medicine in Winston-Salem.

Eleanor McConnell, Hillsborough, was recipient of the NCNA Gerontological Nurse of the Year Award. Ms. McConnell is a clinical instructor in the School of Nursing at UNC-Chapel Hill.

Cheryl Thornburg, Lincolnton, also was honored as winner in the annual NCNA-AJN Company Writing Competition. The winning paper was a report on thoracic outlet syndrome.

Awards were made to district associations that excelled in membership promotion. District Twenty-One received the award for greatest percentage increase and District Eleven had the largest numerical increase. Jo Rountree, Sunbury, received the top award for individual membership recruitment activities.

The NCNA Board of Directors Award for Outstanding Service was presented to Gale Johnston and to Wanda Boyette. Both are retiring members of the NCNA Board of Directors. Gale served as vice-president of NCNA during the 1983-85 biennium and, as such, chaired the Committee on Membership, which topped its goal of 3,000 members prior to the 1985 convention—the highest membership level in more than 10 years. Gale's dynamic and enthusiastic abilities were cited as a primary reason for this accomplishment.

Wanda Boyette has served on the NCNA Board of Directors for the past eight years. She has served NCNA in numerous ways and was cited as consistently providing exceptional wisdom and patience in supporting the goals of the nursing profession and NCNA.

A special tribute was made to two long-time NCNA members who have recently retired. Patti Lewis and Audrey Booth were presented a "professional package" of office supplies embossed with NCNA logos to remind them that retiring from work should not mean retiring from NCNA. They have both provided invaluable service and leadership to NCNA through many years.

The Board of Directors also presented three Certificates of Commendation at the 1985 Awards Banquet. Betty Trought's numerous activities as advocate for nursing and NCNA were cited. Under Betty's leadership, an ad hoc committee is engaged in a difficult task—drafting guidelines useful to both nurse managers and staff nurses in giving, accepting or rejecting work assignments.

Throughout her nursing career in North Carolina, Betty Erlandson has been a verbal and visible advocate for membership in the professional organization. Betty received the Certificate of Commendation for her role in achieving significant membership gains.

Michael Crowell served as attorney-lobbyist for NCNA during the past year. Through many trying times, he rendered special service to NCNA and made contributions with empathy and respect for nursing. For his valuable service, Michael was awarded the Certificate of Commendation.

With all of these warm fuzzies floating around, Judy Seamon was not the least bit surprised when Hettie Garland stood up and began to make some very flattering remarks about Judy's leadership ability, her professional demeanor, etc. However, Hettie's tribute quickly deteriorated into a

Recognition: Audrey Booth, left, and Patti Lewis, right ...

Award winners: (photos left to right) Jane Ray presents the Medical-Surgical Nurse of the Year Award to Laura Coker; Sharon Sells presents the Gerontological Nurse of the Year Award to Ellie McConnell; Jack McGee presents the NCNA-March of Dimes Maternal-Child Nurse of the Year Award to Maida Dundon; Hettie Garland presents the NCNA-AJN Company Writing Award to Cheryl Thornburg.

satire when she commended Judy's unique organizational skills. For those of you who don't know, Judy is NOT the most organized person in the world, a fact she is frequently teased about. That was just the beginning of a surprise roast of President Judy Seamon. A well-coordinated team of colleagues and family then participated in "Top Secret Mission: Operation Turkey Roast."

Laughter filled the ballroom as family, friends and colleagues shared funny stories about our noble leader. And the best part of it all was that Judy Seamon was laughing as hard as anyone in the room. Her ability to laugh at herself is yet another trait to admire! The roast ended on a grand note as Hettie Garland presented Judy with the NCNA Board of Directors Award for Outstanding Service. Her talent, time, energy and financial resources have been given freely and willingly during her tenure as the chief elected officer of NCNA. "Sailing with Seamon" was a wonderful voyage.

At approximately 11:45 a.m., on Saturday, October 26, Hettie Garland received the NCNA gavel and performed her first official function as NCNA president by declaring the 1985 House of Delegates adjourned. Nurses from across the state headed home with new visions of "Professional Power: Pathways to Progress", running through their heads and fatigue running through their bodies. Rest up, nurses. The 1986 NCNA Convention is October 22-25, at the North Raleigh Hilton. See you there!

Deceptive Mail

In various parts of the country nurses have received a very deceptive piece of mail. It announces that the American *Nursing* Association members "in your area voted in favor of the nurses benefit and retirement program."

Be advised that this mail is **not** from ANA. It promises that a representative will contact you. The object, of course, is to sell you insurance. This organization (if there really is such a thing) is in no way connected with ANA.

MEMBERSHIP REWARD AND RECOGNITION AWARDS: Sue Herring, President of District 21 receives award for greatest percentage increase; Kay Helfrich and Diane Horton, on behalf of District Eleven, receive award for greatest numerical increase; Jo Rountree of Sunbury was recipient of the individual membership award.

American Nurses' Association
1986 Convention / June 13-19 / Anaheim, California

NLN Board supports ANA entry position

The National League for Nursing Board of Directors has announced the following action taken at its meeting on October 31,-November 1:

"NLN supports two levels of nursing practice, professional and associate. Further, NLN supports (its) councils working closely with the American Nurses' Association cabinets to help define the scope and practice of nurses within these levels."

NLNs stated its action is in response to the need to prepare nurses "to enter a dramatically changing health care system that will demand greater independence and accountability of nursing, as well as the need to resolve public confusion over the current multiplicity of entry levels into nursing practice ..."

"This represents significant progress, a joining together of two major national nursing organizations to resolve the greatest area of confusion and dissension in nursing over the past two decades."

The American Association of Nurse Anesthetists also have announced that its Board in September voted unanimously to support the ANA resolution on titling.

Message from the President
Hettie L. Garland

Our 1985 convention is now part of the recent past, but I believe that the energy and enthusiasm generated in Winston-Salem will last a long time. I again salute the Convention Program Committee for a superb convention. The comments I heard from the participants probably summarize how we all feel—that convention is a time to greet friends and colleagues, to reduce the sense of isolation (and sometimes stagnation!) that we may feel on a day-to-day basis, and to participate in identifying issues and concerns and developing positive solutions. The forums presented opportunities for significant discussions, and the House of Delegates dealt with some critical issues with professionalism and vision for the future.

The dues increase highlighted a significant area of concern for our colleagues who are underemployed or have lost their positions in health agencies. This symbolizes, in part, the rapid changes occurring in health care delivery and the impact of these changes on our profession. They also symbolize the need for a strong professional association to respond to these changes.

I also salute those members who worked very hard to recruit new members, allowing us to exceed our 3,000 member goal.

Since the most effective recruitment method is one-to-one contact, these nurses have invested a lot of time and enthusiasm in promoting NCNA. Congratulations!

The 1985-87 Board of Directors met on November 14-15 for the board orientation and first business meeting of the biennium. The board developed plans for implementing the goals, priorities, resolutions, and main motions passed by the House of Delegates. The board also identified members to serve on commissions and committees. Over 100 consent-to-serve forms had been received through the *Tar Heel Nurse* or turned in at convention! The appointments should be confirmed within the next few weeks. We feel that we are off to an excellent start in continuing our Pathway to Progress!

January 9, 1986, is NCNA Orientation Day for commission and committee members—so those of you who are involved, please mark this date on your calendar. This is an important day to begin work for the next two years. We also promise an exciting day for all.

I look forward to working with you during the next two years. Together we should be able to accomplish anything!

ACTIONS OF THE BOARD

● Approved preparation of financial data for presentation to the membership at the 1985 convention.
● Approved the Peer Assistance Program.
● Approved an amendment to personnel policies regarding compensatory time.
● Approved a revised fee structure for review of continuing education offerings.
● Deferred preparing a brochure on minimum employment standards for registered nurses and distributing it to employers pending outcome of the dues increase proposal.
● Voted that NCNA direct a complaint to appropriate agencies about EMS regulations for mobile intensive care nurses and the manner in which new regulations were put into effect.
● Appointed Mary Lou Moore as NCNA representative on the Coalition on Adolescent Pregnancies.
● Approved seeking consent from several nurses to allow their names to be submitted to the ANA Nominating Committee for the 1986 ANA ballot.
● Selected individuals to receive 1985 Board of Directors awards and citations.
● Approved establishing a Community Health Nurse of the Year award beginning in 1986.
● Voted to become self-insured for glass damage on headquarters building as a cost containment measure.
● Voted to supplement contributions for printing of minimum employment standards in brochure form.
● Endorsed plans from the Membership Committee for a recruitment project in 1986.
● Directed that the Ad Hoc Committee on Nurse Managed Gerontological Health Facility explore funding from a foundation.
● Endorsed reappointment of Frances Waddle of Oklahoma to the Board of Trustees of the Commission on Graduates of Foreign Nursing Schools.

Nursing board gives election results

Evelyn Schaffer, Salisbury, nursing director at Rowan County Health Department, and Clara B. Williams, Goldsboro, faculty member in the nursing program at Wayne Community College, were elected to the North Carolina Board of Nursing in elections held in the fall.

Their terms are for three years. Both are NCNA members.

LPNs in the state elected Christine G. Jones and Nancy V. Cook to the Board.

MEMBERSHIP THERMOMETER

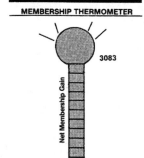

3083

Net Membership Gain

2740

We made it by convention time! Membership as of November 1, 1985, was 3,083. We're on a roll—let's keep going!

Political action book

NCNA has available for sale 10 copies of *Political Action Handbook for Nurses*, at $20 each.

on Districts

by Betty Godwin

The Council of District Presidents has elected new officers: (left to right) Eris Russell, vice-chairman, Bette Ferree, Board of Directors representative; Gwen Waddell, chairman; Kay Jackson, secretary; Estelle Fulp, Board of Directors representative.

The Council of District Presidents met on October 23, 1985 just prior to the beginning of the 1985 convention. The district biennial reports were used to determine the agenda. Council members shared strategies that were found to be effective solutions to common problems.

Topping the list of agenda items was discussion of membership enhancement. Kay Jackson, president of District Three, shared a membership marketing plan developed by her district. The plan began with the establishment of the membership committee and included strategies to enhance member recruitment, retention, and involvement. Annie Hayes, president of District Sixteen, shared the success of developing a yearly theme for program top-

ics to increase participation. This district's theme is volunteerism. Other districts, such as District One, have also used this approach. District One's theme is "Options for Growth: Personal and Professional Development."

The Council voted to endorse a statewide public education effort, "Seatbelts for Safety." Each district has been sent information from the N. C. Seatbelts for Safety group to use in public education activities. Each district is designing its own educational activities. This statewide effort, targeted for December, is providing a much needed public service and yielding public visibilty for nursing as a health promotion oriented profession.

Rates increase for liability insurance

Maginnis and Associates, the insurance company providing professional liability insurance endorsed by NCNA, has announced increases in premiums for this coverage effective January 1, 1986.

The premium increase amounts to about 40%.

Limits	Old	New
$2,000,000/$600,000/$200,000	$25	$35
$1,000,000/$1,000,000/$1,000,000	$38	$53
$1,000,000/$3,000,000/$1,000,000	$43	$58

The Maginnis announcement stated that the increase has "very little to do with actual increases in losses." Factors causing the premium increase includes higher administrative costs and a 300% increase in reinsurance costs.

ABOUT PEOPLE

Hilda G. Newton, nursing director, Gaston County Health Department, was honored recently by the Department for receiving a 1985 award from the N. C. Public Health Association ... **Mary Alice Withers,** vice-president for nursing at Valdese Hospital, is Burke County's 1985 "Woman of the Year." She is a town alderman in Drexel. At the award banquet, **Carol Koontz,** NCNA board member and member of the Valdese nursing staff, shared in the presentation ceremonies. The award is an annual presentation of the Morganton Business and Professional Women's Club ... **Dr. Barbara Germino,** Chapel Hill, spoke on the impact of cancer on families at the Fourth National Conference on Community Cancer Care, Indianapolis, IN. She also participated as a discussant in the recent National Council of Family Relations meeting in Dallas, Texas. Dr. Germino, **Dr. Mary Champagne** and **Beverly Havens,** NCNA members, were among UNC-CH faculty members recently receiving grant awards from the American Nurses' Foundation ... **Dr. Cindy Freund,** Chapel Hill, last month presented her research on "Chief Nursing Officer and Chief Executive Officer Decision-Making Styles" at the SREB research conference in Orlando, FL ... At the November meeting of the Wake County Mental Health Association, **Carolyn Billings** was honored with presentation of a plaque naming her 1985 Volunteer of the Year. The Administrative Committee which she chairs was recognized as the most productive committee of the year. Billings is a member of the NCNA Board of Directors ... **Gail Hardy Russ** has been appointed to a Legislative Research Commission Study Committee on Life Care Arrangements ... **Dr. Patricia A. Chamings** has assumed duties as dean of the School of Nursing at UNC-Greensboro. She formerly was assistant dean of the baccalaureate program at the Nell Hodson Woodruff School of Nursing Emory University ... The UNC-G School of Nursing was scheduled to hold a retirement reception on December 13 for **Betty R. Erlandson** ... The current issue of the Swedish publication *Landstrings-Varlden* features the text of a lecture given at Uppsala University by **Dr. Laurel Archer Copp,** dean of UNC-CH School of Nursing. Dr. Copp also lectured at the University of Lund while in Sweden during the summer ... Another UNC-CH faculty member, **Dr. Anne Hopkins Fishel,** presented a paper, "The Impact on Divorce on Women: Counseling Strategies," in October in Atlanta at the Seventh Southeastern Regional Conference for Clinical Specialists in Psychiatric-Mental Health Nursing ... Two NCNA members recently were honored by the UNC-CH School of Nursing Alumni Association—**Betty Baines Compton** was *(continued on page 7)*

Actions of 1985 House of Delegates

NCNA GOALS FOR THE 1985-87 BIENNIUM:

1. Sustain and strengthen NCNA's role as spokesman for nursing in all areas, including the legislative arena, that affect health care, and provide guidance in the framing of the legal base for the practice of nursing.
2. Increase the number of nurses who participate in the shaping of the nursing profession.
3. Promote and protect high standards of nursing practice and education.
4. Advance the professional status of nursing in the workplace and the economic position of nurses commensurate with professional responsibility.
5. Strengthen district/state communications and relationships to build a stronger organization of better informed members.
6. Participate actively in shaping health policy and setting trends that improve the standards and availability of health care services for all people.

PRIORITIES:

1. Increase membership by recruitment and retention.
2. Stabilize the financial base of NCNA.
3. Increase services to facilitate leadership development and district growth.
4. Bring together concerned groups of both nurses and non-nurses to develop an action plan for implementing two levels of nursing practice in North Carolina.
5. Increase the visibility of NCNA as a political force.
6. Protect all arenas of nursing practice, including specialty practice, through a strong legislative program, monitoring of regulatory agencies and support of appropriate legal action in litigation.
7. Support the advancement of the professional and economic status of nurses commensurate with their professional responsibility.
8. Evaluate nursing's current and potential role and contribution to safe and effective health care for special populations, especially the elderly.
9. Increase the visibility of NCNA as an ANA accredited approver and provider of C.E.

1986-87 LEGISLATIVE PLATFORM:

The North-Carolina Nurses Association endorses legislation and regulatory authority to:

- Protect the public through maintenance of a strong Nursing Practice Act and through authority for the Board of Nursing to regulate the practice of nursing and all of its specialties and to set standards for nursing education programs.
- Protect the rights of patients and their families to safe, affordable, and accessible health care.
- Allow consumers direct access to the qualified health care provider of their choice by removing barriers restricting consumer choice.
- Provide for adequate health care to populations with recognized, special needs, such as the growing number of older citizens.
- Protect the right of citizens to a safe, healthy environment.
- Improve the work environment, the economic base, and the professional and legal status of nurses.
- Strengthen opportunities for individuals to achieve the educational preparation essential for competent nursing practice.
- Provide expertise on health care issues by inclusion of qualified registered nurses on advisory and policy-making bodies.

RESOLUTIONS ADOPTED:

1. SMOKING

WHEREAS, The 1984 ANA House of Delegates adopted a resolution calling on ANA to recognize the intensity of the problem of smoking among nurses and the need for nurses to be actively involved in smoking cessation; and

WHEREAS, research has shown that the prevalence of smoking is higher among nurses than among women in general, and that proportionally fewer nurses than physicians, dentists, and pharmacists have stopped smoking; and

WHEREAS, nurses as the largest group of health care providers, serve as role models in health maintenance and are in a position to encourage and support smoking cessation as a service to themselves, their clients and the public; and

WHEREAS, tobacco smoking is one avoidable cause of disease and premature death in our society and one of the most important public health issues of our time; and

WHEREAS, there is evidence of increased prevalence of smoking and tobacco-related diseases such as lung cancer in women; therefore, be it

RESOLVED, that NCNA promote increased awareness among nurses and nursing students of smoking as a health threat and the difficulties of reducing the tobacco habit, and be it further

RESOLVED, that NCNA encourage nurses and nursing students to stop smoking; and be it further

RESOLVED, that NCNA promote non-smoking policies at NCNA meetings and conventions; and be it further

RESOLVED, that NCNA encourage and assist nurses to appropriately counsel patients as to the risks of smoking, and assist or refer those who desire to stop smoking; and be it further

RESOLVED, that NCNA urge other nursing organizations to join this position of discouraging smoking; and be it further

RESOLVED, that NCNA send copies of this resolution to health professions, organizations and groups concerned with smoking or the public health.

2. GRADUATE STUDY IN NURSING

WHEREAS, the promotion and protection of high standards of nursing practice and education is one of the six priorities established by the NCNA Board of Directors for this biennium; and

WHEREAS, nursing practice in the 1980's is more complex and demanding than at any previous time in the history of nursing; and

WHEREAS, the degree of specialization in nursing education and practice is developing at an unparalleled pace; and

WHEREAS, graduate study in nursing in North Carolina is more readily available with a good selection of areas of concentration—clinical specialties, education, administration; and

WHEREAS, graduate study in nursing at the master's level is only attained in schools of nursing; therefore, be it

RESOLVED, that NCNA inform the public as well as the profession that preparation for advanced nursing practice is gained through graduate study in nursing; and be it further

RESOLVED, that NCNA advise members and other qualified, interested candidates to pursue graduate study in nursing programs offered by NLN approved schools of nursing which will prepare them for positions in advanced nursing practice and education.

3. ELIMINATING DUPLICATION OF SERVICES

WHEREAS, the federation model has been in effect for the past three (3) years; and

WHEREAS, this model returns much of the provision of membership services to the state association; and

WHEREAS, there is now a duplication of member services by the national and state associations; and

WHEREAS, this duplication is a poor utilization of our financial resources; and

WHEREAS, forty-eight (48) percent of each dues dollar is being retained at the national level; and

WHEREAS, NCNA is operating with a financial deficit which necessitates a dues increase; therefore, be it

RESOLVED, that the Board of Directors direct the Finance Committee to identify areas of duplication and delineation of services with associated costs; and be it further

RESOLVED, that the Finance Committee report to the NCNA Board of Directors by the 1986 NCNA convention; and be it further

RESOLVED, Board of Directors report to NCNA House of Delegates at its next meeting; and be it further

RESOLVED, that the information regarding duplication of services with the corresponding cost be disseminated to constituent associations prior to the next ANA convention.

(Resolution #4, "Nomination of ANA Delegates," did not pass.)

5. TERMS OF ANA DELEGATES

WHEREAS the North Carolina Nurses Association bylaws state that all members are eligible to serve as delegates to the ANA House of Delegates; and

WHEREAS, the representation from the state constituencies is determined by the ANA bylaws; and

WHEREAS, NCNA needs to support both a balance of leadership continuity and development of new leaders to be effectively represented at the ANA House of Delegates; therefore, be it

RESOLVED, that the Bylaws Committee be directed to develop a bylaws amendment limiting ANA delegates to *two* consecutive terms, with the exception of the president serving as delegate-at-large by virtue of that office; and be it further

RESOLVED, that this amendment be presented to the 1986 NCNA House of Delegates.

6. PREPARATION AND REIMBURSEMENT OF ANA DELEGATE ALTERNATES

WHEREAS, alternates in attendance at the ANA House of Delegates may be called upon at the site to be seated as a delegate; and

WHEREAS, ANA alternates are expected to demonstrate the same characteristics, behaviors, level of commitment, and attendance as a delegate attending the House; and

WHEREAS, ANA alternates are expected to pay audit and registration fees at the ANA House of Delegates; therefore, be it

RESOLVED, that one alternate receiving the highest number of votes and attending the ANA convention receive the same materials, preparation, and reimbursement as the elected delegates.

Motions Passed:

● Requested Board of Directors to direct the Commission on Member Services to look into the economic dilemma facing nurses and to develop strategies to respond to their needs, and report back to the 1986 House of Delegates.

● Voted that the Board of Directors and Finance Committee examine the feasibility of some alteration in NCNA dues structure, such as but not limited to a sliding scale and a category for financial difficulty for membership, and report recommendations to the membership in the *Tar Heel Nurse* before the House of Delegates meets in October 1986 and report to the House of Delegates at the 1986 convention.

● Directed that the Board of Directors and Finance Committee promulgate a two-year financial plan which is updated and presented to the House of Delegates annually.

● Increased annual dues to $150.

Membership Recruitment Contest to Begin

Grab your membership applications—the Membership Committee has a new recruitment contest for you! It will begin January 1, 1986, and end October 1, 1986. Prizes will be given to the top three participants who each recruit more than **25** new members or 25 full member equivalent.

Prizes include:

First prize—Airfare for two to **New York City** on Eastern Airlines

Second prize—A **free** year of NCNA membership (a $150 value)

Third prize—A $50 gift certificate.

Please read the rules carefully. New member applications that do not meet the contest criteria will not be counted.

1. Contest participants must have their names clearly written on the new member's application. Applications received without a recruiter's name cannot be counted. Only **individual** recruiters are eligible.
2. New member applications must be mailed to NCNA, P.O. Box 12025, Raleigh, N.C. 27605. It is the recruiter's responsibility to assure that the application is *not* mailed to ANA before it is processed by NCNA.
3. A **new** member is defined as one who has not been a NCNA member within the last six months or who has not

transferred membership from another state.
4. To be included in the contest, new member applications must be received at NCNA between January 1, 1986 and October 1.
5. New member recruit applications are not transferable from one recruiter to another.
6. Winners will be announced at the 1986 NCNA convention.

About People — from page 5

named Alumnus of the Year and **Dr. Joan M. Ganong** received honorary membership ... **Ruth Edwards**, member of District Thirteen, has been appointed by Governor Jim Martin to the Mental Health and Mental Retardation Commission ... **Sandra Wilkes**, also a District Thirteen member, has been appointed by the Division of Mental Health/Mental Retardation/Substance Abuse Services to a committee to study issues related to the involuntary client's right to consent or to refuse specific treatment measures ... **Ruth E. Long**, member of District Eleven, has been appointed by Durham County Commissioners to the Durham County Mental Health Board.

NCNA OFFICERS
1985-87

Board of Directors

President
Hettie L. Garland, 22 Woodbury Road, Asheville 28804

President-Elect
Jo Franklin, Route 8, Box 376-B, Salisbury 28144

Vice-President
Davy F. Crockett, 453 Valleymeade Drive, Kernersville 27284

Secretary
Joyce H. Monk, 103 Pinecrest Drive, Farmville 27828

Treasurer
Sheila P. Englebardt, 818 Walker Avenue, Greensboro 27403

Directors
Carol E. Koontz, Route 11, Box 189, Morganton 28655 (term expires 10/87)
Connie B. Wolfe, P. O. Box 2724, Shallotte 28459 (term expires 10/87)
Joan C. Bounds, 1800 Stage Road, Durham 27703 (term expires 10/89)
Sandra W. Randleman, 965 Dawnlea Drive, Lewisville 27023 (term expires 10/89)
Linda B. Wright, Chairman, Commission on Education
103 Brown Avenue Morganton 28655
Rachel H. Stevens, Chairman, Commission on Health Affairs
219 Churton Street, Hillsborough 27278
Carolyn V. Billings, Chairman, Commission on Member Services
3410 Hillsborough Street, Raleigh 27604
Mary Lou Moore, Chairman, Commission on Practice
701 Austin Lane, Winston-Salem 27106

Representing Council of District Presidents:
Estelle Fulp, 2836 Wycliff Road, Raleigh 27607
Bette Ferree, 3708 North Shore Drive, High Point 27260

ANA Delegates

Hettie L. Garland, 22 Woodbury Road, Asheville 28804
Judith B. Seamon, P.O. Box 3486, Morehead City 28557
Roberta Leigh Andrews, P.O. Box 1206, Manteo 27954
Barbara Jo McGrath, 3685 Kale Drive, Lumberton 28358
Russell E. Tranbarger, 4805 W. Friendly Ave., Greensboro 27410
Sheila P. Englebardt, 818 Walker Avenue, Greensboro 27402
Sarah P. Brown, 7316 Lake Tree Drive, Raleigh 27609
Davy F Crockett, 453 Valleymeade Drive, Kernersville 27284
Jo A. Franklin, Route 8, Box 376-B, Salisbury 28144
Vida K. Jackson, 514 Lester Lane, Winston-Salem 27103

Alternates

Margaret Bye, Wake AHEC, 3000 New Bern Ave., Raleigh 27610
Edward M. Stroupe, 518 N. Mendenhall St., Greensboro 27401
Sandra Randleman, 965 Dawnlea Dr., Lewisville 27023
Connie B. Wolfe, P.O. Box 2724, Shallotte 28459
Estelle M. Fulp, 2836 Wycliff Rd., Raleigh 27607
Betty B. Garrison, 2825 Eastburn Rd., Charlotte 28210
Therese G. Lawler, 109 Cheshire Dr., Greenville 27834
Johnea Kelley, 1708 Roxboro Rd., Durham 27701
Rebecca Pitts, 217 Country Club Dr., Asheville 28804
Rebecca W. Carnes, 145 Windsor Circle, Chapel Hill 27514

Nominating Committee

Gwendolyn Waddell, 2110 N. Lake Shore Dr., Chapel Hill 27514, Chairman
Wanda Boyette, Assistant Administrator, c/o Sampson County Memorial Hospital, Clinton 28328
Debbie Craver, Route 8, Box 52, Lexington 27292
Rachel Funderburk, Rt. 10, Box 386, Morganton 28655
Eris Russell, P.O. Box 98, Black Mountain 28711

Collective Bargaining Representative

John J. Chetney, Jr., 2836 Chapel Hill Rd., (24-H), Durham 27707

Officers of Structural Units

DIVISIONS

Community Health

Chairman—Shirley Mozingo, Route 3, Selma 27576
Vice-Chairman—Joanne Corson, 1109 Gunnison Place, Raleigh 27609
Secretary—Margaret Brake, 517 S. E. Maynard Rd., Cary 27511
Nominating Committee—
Lou Brewer, Chairman,1316 Rainwood Ln., Raleigh 27609
Hilda Newton, 1115 Woodvale Ave., Gastonia 28054
Diane Crouse, P.O. Box 439, Lexington 27292
CE Approver Unit Representative—Annie Hayes, Rt. 5, Box 396, Whiteville 28472

Gerontological

Chairman—Sharon Sells, P.O. Box 25, Stanfield 28163
Vice-Chairman—Betty Mauney, 5844 Kinghurst Dr., Charlotte 28212
Secretary—Linda Howard, 1407 Brittle Creek Dr., Matthews 28105
Nominating Committee—
Mary McIntyre, Chairman, 401 Church St., Nashville 27856
Voneva Nunn, 1531 Carmel Rd., Charlotte 28226
Marilyn Wood, 416 Skeet Club Rd., High Point 27260
CE Approver Unit Representative—Marge Bye, Wake AHEC, 3000 New Bern Ave., Raleigh 27610

Maternal-Child Health

Chairman—Judy Barnes, 2709 Hodges Rd., Kinston 28501
Vice-Chairman—Cynthia Luke, 317 Nottingham Ln., Wilmington 28403
Secretary—Elaine Hunkins, 707 Walker Ave., Greensboro 27403

Nominating Committee—
Janice Leggett, Chairman, P.O. Box 2593, Greenville 27836
Martha Eakes, 5809 Cardinal Way, Greensboro 27410
Maida Dundon, 6277 Styers Ferry Rd., Clemmons 27012
CE Approver Unit Representative—Vickie Healey, 108 Stoneridge Dr., Chapel Hill 27514

Medical-Surgical Division

Chairman—Jane Ray, 2611-D Suffolk Ave., High Point 27260
Vice-Chairman—Deborah Ann Reed, 1706 Burnely Dr., Cary 27511
Secretary—Shirley Jenkins, Rt. 3, Box 236-1, Apex 27502
Nominating Committee—
Theresa Tranbarger, Chairman, 4805 W. Friendly Ave., Greensboro 27410
James Henry Brown, 41 Northwood Dr., Wilmington 28405
Vercie Hardee, 4612 Greenbrier Rd., Raleigh 27603
CE Approver Unit Representative—Ginger Sandlin, 6 Carrington Pl., Chapel Hill 27514

Psychiatric-Mental Health Division

Chairman—Rosemary Strickland, 1508 Imperial Dr., Durham 27712
Vice-Chairman—Mable Carlyle, 807 Holly Ave., Black Mountain 28711
Secretary—Nancy Quinn, 631 Westbrook Dr., Burlington 27215
Nominating Committee—
Dorothy Honeycutt, Chairman, 5937 Carmel Ln., Raleigh 27609
Sandra Wilkes, 12700 Raven Ridge Rd., Raleigh 27614
Jeannie Yount, 202 W. 16th St., Washington 27889
CE Approver Unit Representative—Patricia Hayes P.O. Box 72, Madison 27025

CONFERENCE GROUPS

Specialists in Psychiatric-Mental Health

Chairman—Libba Wells, Rt. 3, Box 440, Hillsborough 27278
Vice-Chairman—Marilyn Earle, 2401 Trusty Trail, Raleigh 27609
Secretary—Margaret Raynor, Rt. 2, Box 20, Garner 27529
Nominating Committee—
  Jo Ann Adams, Chairman, 1001 Manchester Dr., Cary 27511
  Carolyn Billings, 3410 Hillsborough St., Raleigh 27607
  Elizabeth Munsat, 1505 Lamont Ct., Chapel Hill 27514

Primary Care Nurse Practitioners

Chairman—Joyce Nixon, 539 Jasin Dr., Gastonia 28052
Vice-Chairman—Linda Tull, 33 Wildwood Ave., Weaverville 28787
Secretary—Judy Zentner, 341 4th Ave., N.E., Hickory 28601
Nominating Committee—
  Cynthia Van Deusen, Chairman, One Woodlawn, Asheville 28801
  Amanda Greene, P.O. Box 574, Carrboro 27510
  Jo Ann Adams, 1001 Manchester Dr., Cary 27511

SECTIONS

School Nurse Section

Chairman—Christine Fisher, 1404 Edgebrook Dr., Garner 27529
Vice-Chairman—Gayle Brown, Rt. 1, Box 19-C, Hamptonville 27020
Secretary—Carol Cox, 408 Lancelot Dr., Greenville 27834
Nominating Committee—
  Eddie Grubbs, Chairman, 4819 Southwin Dr., Winston-Salem 27104
  Elizabeth Best, 150 Charlestowne Cir., Winston-Salem 27103
  Maida Dundon, 6277 Styers Ferry Rd., Clemmons 27012

Nursing Practice Administrators

Chairman—Kathryn E. Madry, 5515 West Market St., Apt. 313, Greensboro 27409
Vice-Chairman—Margaret Whittington, 4701 Spring Forest Rd., Raleigh 27604
Secretary—Johanna Winchester, 1103 Forest Hill Dr., Greensboro 27410
Nominating Committee
  Avis L. Duncan, Chairman, 1401 Paxton Ct., Greensboro 27405
  Brenda Bessard, 702 St. George Rd., Raleigh 27610
  Linda Ellington, Box 46, Polks Landing, Chapel Hill 27514

FORUMS

Baccalaureate and Higher Degree Forum

Chairman—Emilie Henning, 76 Quail Ridge Rd., Greenville 27834
Vice-Chairman—Lou Everett, 103 Ravenwood Dr., Greenville 27834
Secretary—Sherry Laurent, 7311 Rudwick Ln., Charlotte 28226
Nominating Committee
  Arlene Roberts, Chairman, 81 Fisher Creek Rd., Sylva 28779
  Ruth Mauldin, 1719 Beverly Dr., Charlotte 28207
  Bettie Gordon, 5021 Malibu Dr., Charlotte 28215

Associate Degree Forum

Chairman—Nancy Sumner, Rt. 4, Box 264-BB, Rockingham 28379
Vice-Chairman—Linda Phillips, 815-B Charles Rd., Shelby 28250
Secretary—Donnie Greene, 5308 Maple Ridge Rd., Raleigh 27609
Nominating Committee—
  Sue Morgan, Chairman, Box 995, Waynesville 28786
  Rhonda Ferrell, 509 E. College St., Warsaw 28398
  Wilma Harris, P.O. Box 2327, Elizabeth City 27909

Diploma Degree Forum

Chairman—Loletta Faulkenberry, 3414 Longview Dr., Burlington 27215
Vice-Chairman—Gail Pruett, 3201 Wake Forest Hwy., Durham 27703
Secretary—David Williams, 11 Willow Bridge Dr., #64, Durham 27707
Nominating Committee—
  Rosalind McDonald, Chairman, 404 E. Blount St., Kinston 28501
  Estelle O'Brien, 5475 Yanceyville Rd., Browns Summit 27214
  Donna White, 1330 W. Main St., Clayton 27520

Continuing Education Forum

Chairman—Margaret Bye, Wake AHEC, 3000 New Bern Ave., Raleigh 27610
Vice-Chairman—Carolyn Henderson, 3311 Shannon Rd., Apt. 26C, Durham 27707
Secretary—Ginny Tate, Rt. 1, Box 233, Climax 27233
Nominating Committee—
  Carol Moore, Chairman, 111 Ann St., Wilmington 28401
  Cynthia Luke, 317 Nottingham Ln., Wilmington 28403
  Debbie Moore, 3954 Haithcock Rd., Raleigh 27604

COUNCIL OF DISTRICT PRESIDENTS

Chairman—Gwen Waddell, 2110 Lake Shore Dr., Chapel Hill 27514
Vice-Chairman—Eris Russell, P.O. Box 98, Black Mountain 28711
Secretary—Kay Jackson, 514 Lester Ln., Winston-Salem 27103
Board of Directors Representatives
  Bette Ferree, 3708 North Shore Dr., High Point 27260
  Estelle Fulp, 2836 Wycliff Rd., Raleigh 27607

Appeals court backs nurse anesthetists

On October 2, 1985, the U.S. Court of Appeals for the Ninth Circuit ruled in the case of *Bhan v. NME Hospitals, Inc.*, that nurse anesthetists have standing to sue under federal antitrust law for anticompetitive practices excluding them from the market for anesthesia services.

In March 1983, Manteca Hospital in Manteca, California, terminated its contract under which nurse anesthetists had provided anesthesia services to the hospital, allowing only M.D. anesthesiologists to perform this function. A nurse anesthetist affected by the termination brought suit in 1983, claiming the all-anesthesiologist hospital policy was adopted as part of a conspiracy to eliminate competition in the market for anesthesia services in violation of the antitrust laws. The nurse anesthetist contended that the California Society of Anesthesiologists, a defendant in the suit, urged the hospital to adopt the policy of excluding nurse anesthetists.

The federal trial court had dismissed the lawsuit on the ground that nurses and doctors do not compete. The Court of Appeals reversed the trial court, ruling that nurses have standing to sue under the antitrust laws when they are excluded from practicing as the result of anticompetitive arrangements among hospitals and doctors.

Commenting on the reversal of the district court's decision, the president of the American Association of Nurse Anesthetists, Richard Ouellette, noted that the latest "recognizes what should have been clear all along: that nurses who perform functions also performed by doctors are entitled to the full protection of the antitrust laws. ruling This protection is of great importance to nurse anesthetists and indeed all nurses in an expanded role and we are very pleased with this result."

Help!

An unexpected heavy mailing of the September-October Tar Heel Nurse *has left headquarters without sufficient copies for our files. If you are willing to part with your copy or to xerox it for your own use, we would be most grateful to receive your original copy for our files. We need at least 10 copies right away!*

Still frames from 1985 convention

NCNA staff helped members with almost anything and everything at
the registration desk.

The Peer Assistance Program drew lots of interested members.

Candidates worked the cash bar in this election year.

Speaking out at Forums

Barbara Brown, Keynote speaker

An exciting trade show with more than 60 booths was a real attraction.

Will the new Board of Directors be smiling in October, 1987?

Featured speakers, Cynthia Freund and Willis Goldbeck

Who said nurses don't know how to enjoy leisure time?

The Human Rights Committee breakfast was a *motivating* experience!

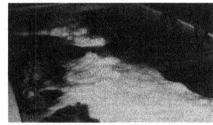

Delegates visited the Credentialing Committee table prior to the House convening.

House of Delegates in action

Potential bidders browse through the Nurse-PAC Celebrity Auction display ...

... and then opened their purses and wallets to the tune of almost $3000.

ADDRESS OF
JUDITH B. SEAMON
President 1983-85

October 25, 1985

In 1981 I asked you to "Sail with Seamon," and you trusted me enough to choose me to be the captain of the "good ship NCNA" during the 1983-1985 biennium. The experience has been one of the most remarkable in my life, and I thank you for such a memorable opportunity. With officers and crew who were committed and supportive, we have met many challenges. Today, I bring to you a report of our voyage.

The priorities adopted by the House of Delegates in 1983, combined with the purposes and functions of NCNA found in our bylaws, provided the direction and destination of the voyage. In my address to the 1984 House of Delegates I presented a progress report on these priorities to that point. Today, I will share the additional activities of the past year to continue to address those priorities.

Priority 1: *To sustain and strengthen NCNA's role as spokesman for nursing in the legislative arena and provide guidance in the framing of the legal base for the practice of nursing.*

1. Offered by subscription a new legislative communication, "Nurses Notes from the Capitol," a legislative update produced every two weeks. The response in numbers and comment was very favorable. All members received the first issue.

2. Another very successful "Day at the Legislature" workshop, during which the districts "mugged their legislators." Our "Mug Your Legislator" project received national recognition in the magazine, *Association Management*, the national publication of the American Society of Association Executives.

3. The introduction of our second Third-Party Reimbursement Bill—SB 470. Everyone involved in this effort—Third Party Reimbursement Committee, our lobbyists and many members—deserve accolades and applause for all they did. We planned well and wisely, we strategized and did all we could and did it right—but all of that was not enough. The circumstances of:

a. a drastically changed composition of the General Assembly;

b. unbelievably rigid opposition and power of the anesthesiologists and Medical Society and initial opposition of the insurance companies and big business; and,

c. an unexpected lack of support of some key figures in the Legislature, allowed the bill to stall in the legislative process and become buried in a subcommittee, where it finally died.

Power and Courage

Be assured that everything was done to first maintain its original good health, then to keep it alive, then to resuscitate it. But, it finally succumbed—because our power could not match the power of the opposition. And, therein is the lesson we must learn and learn well: legislative decision-making requires substantial power complemented by knowing how and when to use it and having the courage to do that.

We tend to learn our greatest lessons from painful experiences. We must learn from this one if we are going to secure the nursing profession within the health care system and carry out our mission of providing the consumer access to the cost-effective care we can provide.

In addition to this monumental effort, our lobbyists tracked a total of 110 bills that could have had an impact on nursing practice. And next session, there will probably be more.

Our regulated profession is always subject to risk and change within the legislative and regulatory arenas, and our presence and influence there is critical. Our profession is known and respected because of your direction, the skillful efforts of our lobbyists, and the willingness of our membership to do their part. We must continue that presence and see that it becomes more forceful for positive change for nursing and health care.

As a result of the monitoring and assertive effort of our lobbyists we now have two NCNA members in key positions on legislative groups. This is reported in detail in your September/October issue of the the *Tar Heel Nurse.*

I wish to give special recognition to Frances Miller, Hazel Browning, and the members of the Third-Party Reimbursement Subcommittee—and especially to Hazel, who with Michael Crowell, carried the responsibility for many weeks for our lobbying effort and suffered the greatest grief at the loss of SB 470.

4. Nurse PAC, because of your generous support last year, has had the resources to send representatives to many of the significant and critical

fund raising events for key political figures, both Democrat and Republican. In fact, we felt reassured when Governor Martin finally commented that "you nurses are everywhere!" Our presence also was noted by others, and most importantly, our name is on the lists of contributors.

Priority 2: *To increase the number of nurses who participate in the shaping of the nursing profession.*

Our membership has exceeded 3,000!—up 11.9% from last year. Take pride in your accomplishments, for most of this is the result of your efforts within your districts with the efforts and creativity of the Membership Committee under the leadership of Vice-President Gale Johnston.

Building our membership will be a continuing priority, and I believe our efforts will be enhanced as we make NCNA an ever more relevant, proactive, and credible force in health care and society in North Carolina because everyone wants to be on the winning team.

We are ecstatic over exceeding 3,000. If we had 4,500, we would have 10% of the nurses in North Carolina. We're headed in the right direction and building momentum. We must keep rolling!

Priority 3: *To promote and protect high standards of nursing practice and education.*

The Commission on Practice has secured a planning grant for implementation of the ANA Code of Nurses. Plans are in process for this project.

The Commission on Education has produced an informational document, published in the March/April issue of the *Tar Heel Nurse*, on "Opportunities for RNs in Baccalaureate Education in Nursing in North Carolina." The commission also responded to drafts from ANA on the issue of titling and licensure.

Achievement

One of the outstanding achievements in education has been NCNA's securing of ANA accreditation as an approver and provider of C.E. Early in the biennium, this became a priority of the Board of Directors. In response to the Board's direction, the CERP Committee and staff, namely, Assistant Executive Director Betty Godwin and Administrative Assistant Dot Bennett, and our new trusty little IBM PCXT word processor began this monumental project and spent seemingly endless hours of careful work in preparation and completion of this project. The site visitors who came last June made several recommendations and identified the following strengths of NCNA:

1. The obvious commitment by the membership of the North Carolina Nurses Association to provide quality continuing education offerings and programs.

2. The loyalty of the volunteers to serve the North Carolina Nurses Association is obvious in the time and effort which they donate freely to the continuing education efforts of the Association.

3. Given the commitment of NCNA to quality continuing education, the CERP Committee demonstrates a high level of performance.

We all should take pride in such an evaluation because it speaks to the value of concerted and unified effort. I believe special recognition goes to the CERP Committee, and to Betty and Dot, for getting the job done in fine fashion.

Priority 4: *To advance the professional status of nursing in the workplace and the economic position commensurate with professional responsibility.*

The Commission on Member Services has initiated the following activities during the past year:

a. Assisted the nurses at Durham VA Hospital in successfully achieving the level of membership required by the Board of Directors to allow NCNA to represent their bargaining unit. District Eleven also worked closely in this effort. NCNA secured a volunteer negotiator who has been effective in a very difficult situation and demonstrated true commitment for the needs of these nurses.

In addition, the Commission revised the "Minimum Employment Standards for Registered Nurses." Because of budgetary constraints, these have only been published in the May/June issue of the *Tar Heel Nurse.* Outside funding is being sought for the publication of the brochure for general distribution.

The newest project of the commission has been accepting the responsibility, as authorized by the Board of Directors, for the initial fund raising for an NCNA fund for legal action. The Legal Fund is a long-range plan to enable NCNA to intervene in court cases involving critical nursing practice issues. The specific details of this project are reported in the September/-October, 1985, issue of your *Tar Heel Nurse.*

Priority 5: *To support and facilitate the transition of ANA to a federation of SNAs so as to enhance the identity of NCNA and the image of nursing in North Carolina.*

The transition is essentially complete, although some details are still being refined in clarifying the services and functions of the state and national associations. The ANA Board of Directors has moved in a supportive fashion, and the ANA Constituent Forum has clarified its role and is beginning to develop its real potential in the overall function of the state and national associations.

United effort

The investment NCNA has made in this effort has been significant and has been a wise one. We are respected among our colleagues, and the source of that respect is the direction and guidance this House of Delegates initiates for the leadership to implement and the support you provide for the implementations. Clearly, our successes are the result of concerted, united effort.

Priority 6: *To strengthen district/state communications and relationships to build a stronger organization of better informed members.*

The Board of Directors has continued its "personal board member" project and I hope you have found it helpful. We feel it has been most beneficial to us.

District mailings have been coordinated on a biweekly schedule. A special feature, "Focus on Districts," has been in each issue of the *Tar Heel Nurse.* This district news column has been the cooperative effort of the assistant executive director and the Board representatives of the Council of District Presidents.

In June, the second annual Leadership Day was conducted by the Council of District Presidents.

Finally, the Ad Hoc Committee on Structure has addressed district needs extensively in its proposed revision of NCNA structure.

The resolutions passed by the 1983 and 1984 House of Delegates have been implemented in the following ways:

1. Care of the Older Citizen—

The Gerontological Division has continued to be active in gathering data and networking with many groups.

Currently, a new ad hoc committee is studying the feasibility of developing a model nurse-managed gerontological health care center. This is an exciting prospect, and the talent and expertise we have in this organization is truly awesome. Meeting the health care needs of the aging is a frontier that nursing must claim.

2. Action on Alcohol and Drug Misuse among Nurses—

The special Peer Assistance Program Committee has developed an excellent program to address this crucial need. Please know this program is the result of years of work and refinement. It had a difficult birth, but the "baby" is outstanding. Special recognition goes to the committee and its chairman, Hettie Garland. We now have the program, but there are no funds to implement it unless we can find outside funding.

3. Third-Party Reimbursement —

The report on this issue was presented earlier. We will continue efforts to remove this barrier to nursing practice.

4. Registered Nurses Appointed to Local Boards of Health—

Legislation was secured in 1983 to include nurses on local boards of health. This is an activity that required and has received in most instances response and involvement of the districts. Districts must continue to monitor this closely and lobby for qualified nurses to be appointed.

5. NCNA—Encourage Political Activity—

Some of these efforts have been addressed. This is another continuing effort.

6. Registered Nurses Appointed to Hospital Boards of Trustees —

Again this requires district involvement and influence for it happens at a local level. A lot more must be done to make this a reality.

Control of practice

7. Self-Direction of Nursing Service Departments —

The responsibility for implementation of this resolution was given to the members of NCNA. The resolution expresses the commitment of NCNA to the concept of nursing practice being controlled by nurses. This concept is reflected in the Association's newest revision of Minimum Employment Standards for Registered Nurses. We hope all members will become familiar with these standards and support their implementation in the work place.

8. Preserving the Statutorily Defined Boards of Health, Social Services, and Mental Health —

This was a hot issue in the 1985 General Assembly and became unbelievably convoluted and complicated. NCNA lobbyists worked closely with other groups to accomplish the charge of this resolution. The outcome was that Mecklenburg County remains the only county where county commissioners have taken over the responsibility for health, social services, and mental health boards, and a two year moratorium was secured on any other county doing likewise. A detailed report of this can be found in your 1985 July/August *Tar Heel Nurse.*

9. Baccalaureate Education for RN Graduates of Associate Degree and Diploma Programs —

The disposition of this has already been addressed.

10. RN Work Assignments —

The House of Delegates will receive a report on progress related to this resolution, and the work done so far will be discussed at a forum during this convention.

11. Endorsement of a Presidential Candidate for ANA Board —

The charge was completed and the related action of the ANA House of Delegates has been reported by ANA.

Other Actions:

Directed the Board of Directors to take some initiative to be a catalyst for addressing the need for a systematic statewide approach for nursing education in North Carolina.

An ad hoc committee was appointed. Its report was received by the Board of Directors and referred to the Commission on Education.

Having completed the business of reporting and updating you on the activities of the 1983-1985 biennium, it is traditional for the outgoing president to share with you what he or she envisions for the future of nursing and NCNA. I wish to participate in that tradition now.

Original missions

Nursing and its professional organization—both state and national—have a rich heritage. The nurses who founded our profession and our professional organization were the *best* of their time—nurses with vision of what nursing was, even at its inception. They responded to the demands of the times which shaped individual needs for health care as stated in, *One Strong Voice, The Story of the American Nurses Association: "In adopting the demands for health care, pioneer nurses began to express concern for the individualistic needs of the sick. This was* and *is* nursing's unique contribution to health care."

While many things have changed, I believe this original mission of nursing remains valid. It is as relevant today as it was in the 1800's.

Truly what is happening in health care today is revolutionary, given the technological advances, economic constraints, consumer expectations, and the continuing and growing human need. Yet the mission—the original objective—of nursing remains, and this is captured beautifully in Donna Dier's description of nursing as serving, caring, and knowing. She specifically states: "There is no point to nursing unless it is to serve ... above all nursing is caring."

I submit to you that no matter what other reponsibilities nursing assumes—it must always keep caring as its hallmark, for that quality and value will always be contemporary.

With these thoughts in mind I envision and hope for nursing and for NCNA that we will always focus upon the original mission—the original objective—of our profession. For that objective will serve as our guidance system for all we must do in contemporary reality.

We must have vision, just as our predecessors did, for what nursing is and will become. And we must share it with our colleagues, just as it has been shared with us.

Further, I believe we must understand the concept and characteristics of professionalism and accept the fact of our professionalism. Donna Diers states in her paper, "To Profess—To be a Professional": "I will take the position that we are no longer searching for our profession, we already have it."

And if you look at the characteristics of a profession—you will agree:

1. involving a high degree of individual responsibility;
2. possessing a body of specialized knowledge and skills;
3. providing a practical and definite service—a unique service to society;
4. being characterized by self organization and self government with appropriate public safeguards;
5. having a code of ethical conduct;
6. having motives that tend to be altruistic; and,
7 having specialized educational and training programs.

Nursing is clearly a profession—and nurses must conduct themselves with professional demeanor.

My hope is that we will approach the weighty issues of today and tomorrow in a professional manner, always seeing how we fit into the overall picture of health care and society and remembering that nursing does not exist in a vacuum.

Futuristic issue

Such weighty issues surely include the successful resolution of entry into practice in a manner that will secure the profession for future nurses, remembering that this is a *futuristic* issue for persons now in the fourth grade. It is not an issue for those of us who have entered into practice except in our responsibility to resolve it for future nurses.

Just as critical is the resolution of the entire credentialing issue which incorporates third-party reimbursement and other barriers to practice and future membership in the professional organization. Again I remind us of our original mission and its underlying principles, for in resolving either of these issues we must be true to those principles if we are to be responsible to our future.

I hope that we would learn the true meaning of power and use it in a responsible fashion for the good of the people we serve and to whom we provide that unique care called nursing. Surely that includes political power, for we must be among the decision makers—serving in that capacity or having their ear for input that will effect change.

I would hope that we will convince our colleagues of their privilege and responsibility to be a part of their professional organization and have a voice in shaping their profession. I believe there is merit in focusing our energies on nurses who see themselves as professionals or can catch that vision and urge them to join our ranks, and then as an organization accomplish our task proficiently. I believe we have to accept the fact that there are nurses who are content to see nursing as an occupation and nothing more. Perhaps we should let them function in that manner, always being ready to welcome them but not spending precious energies trying to impose a value they do not share.

I hope we will care more for ourselves and our colleagues. We are expert in caring for our patients, but not so expert in caring for ourselves and each other. The problems of the image of nursing will correct themselves when we learn to care for ourselves and our colleagues as we care for others. And, further, I believe when we learn to really care for ourselves and our colleagues, our caring for others will be greatly enhanced, and we will experience true professional dimension.

Caring for self

To summarize, I envision nurses and NCNA members having vision, being truly professional, always keeping in focus our original mission, seeing ourselves within the real context of society, increasing our numbers, and caring for ourselves and our colleagues as we care for others. NCNA is an organization of premium quality because of the people who will be its members. To paraphrase the president of the New York State Nurses Association, "NCNA is not a solution, but a vehicle; not an achievement but a tool." Through this organization we can travel where we must go and design what we must do. This is our mission.

My address would be most incomplete without the proper acknowledgments and recognitions.

First, I wish to thank and recognize the person who has been and is my "Rock of Gibraltar," who encouraged me to seek this office when the opportunity was offered, who has been unswerving and generous in his support during my term and has freely offered whatever I might need. He has had my car ready to go—sometimes running facing out of the driveway, always warmed up in the winter and cooled down in the summer and handed me my coffee when I left early in the morning. When I arrived home, many times late and really weary, he's been there to greet me with my favorite evening beverage and a big hug and ready ear. He's willingly used his political network and offered his political expertise when NCNA needed it. He's lectured me on what I needed to do and what nursing must do to stay current. He has been my source of renewal as well as surrogate homemaker and single parent to our children. Basically, he has made it possible for me to fulfill this responsibility in an unrestrained manner. Please join with me in recognizing my husband and a truly committed champion of NCNA, Tony Seamon.

In addition, I wish to express my deepest gratitude to a remarkable and wonderful staff. I truly marvel at their commitment and expertise. You must be on the daily scene frequently to really understand how much they do for our organization. They have been gracious, caring, efficient, humorous and always willing for the elected officials to be in the sunshine, frequently sunshine they have made possible.

Thanks in generous quantities go also to the Executive Committee, for all those extra meetings and willingness to shoulder extra responsibility when our situation required it, and to the Board of Directors for dealing with long hours of packed agendas and the determination to do our job well.

Thanks to the commission and committee chairs and members for all of the miles and hours you invested on behalf of this Association.

And, finally, thanks to the delegates and members they represent. You accept the responsibility for giving NCNA its direction and determining its future. You now face some monumental decisions that will indeed affect the future of NCNA and nursing in North Carolina.

Thank you for "Sailing with Seamon." Being your president has been the finest honor of my professional career. □

Unity Boulevard: Expressway to Power
Cynthia M. Freund, RN, PhD

This address, abridged for publication, was delivered at the 1985 convention. Dr. Freund is chairman of the Department of Core Studies, UNC-CH School of Nursing.

Let me start off by commending the planners of this convention's program. I think they were very creative in the way they linked some very key concepts together. Listen to the session titles: Power Avenue: Roadway to Professionalism; Politics Parkway: Route to Influence; and my topic, Unity Boulevard: Expressway to Power. The sessions are tied together with a convention theme—Professional Power: Pathway to Progress. I was not privy to the planners' discussions, so I don't know how explicitly they thought about the conceptual scheme they gave us, but I want to take a moment to examine it—both for its merits and as a foundation for this paper.

Note that in the title, Power Avenue: Roadway to Professionalism, the convention planners did not say expressway to professionalism, but rather roadway to professionalism. True professionalism will not come easily or quickly. We cannot mandate it. We cannot legislate it. We cannot avoid the stop and go lights and the detours. We cannot cut ourselves an expressway through mountains and over rivers to get there tomorrow. All professions evolve over time. The journey to professionalism is indeed a long roadway, but, and this is an important but, if we accumulate power along the way, we can increase our speed and hasten the journey to our destination, professionalism.

I do not mean to imply that power is the only way to professionalism. It is not; there are other ingredients, such as the development of our own body of knowledge, not everyone else's knowledge that we call our own; monopoly over our services, that is, providing services that only we can provide; research-based practice and not conventional wisdom-based practice; and finally a professional state of mind (which is my bottom line and I will elaborate on it later). The point is, power is not a sufficient

condition for professionalism, but it is a necessary one.

Our convention planners also introduced the notion of Politics Parkway: Route to Influence. I always use Harold Lasswell's 1936 definition of politics—the process of deciding who gets what, when and how—because it succinctly tells it like it is. Madeline Leininger (1978) defines politics as "the art of influencing another's thoughts and actions for individual self-interests, group needs, and/or societal goals". Indeed, politics is a process of influence. There are a multitude of definitions of power; all definitions of power, however, encompass the ideas of influencing others, convincing them to do what they otherwise might not do on their own, and overcoming resistance. Power and politics are intertwined. Discussions of power invariably relate to politics, even if politics is not explicitly labeled as such, and the converse is also true—discussions of politics move over into power. In tying all this together, let us think of politics as the use of power to influence others in deciding who gets what, when and how for either our own self-interests, group needs and/or societal goals.

Political efforts

Let us note that our convention planners put politics on a parkway. Parkways are built not to bypass everything but rather to go through everything. They are built so that a traveler can take in all the sites and vistas along the way. All too frequently, politics is thought of as that which occurs in Washington and our state capitols. But, if we think about it, we all know that we engage in politics in various other places—at our workplaces, at our places of fun and leisure, and even at home. We just call it something different—family dynamics, group dynamics, bureaucracies, corporate culture, professional turfdom, etc. The point is, if we are to influence, we must politick at all points along the parkway. Yes, we must direct our politics, our influence efforts, at legislators and policy-makers, but we must also direct our politics at home, within our own ranks, at our workplaces and with the other players within the health system. We cannot afford to decrease our political efforts with legislators and policy-makers, but I contend that we must increase significantly our political efforts within our own ranks.

Finally, the analogy for my topic, Unity Boulevard: Expressway to Power, is in my mind quite clear. With unity, we will truly be on an expressway to power. Without unity, our route to power will be along a country road, slowing to a snail's pace through small towns, picking up a little speed on the open road; but in comparison to an expressway, the trip will be quite slow. The real questions are: is unity possible, what price do we pay for unity, and how do we achieve it? These are the questions I will address, but before I do, let me finish our examination of the convention's theme—Professional Power: Pathway to Progress.

We are all into whatever we are into for some purpose, and that we have labeled "progress". I have interpreted progress to mean, in its ultimate last-order sense, the health improvement and betterment of society. I have also interpreted progress to mean, in its immediate and first-order sense, our own vested interest. It is about time that we as a profession acknowledge, and admit without guilt or apology, that our own vested interest is of paramount importance. If we believe that what we do affects the health and well-being of society, then we have to protect our vested interest, unashamedly. It may appear to others, and even to ourselves, that we are being self-serving. However, I would argue that we must be self-serving. How can society reap the benefit of what we have to offer if we do not preserve our vested interests, in essence our very existence? To follow Mr. Goldbeck's distinction, our vested interest does not have to be nor should it be our pocketbooks, our economic gain. But, our vested interest is preserving our rightful place in the system so that we can continue to give society that which for centuries we have done so well. Our vested interest is the first-order effect leading to the last-order effect, the betterment of society.

Collective power

Professional power is our pathway to progress. Note that we are talking about professional power, not just power of any sort. Professional power implies both a certain degree of professionalism and collective power—which is different from individual power or even power dispersed over a number of individuals. Power both contributes to our professionalism and becomes a part of it. The cause becomes part of the effect. Collective power leads to increasing professionalism, which in turn, brings increased professional power. We then use our professional power, through the process of politics, as well as other processes such as scientific and educational ones, to affect progress, both for our profession and society.

In this model, I am suggesting that unity, which I interpret to mean collective power, is one of the necessary conditions for professional power. I have added one piece to the model—Professional Solidarity: A State of Mind. I will present an argument to suggest that solidarity among ourselves, a state of mind, is the common denominator leading to collective power.

I want to put the issue of unity or collective power into the context of a larger goal. No matter how much we value increasing professionalism, no matter how much we want to influence politicians—for our own purposes or for society—no matter how much we want to achieve progress, however defined, unity or collective power is a necessity for the fulfillment of these needs and desires. Of course we will make some progress without unity; we already have, but it will be progress in small letters, not capital letters. It is within this context that I take the view that unity is a necessary means to a much larger end, and not a goal in and of itself.

I will use the terms unity and collective power interchangeably. When I say unity, think collective power; when I say collective power, think unity. I also ask you to accept this model as it is, for the time being. It is not perfect or refined and it is certainly untested. I have presented it merely as a contextual model so that we have a common frame of reference; so that we talk about unity as a critical means to much greater ends, such as increasing professionalism, professional power, political clout and progress ...

Soft side

As I was mulling around trying to get this paper together, what I discovered, and what I should have known, that there was what I call a hard side and a soft side to this issue of unity. The hard side is the logic, and even the theory, but most importantly, the raw logic of the issue. "Yes, we believe in unity; it is important." The soft side is the 'but if' side, the logic colored by emotions and subjectivity, particularly in regard to specific issues. "Yes, we believe in unity, but if ...", and then we list a variety of issues with which we do not agree. Unity, yes, but if the association, the leadership, they—whoever they are—does this, that or the other thing, we will not contribute to that unity—to the collective power. The hard side is the raw logic that tells us, yes, unity is important. The soft side is the particular issue, the emotion, the subjectivity and the divergent individual opinion that clouds the logic and infringes on our unity and collective power.

This is why I added Professional Solidarity: A State of Mind to the model of the convention theme, and why I deliberately chose the word 'solidarity.' Collective power unit—in its primal form, is numbers and money. More money can make up for fewer numbers and more numbers can make up for less money. But, without solidarity among those who are part of the collective, money and numbers are irrelevant.

The word solidarity has been popularized and nationalized recently. None of us here are so old—or too young, whichever you prefer—that we cannot recall the recent news about the solidarity movement in Poland and now more recently in South Africa. When we think of these solidarity movements certain images come to mind. In particular, we think of individuals who risk their livelihood and very existence to support a cause that will, in the long run, benefit the whole. Individual interests which may have been as basic as food on the table or life itself were and are subsumed in favor of the good of the whole.

Professional solidarity will not demand that from us. I am suggesting that, for us, solidarity is a state of mind. It is sort of like citizenship. We belong to a pluralistic society, and our citizenship implies our endorsement of pluralism. We vote on issues, we elect people to represent us and make decisions for us—for the benefit of the whole—and we hope that more often than not we are the whole. We know, of course, that our country has done and will do things with which we may not agree as an individual and that our representatives will make decisions for the benefit of the whole that do not benefit us as individuals. But, we do not renounce our citizenship. We do not drop out of the societal collective. We may fight, campaign and work to change that with which we do not agree; we may also do nothing and just not like it. If we felt morally indignant and outraged, we might revolt or move to another country, but short of that, we hang in there, in the spirit of citizenship and in support of the principles of majority rule, pluralism and solidarity.

If everyone who calls himself or herself a nurse would view our profession with a similar spirit of solidarity, we would be golden. We would have numbers, we would have money, we would have a strong collective voice to back up our numbers and money. We could have collective power which would hasten our journey to professionalism; we would be able to influence others; we would make progress. Following up on Mr. Goldbeck's remarks, I believe that with solidarity will come clarity regarding our direction and vision. Without solidarity, our focus will be diffused and we will lack power.

Professional commitment

I am not equating solidarity with membership in NCNA, ANA or any other professional association for that matter. In my frame of reference, solidarity implies something much broader and more encompassing. Professional solidarity is a commitment to our profession and its goals; it is support of the whole with one collective voice; it is an exquisite professional state of mind. With such a state of mind, membership in NCNA, ANA and other professional associations comes naturally, without second thought. Membership is a reflection of solidarity, a professional state of mind. Solidarity may be inclusive of membership in professional associations, but professional solidarity is broader and more encompassing; they are not the same.

At present, our profession is not characterized by a high degree of solidarity. But we can get there. We can all work to nurture a professional state of mind. I will use as examples a few current, and perhaps volatile, issues to demonstrate how we might do this.

To begin with, we have to grapple with a very basic reality. There are 1.6 million of us in this country. How can we realistically expect to present one collective voice representing 1.6 million individual nurses? The 1.6 million of us are different; we are clinicians, teachers, administrators, researchers, etc.; we hold multiple roles in multiple specialties in multiple settings. Because of our sheer numbers, we cannot expect anything but diversity in our roles and responsibilities—and in our vested interests. Furthermore, unlike other professional groups, which happen to be smaller in number, we have various mechanisms for professional socialization. At present, we have three different routes for entry into the profession: the associate degree route, the diploma route and the baccalaureate route—three different routes for basic professional socialization. Then we have even more routes for further socialization. Associate degree and diploma nurses can go on for a baccalaureate in nursing or in another of many different fields. Baccalaureate nurses can go on for a master's in nursing or in another of many different fields. We also have had, throughout our history, a variety of advanced certificate programs. And finally, at the so-called ultimate level of professional socialization—doctoral training—we have three different types of doctoral degree programs within nursing (the PhD, DNSc and ND), to say nothing of the doctoral degrees in many other disciplines that nurses pursue.

Richness in diversity

I do not intend here to pass judgment on what people learn through these multiple educational paths. Because of our numbers and state of development as a science, I believe some diversity adds to our richness as a profession. The important point is that most professions, and I see no reason why we should be different, are characterized by their centrality of mission, their internal consistency. Diversity is their complement not their characteristic. Professions develop and maintain their centrality by their socialization processes, which are consistent and similar within a given profession. In 1985, nursing stands as a profession characterized by its diversity, not its centrality or consistency.

Given our numbers, 1.6 million, and given our variety of socialization processes, which bring us diversity and not centrality, and given our multiple roles and responsibilities, is it surprising that we have difficulty achieving unity and speaking with one collective voice? I suggest that disunity is the more natural outcome of such a state of affairs.

I do not mean to be discouraging, just reality-oriented. Nor do I mean to install doom and gloom. There are ways out of our dilemma—not easy ways, but there are ways.

This summer, the ANA House of Delegates went on record to support in each state's Nursing Practice Act. They recommended that the baccalaureate in nursing be the minimum requirement for entry into the profession and for licensure as a registered nurse. Even though we have debated this issue for decades, I hope we will not continue the debate for a couple of more decades. This action is a step toward bringing some consistency to our basic professional socialization processes. The House of Delegates, in essence, recommended that there be only one professional socialization mechanism and only one route to entry into the profession—the baccalaureate in nursing—and note that I have called it entry into the profession, not entry into practice.

How will we fare in trying to achieve this goal? The achievement of the goal is a political process—we will have to influence and convince legislators of the merits of our proposal. In and of itself, that is a most difficult challenge. In order to do that, we will need the unified voice of 1.6 million of us, or at least a plurality, as we are distributed in the 50 states across the country. Is such a unified voice possible or realistic to expect? I do not believe it is realistic to expect such unity to evolve naturally. Every year, associate degree and diploma graduates outnumber baccalaureate graduates 3.7 to 1. If current trends continue, by the year 2000, only 750,000 or 28% of the total nurse supply, which will then be 2.6 million, will hold the baccalaureate in nursing. Let me say it a different way. A little more than a quarter of us—28%, hold a baccalaureate or higher degree. It is clear to me that we must start our politicking at home, within our own ranks, and not with legislators ...

We, as a profession, have made a proposal that appears to exclude 75% of us. I said "appears"; I do not think it really does. Current associate degree and diploma nurses will not be excluded from the ranks of the profession until they die. The proposal is for the future long-range good of the profession as a whole, even though it may appear to benefit the minority at the expense of the majority.

Test of stature

In my view, the only way that we will be able to overcome the odds against getting this proposal through is for each and every one of us to deputize ourselves as emissaries and ambassadors of solidarity. I believe this goal, and our success or lack of success in achieving it, to be the sine qua non test of our stature as a profession. That commands each of us to politick at home.

I will use another volatile issue to illustrate professional solidarity. This issue is the dues increase the House of Delegates has just decided. I find it ludicrous for a House of Delegates to waste its time debating such an issue. Delegates are elected by the membership to debate issues of substance to the profession and to set policy and give direction to the organized entity representing the collective (the association). Dues are not an issue of substance or policy; this is an operational issue. How can we expect the association—or any organization—to operate with a 1980 budget in a 1985 economy? ... No business or organization survives operating on 5-year old budgets.

It is time that as a profession we came of age. I take as a sign of professional maturity the House of Delegates' approval of the $35 dues increase. After all, a $35 increase does not even match the cumulated inflation rate over the past 5 years. I would also take as a sign of enlightened professional wisdom an amendment to the bylaws that permitted an automatic annual dues increase tied to the rate of inflation.

First, it just makes good business sense. Second, it really is time we grew up. Children and adolescents go to their parents and ask for more moey when the price of milk or lunch go up at school, or tennis shoes cost more, or whatever. That is what we are doing here ... But third, and most importantly, instead of debating dues, we could direct our attention to issues of professional substance. Do we want to launch any new initiatives—what are they and to what purpose? Do we want to discard any ongoing programs? These are substantive issues that we are distracted from because we are debating whether we can do as much or more with less—a rather pointless debate. Our power is defused because we are focusing on mere operational issues, and not on issues of substance about our future and our direction. Finally, an automatic dues increase would be painless ...

Just as I would take as a sign of professional maturity approval of the dues increase and as a sign of professional wisdom a yearly automatic dues increase, I would take as a sign of professional solidarity no loss in membership due to either. I am not so foolish as to think we won't lose members with a dues increase. There are the softsiders who will say: what is the association doing with my money; I don't agree with what the association is promoting; what does the association do for me, etc. ... If we all left here and went-home with a spirit of solidarity, in support of a collective entity, and in support of a dues increase to strengthen our collective power and profession, in support of an action that is good for the whole, we might not end up losing members. Once again, professional solidarity will come from politicking at home.

Balance

At what price do we achieve solidarity, unity and collective power? The price is diversity, and we must be cautious to preserve diversity while building unity.

Diversity within the profession, like unity, has value. However, the more we have of one, the less we have of the other. The issue is one of balance—balance between unity and diversity.

If we, as a profession, have a truly professional state of mind, we will not only tolerate diversity within, we will respect it. We will encourage divergent opinion and new ideas; we will nurture open and free debate. We must value our diversity within our own ranks, BUT, when it comes to long range decisions and the direction of the profession, we must value above all else that which benefits the whole. As individual professionals, with a professional state of mind, we must learn to respect our differences and argue them out but put them aside when it comes to our collective voice. If each of us is willing to put aside our own individual 'but its' and 'yes buts' in favor of our profession's internal consistency, our centrality, we will have achieved professional solidarity.

These are ways that we who belong to a professional association can demonstrate our solidarity, but how do we inspire solidarity among the rest of the nursing population? For one thing, we must start at the beginning, with those who are learning to become nurses. I know all too well that we have more and more to teach students in less and less time, and that our prime goal is to teach students to be able and competent clinicians. But, we are preparing them to be professional nurse clinicians not just any type of clinician. We must emphasize the clinician aspect, which is how to think and do. But we must also emphasize the nurse aspect, which is identity with a group that has a central mission, and the professional aspect, which is a state of mind and commitment to a larger whole. We are not, or should not be, preparing students for a clinical occupation but for a professional life.

To the teachers out there, how many of your students are aware of the issues being discussed at this convention, of the actions taken by the ANA House of Delegates last summer? How many are aware of the fact that business coalitions dealing with health even exist? How many are aware of what's happening in Washington regarding payment mechanism for home health, nursing homes and outpatient or primary care, and of the issues raised by Mr. Goldbeck yesterday? There is even a better question—how many faculty know about these issues, for if they don't students surely won't learn them, at least not from faculty. If faculty take a limited view of a clinical or a professional's role, if faculty do not expose students to the larger professional issues, if faculty are ignorant of the issues themselves, how can we expect anything more of our students and graduates? We may end up preparing capable and competent clinicians, clinicians who do their job or occupation quite professionally, but we are not preparing professionals. If we want to prepare professional nurses, we must raise the consciousness of our students regarding true and full professionalism. Preparing professionals will not require any major curriculum change nor should it be left only to those who teach the trends and issues courses. It will require from all of us as teachers a commitment to inspiring a professional state of mind in our future generations. It is not only the teachers and academicians who have a role—we all do.

Politicking at home

We no longer have a shortage in nursing. Nursing service administrators now have the luxury of being selective in their hiring process. They could now hire those who are not only competent clinicians, but who also demonstrate a commitment to the long-range good of the profession.

You see, to get others to buy into our cause, we can use our logic and enthusiasm to convince them, we can cajole, and if that doesn't work, we should be willing to be a little coercive—perhaps in subtle ways, but coercive nonetheless. The bottom line is that each and every one of us must be committed to doing whatever, whenever and wherever to develop professional solidarity within our own ranks. We must do our politicking at home. Then, and only then, will we have the unity or collective power to increase our professionalism. It is a cycle, but not a vicious one. Solidarity will enhance our collective power which in turn will increase our professionalism which in turn will enhance further our solidarity, power and professionalism. Solidarity is contagious, once started. History and theory will help, but only if we are of a professional state of mind ...

My message has not been, "Join the association, be a member". Most of you are. My message is this: "Consider yourselves ambassadors, missionaries, apostles, zealots—whatever hat fits best—for professional solidarity." Our solidarity and collective power—our unity—is not an end in and of itself, nor is it to get what each of us wants from legislators and policymakers. The purpose of our solidarity is to hasten our journey to true and full professionalism, and progress for our profession and society.

I do not discount the importance of politicking with legislators, policymakers, the business community, third-party payors and other health care providers. These activities are crucial, but I have left others to talk about that. I have chosen to emphasize our politicking at home, within our own ranks. We must not leave here and direct all our efforts outward; each of us must see that we have political work to do at home. If we don't start at home, we will never start the spiral towards increasing our collective power. If we don't start at home, five, 10, and 20 years and into the 21st

century, Mr. Goldbeck can return and ask us the very same question he asked us yesterday. I quote: "I know you should fit in, but where do you fit in?"

Of course we fit in, but not if we are fractionated. I heard at the House of Delegates this morning some signs of being fractionated—staff nurses againt administrators. There are other potential fractions—service vs. education, AD and diploma nurses vs. baccalaureate nurses, the employed vs. the unemployed. Please let us not fractionate ourselves and dilute our collective strength. My message is really quite simple: Let us politick at home in the spirit of solidarity. Let us respect and debate our differences, but move beyond them when it comes to the long-term good of the whole. I know the nurses of this state have, on many occasions, come together to demonstrate their collective strength to the state legislature. Let's capture that energy and use that same skill to develop our own internal solidarity. It is a means to an end. We will not only help ourselves; we will truly 'fit in' so that we can both shape the health system and improve the health of the society we serve. ☐

NEWS BRIEFS

American Academy of Nursing 1985 Media Awards

• "Why Me" aired as the ABC Monday Night Movie on March 12, 1985, received an award for a positive fictional portrayal of nurses and nursing. Based on the book, "Why Me," by Leola Mae Harmon, RN.

• "Code Gray: Ethical Dilemmas in Nursing," received an award for documentation of true-to-life situations of nurses facing ethical dilemmas. Christine Mitchell, RN, BSN, served as the film's consultant, associate producer, and narrator.

• Linda Kay Goodwin, RN, BSN, received recognition for her weekly newspaper column, "Hang in for Health," that appears regularly in the Sunday edition of the *Parkersburg News* in West Virginia.

Entry forms for 1986 may be obtained by writing to: American Academy of Nursing, 2420 Pershing Road, Kansas City, Missouri 64108.

Publications

• *A Guide for Community-Based Nursing Services,* supplies timely direction to nurses who are or plan to be providers within a community. Cost is $4.00. Pub. No. CH-12. Send orders to ANA, 2420 Pershing Road, Kansas City, Missouri 64108.

• *Boards of Nursing,* details the composition, member qualifications, and the statutory authority of each state board of nursing in the United States, Guam, and the Virgin Islands. Cost is $6.00. Pub. No. D-85. Send order to ANA, 2420 Pershing Road, Kansas City 64108.

• "Home Parenteral Nutrition," is a comprehensive new videotape program to help nurses prepare patients for home parenteral nutrition. Video may be rented for $60 or purchased for $250. It is also available for free preview by qualified organizations considering purchase. For details write AJN, Educational Service Division, 555 W. 57th Street, New York, NY 10019; or call 1-800-223-2282.

Call for Abstracts

• "Nursing Perspectives on Adaptation to Chronic Illness," the 12th Annual Nursing Resource Symposium Clinical Center Nursing Department, National Institute of

Health, Bethesda, Maryland; May 5, 1986. For information call Dr. Margaret Dear at (301) 496-6012. Abstracts due by January 31, 1986.

Calendar of Events

The following "Calendar of Events" will inform members of meetings of NCNA structural units and other related groups and agencies. All structural unit meetings will take place in headquarters unless otherwise indicated.

Meetings of the NCNA Board of Directors, committees and commissions are open to the membership. Members may attend to see the Association in action and to communicate with the elected and appointed officials. Members planning to attend should notify NCNA at least two days prior to the meeting, so that we can plan for adequate seating and plenty of coffee!

Date/Hour	Event
December 23-27	NCNA Office Closed
January 1, 1986	Holiday, NCNA Office Closed
January 8, 1:30 p.m.	NCNA Executive Committee
Jan. 9, 9:15 a.m.	Orientation Session for new Committee and Commission Members—N.C. State Faculty Club
Jan. 10, 10:00 a.m.	Ad Hoc Committee on RN Work Assignments
Jan. 15-18	N. C. Board of Nursing Meeting
Jan. 16, 1:30 p.m.	Joint Practice Committee, NC Medical Society Building
Jan. 17, 8:00 a.m.	"Discharge Planning: Expanded Role of the Professional Nurse"—Workshop facilitated by Gail Hardy-Russ, Wilson, N.C.
Jan. 23, 1:30 p.m.	Third Party Reimbursement Subcommittee
Jan. 24m 9:00 a.m.	NCNA Board of Directors
Jan. 31, 10:00 a.m.	Medical Surgical Division Executive Committee
Feb. 10, 10:00 a.m.	Council of District Presidents
Feb. 13, 10:00 a.m.	NCNA Executive Committee
Feb. 17	Snow date—Council of District Presidents
Feb. 28, 8:30 a.m.	"Professional Issues in Nursing"—workshop facilitated by Carolyn Billings, M.S.N., R.N.; Greenville, N.C.
Feb. 28, 9:00 a.m.	NCNA Board of Directors
April 24-26	Primary Care Nurse Practitioner Conference Group Spring Symposium
June 13-20	ANA Convention, Anaheim, California
Oct. 22-25	NCNA Convention, Raleigh

DUES RATE SCHEDULE

The new dues rate schedule became effective with December 31, 1985, renewals and for new memberships on or after December 1.

. Members who are on the electronic dues payment plan (bank draft) have already received notice that the new dues rate is effective with their December payments. When a member signs

the EDPP authorization on the membership application form, a part of the agreement states: "ANA is authorized to change the amount by giving the undersigned thirty (30) days written notice." Since bank draft dues payment is processed through a national bank system clearinghouse arrange-

ment, no new authorization for the new dues amount is required of the member.

ANA's Central Billing System allows those paying dues in three installments to complete the installments for a membership year begun prior to December 1 at the old dues rate.

DUES RATE SCHEDULE

	annual payment	installment payments first payment	2nd/3rd payment	EDPP monthly bank draft
Full dues	$150.00	$53.50	$50.00	$12.50
1/2 rate*	75.00	28.50	25.00	6.25
1/4 rate**	37.50	16.00	12.50	3.13

*New grads (eligible during first six months after graduation); RN full-time students; RNs not employed; RNs 62 or older and earning no more than Social Security allows.
**RNs 62 or older and not working, or totally disabled.

Workshop Calendar

January 17, 1986, 8:00 a.m.-4:00 p.m., Wilson Memorial Hospital Auditorium, Wilson, N.C.

"Discharge Planning: Expanded Role of the Professional Nurse," Gail Hardy. Produced in association with Area L AHEC and Districts Eighteen and Twenty.

February 28, 1986, 8:30 a.m.-4:00 p.m., Willis Building, Greenville, N.C.

"Professional Issues in Nursing," Carolyn Billings, M.S.N., R.N. Produced in association with Eastern AHEC and Districts 18, 20, 21, 30

Date TBA, Greensboro, N.C.

"Marketing Institute"

The first two workshops for 1986, "Discharge Planning: Expanded Role of the Professional Nurse" and "Professional Issues in Nursing" were previously offered in 1985. The participants rated each workshop as exceptional!

"Discharge Planning" is a one-day program in which Gail Hardy focuses on practical applications of discharge planning. A copy of the brochure may be found in the 1985 May/June issue of the Tar Heel Nurse. As stated on that brochure, Gail Hardy has enormous energy and dedication and is nationally recognized as an expert on continuity of care and discharge

planning. She relates the nurse's role in discharge planning to DRGs, JCAH Standards, quality assurance, etc. The fee will be $30 for members and $40 for non-members.

"Professional Issues in Nursing" is a workshop that all non-members need to attend. If the cc-sponsoring districts can convince potential members to attend, these nurses will walk away as believers in professionalism through unity that can occur within the professional organization. Carolyn Billings uses an informal people-oriented approach to involve participants in the workshop. Carolyn involves participants in exploration of the application of The Code for Nursing into clinical practice and the need to care for each other as well as themselves. The registration fee will be $20 for members and $30 for non-members.

Use the response form below to request brochures.

Holiday Closing

Headquarters will be closed December 23-27 for the holidays and for staff to use up accrued vacation. Headquarters also will be closed on January 1, 1986.

The staff wishes for each of you a happy holiday season!

Response Form .... Clip and Return .... Response Form

Name _____

Address _____

Please send me brochures on the following programs. (Choose as many as you like)
____ "Discharge Planning: Expanded Role of the Professional Nurse"
____ "Professional Issues in Nursing"
____ "Marketing Institute"

Return response to: ATTN: Betty Godwin, NCNA, P.O. Box 12025, Raleigh, NC 27605

NEWS NOTES FROM:

Primary Care Nurse Practitioner Conference Group

Joyce L. Nixon, Chairman
Primary Care Nurse Practitioner Conference Group

To those of you who have wondered if we're alive and well—well, we are! The new Primary Care Nurse Practitioner Conference Group (PCNPCG) officers look forward to serving you over the next two years. They are Joyce Nixon, FNP, chairperson; Linda Tull, FNP, vice-chairperson; Judy Zentner, FNP, secretary. These three people are enthusiastic about the prospects of accomplishing certain goals over the next two years under the sponsorship of NCNA. Results of the PCNPCG election results are announced elsewhere in this issue.

Linda and I attended the NCNA convention in Winston-Salem in October and took note of the concerns of fellow members who attended also. Perhaps some of these concerns are yours, too. Here are some of the major needs confronting us:

1. A need for improved communications among NPs across the state. It has been noted for some time that frequently some NPs are functioning in an isolated manner and unaware of current professional, political and clinical changes which would affect their NP positions. Communication, even to those seeking it, has sometimes been carried out rather disjointedly and spasmodically. No one person has been to blame.

2. A need for better unity/cohesion/networking among North Carolina NPs. As communications improve I see this second need also improving.

3. A need for increased membership of NPs in their professional organization—NCNA. As this is accomplished, both communication and unity will be facilitated and expedited. We who are members must diplomatically and effectively convince our fellow non-members that communication, unity and *power* to accomplish our goals and objectives are achieved most readily through our strong, sponsoring professional organization—NCNA. It is NCNA who lobbies for our rights in the legislative halls. It is NCNA who keeps the eye on those legislative bills which could undermine our goals. It is NCNA that seeks to give us topnotch C.E. It is NCNA that informs and lends support to the cause of the NP in a holistic manner—taking into consideration all our particular needs. We owe strong allegiance to NCNA, for herein lies much of our viability as a functioning health care group.

4. A need for improved election procedures and participation for officers of the PCNPCG. A better understanding of NCNA Bylaws and Guidelines for elections will improve this, and as membership into NCNA and concomitant and increased attendance at the NCNA fall convention is seen, I foresee a more valid election procedure. A copy of election procedures and absentee voting will be distributed in a timely fashion to all NCNA-PCNPCG members.

5. A need to further encourage and develop the meeting of NPs within their AHEC regions. Already we are seeing this as an excellent way to facilitate the solving of individual and common problems of NPs, whether it be in the area of clinical education or political and professional development. The general structure will look something like this: NPs will be grouped according to AHEC regions. There are nine AHECs in North Carolina. A regional liaison person should be selected to lead his/her particular region. An associate regional liaison person should also be selected along with a secretary. All officers will be members of NCNA and responsible to the chairman of the PCNPCG, Joyce Nixon. A report of activities of the AHEC meetings should be sent to me after each meeting. I then will keep in contact with NCNA and interact with elected NCNA leadership and staff to meet needs, solve problems, address concerns, applaud achievements of the particular AHEC regions. Membership in NCNA will be a prerequisite to be a voting participant of the AHEC NP meetings, since NCNA and the PCNPCG, which is part of NCNA, are the sponsoring, coordinating group for the AHEC NP meeting. However, we hope that all area NPs will want to be involved with any C.E. and issue discussions and eventually will become full-fledged voting members of PCNPCG.

Non-member NPs should be encouraged to join NCNA and thereby help, monetarily, their own cause. Printed communication from NCNA PCNPCG will be sent only to dues-paying members.

NPs will also be encouraged to attend their local NCNA district meetings so as to interact, network, offer NP expertise to their other nursing colleagues, i.e., supporters.

Call me for questions concerning how to get organized through your AHEC.

In the spring of the year at the Nurse Practitioner Annual Symposium, NPs from across the state will assemble, learn, network and give reports of activities from their various AHEC regions. Already your officers and continuing education committee, consisting of Amanda Greene and Jan Wolfe, have met and are excited about what we're going to offer you at the spring symposium. The symposium meeting place itself will offer you the best of leisure, comfort, and beauty while you update your education professionally and clinically. NCNA, of course, sponsors the whole show. Tentative dates are set for April 24-26, 1986. Please hold those on your calendars.

These are only a few of the needs we will be addressing in the next two years as we get ourselves better organized.

Linda and I had an all-day meeting with Frankie Miller, executive director of NCNA, and Hazel Browning, associate executive director, on November 6, 1985. At this meeting we solidified actions needed to accomplish our goals and objectives. Interaction was good, and I feel confident knowing we have the knowledgeable support of NCNA.

I end this note to you by saying that we need to unite and go forward as client and self advocate for improved health care. We are better able to do this as we maintain strong allegiance to one another under the umbrella of NCNA.

Notice to providers of nursing C.E.

Impending changes in the continuing education approval program were noted in the last issue of *Tar Heel Nurse*. These changes are a result of achieving ANA accreditation status.

The two major changes that will affect providers of continuing education are the application fee structure and deadlines for submitting applications. The policy statements for these changes are as follows:

1. Deadline for Applications

Applications are to be received at NCNA six (6) weeks prior to the first offering date. If submitted between four (4) and six (6) weeks, applications will be reviewed for an additional application fee of $10.00.

2. Application Fee for Single Offerings

An application fee is required for each single offering, except those provided solely by NCNA districts. The fee schedule has been established for the next three years as follows:

Effective Dates of Fee Schedule	Received six weeks prior to offering	Received four weeks prior to offering
Jan. 1,-Dec. 31, 1986	$50	$60
Jan. 1,-Dec. 31, 1987	$57	$67
Jan. 1,-Dec. 31, 1988	$65	$75

- A check made payable to NCNA is to be submitted along with the completed application. Applications are not reviewed until the fee is received.

- Application fees are non-refundable

The fee structure is based on an analysis of actual cost of the review and approval program. The submission deadlines are essential in order for applications to complete the *entire* process *before* the first offering date. NCNA can no longer approve programs that have begun or have been completed, even though the application was received at headquarters prior to the first offering date.

Implementation of these changes may not come easy for all providers. However, the efforts will be rewarded. NCNA approved credit is now accepted nationwide.

Legal References Manual

The North Carolina Medical Records Association has published a *Legal Reference Manual* to be used for reference and to provide guidance relative to legal issues affecting medical record practices in the state. Written by Julie Burton, RRA, the manual is priced at $36 and may be ordered from Tricia Byers, 4902 Lawndale Drive, Apartment 706, Greensboro, N.C. 27405.

Calendar of continuing education offerings approved by NCN

Date	Credit	Offering
11/01/85	6 c.h.	"Basic Fetal Heart Monitoring," Watauga County Hospital, Boone (#5432)
11/01/85	9.5 c.h.	"Piedmont Oncology Association 50th Annual Symposium," Winston-Salem (#5427)
11/02/85	7 c.h.	"Advanced Intrapartum Fetal Heart Rate Monitoring," Watauga County Hospital, Boone (#5433)
11/04/85	6 c.h.	"The Legal Implications of Charting," Sally S. Todd, Fayetteville (#5396)
11/04/85	6 c.h.	"ABC's of Finance for Nurse Managers," Sally S. Todd, Fayetteville (#5397)
11/04/85	6 c.h.	"Volunteerism: The Nurse as a Volunteer," NCNA District 16 (#5450)
11/05/85	6 c.h.	"Current Issues in Perinatal Nursing," Forsyth Memorial Hospital, Winston-Salem (#5451)
11/07/85	7 c.h.	"Promoting Healthy Lifestyles Among Health Professionals," N.C. Public Health Nursing Administrators (#5368)
11/07/85	2 c.h.	"Neuro-Linguistic Programming," John Umstead Hospital, Butner (#5457)
11/08/85	31.5 c.h.	"Advanced Cardiac Life Support," Salem Nursing Education Consultants, Winston-Salem (#5459)
11/08/85	7.5 c.h.	"Management of Patient with End Stage Renal Disease: A Team Approach," Forsyth Memorial Hospital, Winston-Salem (#5426)
11/08/85	3 c.h.	"Helping the Student Nurse Think Analytically," ADN Council, Statesville (#5448)
11/09/85	5 c.h.	"An Introduction to Therapeutic Touch," Wingate College, Wingate (#5453)
11/12/85	2 c.h.	"Immunosuppressant Medication Used in Organ Transplantation," Old Salem Chapter AACN, Winston-Salem (#5462)
11/13/85	6 c.h.	"Renal Update '85" Chi Eta Phi Sorority, Iota Chapter, Charlotte (#5478)
11/13/85	2 c.h.	"Rheumatoid Arthritis: An Update," Medi-Save Pharmacy, Charlotte (#5373)
11/19/85	7.5 c.h.	"Neurological Perspectives: An Overview," Charlotte AHEC, Charlotte (#5454)
11/20/85	1 c.h.	"Respiratory Emergencies in Children," Metrolina Chapter of Emergency Nurses Association, Charlotte (#5444)
11/20/85	1 c.h.	"Alzheimers," NCNA District 18 (#5445)
11/20/85	3 c.h.	"Understanding the Communication Impaired," Yadkin County Home Health Agency, Yadkinville (#5466)
11/20/85	14 c.h.	"Respiratory Core Curriculum," Pitt County Memorial Hospital, Greenville (#5467)
11/20/85	1.5 c.h.	"Perioperative Care of the Patient with Obstructive Lung Disease," Piedmont Chapter of N.C./Association of Post Anesthesia Nurses, Charlotte (#5470)
11/21/85	2 c.h.	"Legal Aspects of Charting," NCSU Student Health Services, Raleigh (#5460)
11/21/85- 1/09/86	1 c.h./ session	"Legal-Ethical Issues in Nursing Practice ... A Series," Columbus County Hospital, Whiteville (#5483)
11/22/85	7 c.h.	"Stroke: Acute Care—Discharge Planning—Rehabilitation," Wilmington AHEC, Wilmington (#5465)
11/22/85	6 c.h.	"Group Psychotherapy: Tasks and Techniques," Charter Pines Hospital, Charlotte (#5394)
11/29/85	17 c.h.	"The Way of the Dream," C.J. Jung Society of the Triangle Area, Chapel Hill (#5471)
11/30/85	2 c.h.	"Update on Tracheal Care in the Home", Forsyth County Health Department, Winston-Salem (#5464)
12/01/85	2 c.h.	"Emergency Cardiac Defibrillation of Adult Patients," Wilkes General Hospital, N. Wilkesboro (#5469)
12/03/85	3 c.h.	"N.C. Nursing Practice Act Interpretation of Category I and II Nursing Practice," Columbus County Hospital, Whiteville (#5480)
12/05/85	1 c.h.	"Risk Factor Modification for Coronary Artery Disease: An Update," NCNA District Nine (#5377)
12/06/85	5 c.h.	"Potpourri of Orthopedic Care", Moore Memorial Hospital, Pinehurst (#5473)
12/10/85	2 c.h.	"The Supervisor's Role", N.C. Division of Health Services, Fayetteville (#5475)
12/12/85	4.5 c.h.	"Rape Crisis Workshop", NCSU Student Health Services, Raleigh (#5483)
12/13/85	4.5 c.h.	"Update on N.C. Organ and Tissue Program", E. Newton Smith Public Health Center, Fayetteville (#5481)
12/21/85	17 c.h.	"Trauma Core Curriculum", Pitt County Memorial Hospital, Greenville (#5472)
1/12/85	1 c.h.	"Aging: The Poetry, The Process, and The Problems," NCNA District Three (#5461)
1/12/85	4.5 c.h.	"Core of the Student in Emergency Crisis", NCSU Student Health Services, Raleigh (#5474)
1/09/86	1 c.h.	"Family Members' Concerns After Cancer Diagnosis," NCNA District Nine (#5378)
1/13/86	2.5 c.h.	"Your Dental Health," NCNA District Thirty-Three (#5415)
1/14/86	2 c.h.	"Overview of N.C. Nursing and the Law," Wake Technical College, Raleigh (#5468)
2/06/86	1 c.h.	"Health and Wellness through Stress Management," NCNA District Nine (#5379)
10/12/86	14.5 c.h.	"Monitoring the Critically Ill", Nurse Ed Company (#5482) Asheville (#5482)

NORTH CAROLINA
NURSES ASSOCIATION
P.O. Box 12025
Raleigh, North Carolina 27605

Vol. 47, No. 6   November-December 1985

Official publication of the North Carolina Nurses Association, 103 Enterprise St., Raleigh, N.C. Tel. (919) 821-4250. Published 6 times a year. Subscription price $12 per year, included with membership dues. Indexed in *Cumulative Index to Nursing and Allied Health Literature* and available in MICROFORM, University Microfilms International.

HETTIE L. GARLAND .... President
JO FRANKLIN .... President-Elect
DAVY F. CROCKETT .... Vice-President
JOYCE H. MONK .... Secretary
SHEILA P. ENGLEBARDT .... Treasurer
    · STAFF
FRANCES N. MILLER ..... Executive Director
HAZEL BROWNING ..... Assoc. Exec. Director
BETTY GODWIN .... Asst. Exec. Director
PATRICIA W. BRYAN ..... Administrative Asst.
DOROTHY BENNETT .... Administrative Asst.

ISSN 0039-9620

Tar Heel Nurse

Vol. 48, No. 1   OFFICIAL PUBLICATION OF THE NORTH CAROLINA NURSES ASSOCIATION   January-February 1986

Two NCNA members candidates for major ANA offices in '86

Two NCNA members are candidates for major office in ANA elections to be held at the June convention in Anaheim, California.

McGrath   **Freund**

Barbara Jo McGrath, NCNA president in 1981-83 and nursing education director for Fayetteville AHEC, is a candidate for ANA Board of Directors. She was chair-

man of the ANA Nominating Committee in 1984-85.

Cindy Freund, director of Core Studies at UNC-CH School of Nursing, is a candidate for the ANA Cabinet on Nursing Education. She was a major speaker at the 1985 NCNA convention, is serving on the Ad Hoc Committee on Nurse-Managed Gerontological Health Facility, and currently serves on the General Medical Data Base Study.

To help McGrath and Freund in their campaigns, personal contributions directed to Barbara Jo McGrath, 368 —, —, 28358; Cindy —, —, Court, Chapel Hill —, —, associa— —, port cand—

Spring Symposium to feature first annual Audrey Booth Lecture

A very special event will kick off the 1986 Spring Symposium for the NCNA Primary Care Nurse Practitioner Conference Group (PCNPCG).

The continuing education program will begin with the First Annual Audrey Booth Lecture, named in honor of a nurse who has provided significant leadership and guidance to the Conference Group since its inception.

Appropriately, Dr. Loretta Ford will present the lecture. Dr. Ford is dean of the School of Nursing and director of nursing at University of Rochester Medical Center, Rochester, New York. Her studies define roles for nurses in health care and foster participation in the creation of these practitioner program at Colorado.

The half day program is scheduled and will take place at the Conference Center, a waterfront facility — pleasure, so — recommended. Symposium — NCNA members — members.

— designed to address current topics including treatment of pediatric disorders, AIDS, hypertenison, methods for dietary counseling, prescribing of contraceptives, a sports medicine module, and a focus on nurse entrepreneurs. The Conference Group will hold a business meeting during the symposium, and time is allowed for regional nurse practitioner meetings for networking and planning. A trade show on Friday will be an added feature of the program.

Nurse PAC prepares for E—

Nurse PAC Chairman Judy Seamon reports that plans are underway for Election '86· Nurse PAC committee members met on February 18 to finalize a candidate questionnaire and establish a timetable for endorsements prior to the May primary.

A process similar to the one used in 1984 is being used for candidate interviews. This process utilizes nurse interviewers in every district. District presidents assist by identifying interested nurses in their areas. "The candidate interview is an excellent opportunity for nurses to become involved in the political process," says

Chairman Seamon.

Any candidate who is a nurse in his or her district— candidate questionnaire by— questionnaire responses are— Nurse PAC will meet to cons— dorsements. The questionnaire is o— piece of information taken into consi— tion. In addition, the committee looks at v— ing records of incumbents and nurse— interviewers and district recommendations.

Nurse PAC's endorsements will be announced in late April.

NCNA members named certification examiners

Several NCNA members are serving on ANA's certification committees of examiners. They were appointed in November, 1985, by the Interim Board on Certification from recommendations made last August by NCNA.

NCNA members who have notified headquarters of their appointment are:

Ed Kirkpatrick of Jamestown, Medical-

Surgical Nursing Practice Committee, Medical-Surgical Nurse Subcommittee;

Rebecca Pitt of Asheville, Medical-Surgical Nursing Practice Committee, Clinical Specialist Subcommittee;

Sister Edna English of Greenville, Maternal-Child Nursing Practice, Maternal-Child Health Nurse Subcommittee;

Gloria Cheek of Durham, Psychiatric-

Mental Health Nursing Practice Committee, Psychiatric-Mental Health Nurse Subcommittee;

Sheila Englebardt of Greensboro, Nursing Administration Committee, Nursing Administration Subcommittee.

Members of the committees of examin-

(continued on page 9)

CPSIA information can be obtained
at www.ICGtesting.com
Printed in the USA
BVHW040909281118
534010BV00038B/573/P